Contents

2nd Edition

BTEC FIRST Business

Diane Canwell

Jon Sutherland

Nelson Thornes

Published in 2006 by:
Nelson Thornes Ltd
Delta Place
27 Bath Road
CHELTENHAM
GL53 7TH
United Kingdom

09 10 11 12 / 10 9 8 7 6 5 4

A catalogue record for this book is available from the British Library

ISBN 978 0 7487 8394 6

Cover photographs by Digital Vision and Image 100
Page make-up by Pantek Arts Ltd, Maidstone, Kent
Printed and bound in China by 1010 Printing International Ltd

Introduction

The business world is a fast changing environment. Businesses cannot afford to be left behind in this hugely competitive world, they have to either adapt or die. A business has to make its presence known, whether it uses a flier pushed through a letterbox or a flashy television advert. It needs to be online!

Each business needs to know what it is about, what it wants to do and how it will do it. They need to strike up lasting relationships with their customers, control and account for their money and continuously communicate. Their most important resource, experienced managers and employees, need to be well rewarded and looked after, their activities need to be supported and the latest business techniques and equipment should be used.

The business world is not as complicated as you might think, it's about ideas, putting them into action, outwitting the competition and getting the right message across to potential customers.

How do you use this book?

Covering all 10 units of the new 2006 specification, this book has everything you need if you are studying BTEC First Certificate or Diploma in Business. Simple to use and understand, this book is designed to provide you with the skills and knowledge for you to gain your qualification. We guide you through your qualification through a range of features that are fully explained over the page.

Which units do you need to complete?

There are 10 units available for the BTEC First in Business. For the BTEC First Diploma in Business you are required to complete 3 core units and 3 specialist units.

Core Units	Specialist Units
Unit 1 **Exploring Business Purposes**	Unit 4 **Business Communication**
Unit 2 **Developing Customer Relations**	Unit 5 **People in Organisations**
Unit 3 **Investigating Financial Control**	Unit 6 **Providing Business and Administrative Support**
	Unit 7 **Personal Selling**
	Unit 8 **Business Online**
	Unit 9 **Exploring Business Enterprise**
	Unit 10 **Starting a Small Business**

Is there anything else you need to do?

1 Start reading a newspaper with a business news section.
2 Find out what businesses near you do and what sort of jobs they offer.
3 Visit as many different businesses as possible.
4 Use your work placement to collect useful information.
5 Always look for useful information, it's always easier to understand things if they are happening for real!

We hope you enjoy your BTEC course – Good Luck!

Turn over now for your guide to the features of this book.

Features of this book

Learning Objectives
At the beginning of each Unit there will be a bulleted list letting you know what material is going to be covered. They specifically relate to the learning objectives within the 2006 specification.

Grading Criteria
The table of Grading Criteria at the beginning of each unit identifies achievement levels of pass, merit and distinction, as stated in the specification.

To achieve a **pass**, you must be able to match each of the 'P' criteria in turn.

To achieve **merit** or **distinction**, you must increase the level of evidence that you use in your work, using the 'M' and 'D' columns as reference. For example, to achieve a distinction you must fulfil all the criteria in the pass, merit and distinction columns.

Activities
are designed to help you understand the topics through answering questions or undertaking research, and are either *Group* or *Individual* work.

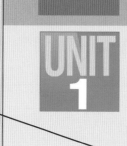

UNIT 1
Exploring Business Purposes

This unit covers:

- the nature of business and ownership
- the classification of business activities
- business aims and objectives in different sectors
- the main functional areas that support business organisations

The business world is complicated and indeed it is often difficult to understand what being in business actually means. On a daily basis hundreds or thousands of businesses touch our lives. These are businesses that sell products or services and many others that support other businesses.

The business world is always changing. Products and services that were popular last year may no longer be in fashion. Businesses need to be aware of this and their changing environment. In addition, businesses operate across the world and must also cope with competition from the world.

grading criteria

To achieve a **Pass** grade the evidence must show that the learner is able to:	To achieve a **Merit** grade the evidence must show that the learner is able to:	To achieve a **Distinction** grade the evidence must show that the learner is able to:
P1 describe different types of business organisations in terms of purpose, ownership, size and scale.	**M1** compare and contrast the ownership, aims and objectives of two selected businesses.	**D1** evaluate how the functional areas contribute to the aims and objectives of the two selected businesses.
P2 describe the primary, secondary and tertiary classifications of business activities using local and national examples.	**M2** explain areas of growth or decline in the primary, secondary and tertiary classifications of business activities.	**D2** describe the purpose of setting aims and objectives for businesses.
P3 describe the purpose of setting aims and objectives for businesses.	**M3** explain the interaction of functional areas and how they relate to each other in two selected businesses.	

activity
INDIVIDUAL WORK (1.1) R. L. Anderson Ltd. manufactures silk flowers. They sell £750,000 worth on average each year. They have calculated that their eight competitors sell between them £6.25 million worth per year. Calculate Anderson's market share.

case study 1.1 — Bertram's Cycles

Bertram's Cycles have three shops in the east of England. They provide an unrivalled selection of cycles and cycling equipment. All stores have highly experienced staff. They offer some of the best discounts on top brands in the country. Bertram's have been in the cycling business for 20 years. The founder, Charles Bertram, was an Olympic cycling medallist. There has not been a question or query about cycling from one of their customers that Bertram's have not been able to answer.

activity
INDIVIDUAL WORK

In groups of two or three, write a short statement of Bertram's main aims and objectives. Compare your statement with those from other groups in the class.

keyword

Profit
– a business's ability to sell its products and services for more than it costs them to acquire or provide those products and services.

Organisations are not just businesses. They are not all concerned with making a **profit**.

One of the best ways to think about organisations is to focus on the fact that they are all concerned with success. An organisation wants to be able to supply its products or services to its customers in the most efficient way. This goal of success can be applied equally to organisations that supply services at no cost to the customer and to businesses that supply products or services at a cost to their customers.

link

Links to Unit 2, page 120.

The Foundation for Small and Medium Enterprise Development
www.fsmed.org

remember

Charities also provide a range of services at no cost to customers.

progress check

1. Define the word 'profit'.
2. What is a mission statement?
3. What is the role of a wholesaler?
4. Give three advantages and three disadvantages of a partnership
5. What is the difference between a plc and a Ltd?
6. What is an SME?
7. To be classed as a medium-sized business, how many people should the business employ?
8. What is a multinational?
9. Give three examples of national businesses.
10. Give three examples of European businesses.

Case Studies
provide real life examples that relate to what is being discussed within the text. It provides an opportunity to demonstrate theory in practice.

An **Activity** that is linked to a Case Study helps you to apply your knowledge of the subject to real life situations.

Keywords
of specific importance are highlighted within the text in blue, and then defined in a 'keyword' box to the side.

Links
direct you to other parts of the book that relate to the subject currently being covered.

Information bars
point you towards resources for further reading and research (e.g. websites).

Remember boxes
contain helpful hints, tips or advice.

Progress Checks
provide a list of quick questions at the end of each Unit, designed to ensure that you have understood the most important aspects of each subject area.

Acknowledgements

Photograph credits:

Digital Vision XA (NT) p3; S Meltzer / Photodisc 17 (NT) p12; F Schussler / Photodisc 17 (NT) p16; Digital Vision 1 (NT) p18; © Stockbyte Platinum / Alamy p25; Corel 736 (NT) p26; Jules Frazier / Photodisc 66 (NT) p34; Ryan McVay / Photodisc 69 (NT) p36; © image100 / Alamy p47; Ryan McVay / Photodisc 71 (NT) p49; Corel 734 (NT) p51; © Vladimir Godnik / Alamy p52; Keith Brofsky / Photodisc 68 (NT) p54; Digital Vision 1 (NT) p55; © Image Source / Alamy p57; Ryan McVay / Photodisc 69 (NT) p61; Corbis RF (NT) p69; Keith Brofsky / Photodisc 68 (NT) p74; Keith Brofsky / Photodisc 55 (NT) p78; © image100 / Alamy p82; Keith Brofsky / Photodisc 68 (NT) p87; Stockbyte 31 (NT) p94; Ryan McVay / Photodisc 69 p106; © Image Source / Alamy p113; Ryan McVay / Photodisc 69 p120; Keith Brofsky / Photodisc 68 (NT) p130; Steve Cole / Photodisc 55 (NT) p133; © Jack Sullivan / Alamy p139; Steve Mason / Photodisc 45 (NT) p149; © Image Source / Alamy p155; Photodisc 22 (NT) p156; Keith Brofsky / Photodisc 55 (NT) p160; Rubberball WW (NT) p169; © image100 / Alamy p173; Ryan McVay / Photodisc 73 (NT) p175; Ryan McVay / Photodisc 68 (NT) p178; John Rizzo / Photodisc 66 (NT) p186; Corel 737 (NT) p190; © Imageshop / Alamy p195; Ryan McVay / Photodisc 76 (NT) p201; Corel 328 (NT) p204; © Andrea Matone / Alamy p207; © Stockbyte Platinum / Alamy p211; Corel 765 (NT) p213; © Adams Picture Library t/a apl / Alamy p213; Ryan McVay / Photodisc 73 (NT) p219; © image100 / Alamy p224; Bananastock TE (NT) p228; Ryan McVay / Photodisc 71 (NT) p235; Rubberball WW (NT) p262; McDonalds (NT) p267; Keith Brofsky / Photodisc 68 (NT) p271; Corel 129 (NT) p279; Photodisc 71 (NT) p281; © Enigma / Alamy p282; © Andrew Palmer / Alamy p287; Nelson Thornes p297; © Barry Mason / Alamy p305.

Exploring Business Purposes

This unit covers:

- the nature of business and ownership
- the classification of business activities
- business aims and objectives in different sectors
- the main functional areas that support business organisations

This unit aims to explain the nature of different businesses, their different aims and objectives, and the different sectors in which they operate. It also examines the fundamental building blocks of a business which, when put in place, help it to achieve its aims and objectives. This unit will help you understand how a business functions and provide you with useful background for future employment or work experience.

This unit is internally assessed and requires you to show your understanding of the nature of business, ownership, how businesses can be classified, the sectors in which they operate, and the main functional areas that support a business.

grading criteria

To achieve a **Pass** grade the evidence must show that the learner is able to:	To achieve a **Merit** grade the evidence must show that the learner is able to:	To achieve a **Distinction** grade the evidence must show that the learner is able to:
P1 describe four different types of business organisations in terms of purpose, ownership, size and scale	**M1** compare and contrast the ownership, aims and objectives of two selected businesses	**D1** evaluate how the functional areas contribute to the aims and objectives of the two selected businesses
P2 describe the primary, secondary and tertiary classifications of business activities using local and national examples	**M2** explain areas of growth or decline in the primary, secondary and tertiary classifications of business activities	
P3 describe the purpose of setting aims and objectives for businesses	**M3** explain the interaction of functional areas and how they relate to each other in two selected businesses	

1

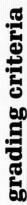

UNIT 1

grading criteria

To achieve a **Pass** grade the evidence must show that the learner is able to:	To achieve a **Merit** grade the evidence must show that the learner is able to:	To achieve a **Distinction** grade the evidence must show that the learner is able to:
P4 describe the functional areas and their main purposes within business organisations		

Business and Ownership

keyword

Profit
– The ability of a business to sell its products and services for more than it cost to acquire or provide those products and services.

Organisations are not just businesses. They are not all concerned with making a **profit**.

Businesses are all concerned with success. An organisation wants to be able to supply its products or services to its customers in the most efficient way. This goal of success can be applied equally to organisations that supply services at no cost to the customer and to businesses that supply products or services at a cost to the customer.

Organisations often call their aims and objectives **mission statements**. A mission statement describes, as clearly and briefly as possible, what the organisation intends to do, how it will attempt to go about it, and states its long-term aims.

case study

1.1

Bertram's Cycles

Bertram's Cycles have three shops in the east of England. The company provides an unrivalled selection of cycles and cycling equipment. All stores have highly experienced staff. The stores offer some of the best discounts on top brands in the country. Bertram's has been in the cycling business for 20 years. The founder, Charles Bertram, was an Olympic cycling medallist. There has not been a question or query about cycling from one of its customers that Bertram's has not been able to answer.

activity

GROUP WORK

In groups of two or three, write a short statement of Bertram's main aims and objectives. Compare your statement with those from other groups in the class.

Purposes of business

As you may now realise, different organisations have different purposes. Their purposes depend very much on what kind of activities the organisation is involved in and how it receives the bulk of its **income**.

Supply of goods and services at a profit

This is perhaps the most common activity undertaken by organisations. Businesses will either produce or buy products and services and then sell them on to customers at a higher price in order to cover their own costs and to make a profit. Many of the products that you can buy in your local high street have passed through the hands of several businesses.

---

activity

GROUP WORK (1.1)

Choose one of the following products and try to work out how many times it would be sold on by organisations before it reaches the high street and is ready to be purchased by a customer:

a) Hamburger.

b) Music CD.

c) Book or magazine.

d) PlayStation game.

Supply of goods and services free

You might ask yourself how an organisation can offer goods and services at no cost to the customer. The simple answer is that the organisation receives the funding it needs to provide those goods and services for free from another source other than the customer.

There are a large number of organisations that receive funding, either from central or local government, to provide services that the customer does not have to pay the organisation for. Other organisations, known as **charities**, also provide a range of services at no cost to customers.

> **keyword**
>
> **Charities**
> – Organisations that exist to provide a service or to support a particular cause.

> **activity**
> **GROUP WORK**
> **(1.2)**
>
> Are the following services provided for free, or are they being funded in some other way?
>
> a) Refuse collection.
>
> b) Parks.
>
> c) Street lighting.
>
> d) Road mending.
>
> e) Supermarket carrier bags.
>
> If you think that any of the above are free, where do you think the money comes from to pay for the service?

Supply of goods and services at cost

Some organisations offer products and services to their customers without making a profit from the sale. It may often be the case that these organisations are able to obtain goods and services that they can then pass on to their customers, as they are difficult to obtain elsewhere. Typical examples include equipment for disabled or older people. It may be difficult for these customers to choose and order particular items they need for their homes. Local and central government therefore act as buyers for these people, and sell on what they have purchased without adding to the cost.

Supply of goods and services for sale at below cost

There are other organisations that offer goods and services at a reduced cost. Rather than supplying goods and services for free, they charge customers a small amount which does not cover the cost of supplying those products or services. These organisations are able to supply at below the cost to themselves because they receive funding from another source to help them do this.

Ownership of business

The type of ownership of a business can give you some clue as to its size. A local plumber, for example, may well be a sole trader. A firm of solicitors or accountants may well be a partnership, and a family-run shop may be a private limited company. A branch of a chain, such as Tesco, is most likely to be a public limited company. You will recognise charities or voluntary organisations as many of them have branches in most towns and cities.

Franchises are more difficult to spot, but these are organisations that have the name of a well-known, national company, but are in fact run by local people.

Cooperatives are more rare and the most common are the various types of cooperative supermarkets, such as Rainbow.

Sole trader

This individual will be responsible for supplying or borrowing all the money required by the business and for actually running the business on a day-to-day basis. Perhaps the most common sorts of sole traders are craftsmen and women – for example, plumbers, decorators, electricians, mobile hairdressers, window cleaners and chiropodists.

Sole-trader businesses cover a very wide range of activities, but they all have some features in common, including the way they are started, and that the business can normally be run by one person, although that person has to be very flexible and needs to be willing to work very long hours.

> **remember**
>
> Sole traders are single-person enterprises and around 63 per cent of all UK businesses are sole traders.

Table 1.1 Advantages and disadvantages of setting up as a sole trader

Advantages	Disadvantages
There are no particular legal formalities to complete before commencing to trade	Capital is limited to the owner's savings or profits or any other money he or she can borrow
There are no particular legal requirements governing the layout of the accounts	The owner has sole responsibility for debts – if the owner does fall into financial difficulties it may be necessary to sell his or her own personal possessions to meet the business's debts
The annual accounts do not have to be audited	Responsibility for a range of activities falls upon the shoulders of the one person who runs the business
The owner has the freedom to run the business in his or her own way	The success of the business is always dependent on how hard the sole trader wishes to work
	Any unforeseen accident or illness could seriously affect the business since all responsibilities rest on the shoulders of that one person

> **activity**
> GROUP WORK
> (1.3)
>
> Consult your *Yellow Pages* directory and try to identify at least 10 local sole traders. What kind of occupations are they? Compare your findings with those of the other groups.

Partnership

A partnership may be formed to overcome the problems that a sole trader can have in raising capital. A partnership consists of between two and 20 people who set up in business together and share the responsibility for that business. Each partner is required to contribute some capital and the profits and the losses are shared between all of the partners. Control of the business is the responsibility of all the partners and decisions made by one partner are always binding on the others.

In partnerships, all partners have what is known as unlimited liability. This means that any debts incurred by the partnership have to be met by all the partners.

Partnerships are commonly found in accounting and legal professions, where specialists in different areas of their profession will join together in a partnership to make the business more attractive to prospective clients.

Table 1.2 Advantages and disadvantages setting up a partnership

Advantages	Disadvantages
It is easier for partners than sole traders to raise capital because all of the partners can pool their resources	Each partner is personally liable for all of the firm's debts
Partners can share their expertise and their workload	Disagreements can arise between partners about the amount of effort that each of them puts in
Partners can arrange to cover one another at times of illness or holidays	Partnerships can only raise limited amounts of capital as compared with businesses
A partnership, like a sole trader, does not have to publish its accounts or have them audited	Decision-making can be slow since all partners have to be consulted
Additional capital can be raised by introducing more partners into the partnership	The death or retirement of a partner can bring a partnership to an end if such a rule is written into the deed of partnership
	All profits must be shared

activity

GROUP WORK (1.4)

Investigate at least five partnership firms in your local area and try to discover the number of partners in each of these businesses. What advantages do they have over sole traders? If you were starting a business, what qualities would you be looking for in your partners? Discuss your findings as a group.

Limited Liability Partnership (LLP)

An LLP is in many ways similar to a partnership, though individual members have lower levels of liability to debts. There are more administrative responsibilities compared with a partnership and the organisation runs rather like a private limited company.

In terms of liability, the Limited Liability Partnership is itself liable, rather than the individual members of the LLP. As a result, LLPs are usually only recommended for profit-running businesses.

Private Limited Company (Ltd) and Public Limited Company (Plc)

The limited company is one of the most common forms of business organisation. A limited company is separate in law from its shareholders and directors.

remember

You can buy a ready-made company for under £150 and these are known as 'off-the-shelf' companies.

Individuals put capital into the business – they are known as shareholders – and they each therefore own part of the business and will share a percentage of any profits that are earned. They elect a number of directors who will actually run the business on their behalf.

Private Limited Company

You can always tell that a company is a private limited company when the word Limited or Ltd is written after the company name. The shares in a private limited company are not freely available to the general public and only the directors agree the transfer of shares. Private limited companies are usually family concerns or were originally so. This is the form of organisation often chosen when a sole trader wants to expand and wishes to retain control of the company.

Public Limited Company

This tends to be a larger company. It will have Plc after the company name. These companies are allowed to raise capital by selling their shares on the Stock Exchange. This gives them greater flexibility in raising capital. They still only need two people to form a Public Limited Company, and there is no stated maximum number of shareholders.

The process of creating a public company is very similar to that of creating a private company. Once a public company has received a Certificate of Operation, it will prepare a prospectus, which is basically an invitation to the public to buy shares. The people forming the company must decide how these shares are to be sold and how many shares will be allocated to each prospective buyer.

The Registrar of Companies will then issue a Trading Certificate. This means that the business is up and running.

activity

GROUP WORK (1.5)

In pairs, one person taking companies that are Plcs and the other taking Ltds, list the main advantages of these types of companies. Take just five minutes to do this, and then together try to agree which has the most advantages. If you agree that Plcs are better than Ltds, think about why some companies remain Ltds. If you think that Ltds are better than Plcs, why do some companies take the trouble to become Plcs?

Table 1.3 Advantages and disadvantages of setting up a limited company

Advantages	Disadvantages
Shareholders have limited liability	The formation and running costs of a limited company can be expensive
It is easier to raise capital through shares	Decisions tend to be slow since there are a number of people involved
It is often easier to raise finance through banks	Employees and shareholders are distanced from one another
It becomes possible to operate on a larger scale since additional shares are offered to the public	All the affairs of the company are made public through the audited accounts and annual returns that the company makes
It is possible to employ specialists	Legal restrictions under the various Companies Acts are fairly tight
Suppliers tend to feel more comfortable trading with legally established organisations	Large companies are often accused of being impersonal to work for and to deal with
Directors are not liable for the debts of the company	Rates of tax on profits are often higher
The company name is protected by law	
There are tax advantages attached to giving shares to employees	
A company pension scheme can give better benefits than those that are available for the self-employed	
The ill-health or death of shareholders does not affect the running of the business	

Public corporation

Public corporations are companies or quasi-corporations controlled by government. Examples include British Nuclear Fuels Plc and Royal Mail. These companies receive more than half their income from sales of goods or services into the marketplace.

Table 1.4 Advantages and disadvantages of being a public corporation

Advantages	Disadvantages
In creating public corporations the government ensures that essential services are provided	Public corporations tend to be large and can be inefficient
The government can use public corporations as part of its overall plans	They are large, impersonal organisations, which makes it difficult to motivate staff
The government can ensure that services are not duplicated	If the corporation makes mistakes which cost them money, additional funding has to be given to the organisation by the government via taxation
If the corporation makes a profit, it can either be reinvested or given back to the Treasury to help reduce taxation	Sometimes the corporations are influenced by political issues

The bulk of funding for public corporations comes direct from government (the Treasury), and as a result the government exercises control over the organisation. A government minister will be responsible for the corporation and will have to answer questions in parliament if there are any problems with the organisation. Corporations have a separate legal identity and a Board and Chairperson are responsible for the day-to-day running of the organisation.

Charity and voluntary organisations

Charities and voluntary organisations share many features. They are generally:

- Set up for charitable, social, philanthropic, religious, political or similar purposes.
- Required to use any profit or surplus only for the organisation's purposes.
- Not a part of any governing department, local authority or other statutory body.

Voluntary organisations have a legal structure or status, being an unincorporated association, or a trust or company limited by guarantee.

The number of registered charities is growing. At the end of 2003 there were 162 104 main charities registered with the Charity Commission in England and Wales; by the end of 2004 there were 163 698. According to the Charity Commission, the total annual income for all the registered charities was £34 863 247 125 or nearly £35 billion in 2004.

> **remember**
> There are thousands of registered charities in the UK. These are all registered with the Charity Commission.

The Charity Commission
www.charity_commission.gov.uk

Franchises

The franchise is a form of organisation that has been imported into the UK and the rest of the world from America, where over a third of all retail businesses are operating on a franchise basis. The main features of franchising are as follows:

- Franchising is hiring out or licensing the use of product lines to other companies. A franchise agreement allows another company to trade under a particular name in a particular area.
- The person who takes out the franchise needs a sum of money for capital and is issued with a certificate from the franchising company.
- Another important feature of the franchise agreement is that the franchisee agrees to buy all of its supplies from the franchisor and the latter makes a profit on these supplies.
- The franchisor also takes a share of the profits made by the franchisee's business.
- The franchisee, on the other hand, benefits from trading under a well-known name and enjoys a local monopoly.
- The franchise agreement allows people to become their own boss without the normal kinds of risk of setting up a business from scratch.

Cooperatives

In the past, cooperatives were found only in agriculture or retailing. More recently there has been growth in the number of cooperatives in services and in small-scale manufacturing.

In a cooperative all the people who form part of that organisation join together to make decisions, share the work and also share the profits.

Size of businesses

The size of a business can be measured in a number of different ways: in terms of the number of people it employs; the number of stores, offices or branches it has; the amount of sales it makes or the amount of profit it makes. It would be wrong to assume that organisations that appear to be tiny, perhaps because they do not employ very many people, are not large businesses, as they may in fact make large profits from what they do.

Small organisations

In January 2004, the UK government changed the description of what they considered to be a small or a medium-sized business. Tables 1.5 and 1.6 show how the size of businesses is measured.

Table 1.5 How small businesses are measured

	Now (from 30/1/04)	Before (before 30/1/04)
Turnover (no more than)	£5.6 million	£2.8 million
Balance sheet (no more than)	£2.8 million	£1.4 million
Employees (no more than)	50	50

Source: The Department of Trade and Industry
Note: A business must satisfy at least two of the given criteria to be considered a small business.

Table 1.6 How medium-sized businesses are measured

	Now (from 30/1/04)	Before (before 30/1/04)
Turnover (no more than)	£22.8 million	£11.2 million
Balance sheet (no more than)	£11.4 million	£5.6 million
Employees (no more than)	250	250

Source: The Department of Trade and Industry
Note: A business must satisfy at least two of the given criteria to be considered a medim-sized business.

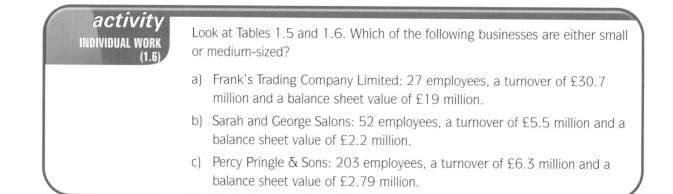

activity

INDIVIDUAL WORK (1.6)

Look at Tables 1.5 and 1.6. Which of the following businesses are either small or medium-sized?

a) Frank's Trading Company Limited: 27 employees, a turnover of £30.7 million and a balance sheet value of £19 million.

b) Sarah and George Salons: 52 employees, a turnover of £5.5 million and a balance sheet value of £2.2 million.

c) Percy Pringle & Sons: 203 employees, a turnover of £6.3 million and a balance sheet value of £2.79 million.

Small to medium-sized organisations

The European Union (EU) defines an SME, or 'small or medium-sized enterprise', as an organisation that employs fewer than 250 staff and has a turnover of less than €40 million (approximately £26 million).

Medium-sized organisations

A medium-sized organisation is defined by the EU as being one that employs more than 250 people and has a turnover of more than €40 million (approximately £26 million).

Many medium-sized organisations operate on a national basis and include travel agents, betting shops and newsagent chains. They are major employers in the UK and are involved in businesses as varied as agriculture, production, construction, retailing, catering, business services and wholesaling.

keyword

Multinational – A business that runs operations in at least two different countries.

Large organisations

There are a great number of different forms of large organisation operating in the UK. Some are UK businesses, whilst others are known as **multinationals**.

Typical large organisations include the following:

- Retail organisations, such as Marks & Spencer Plc, Tesco Plc and PC World
- Computer manufacturers, such as IBM, Apple and Dell
- Oil companies, such as Shell, Esso and BP
- Franchise organisations, such as The Body Shop, McDonald's and Pizza Hut
- Manufacturing organisations, such as General Motors (Vauxhall), Nissan and Ford.

---

activity
GROUP WORK
(1.7)

In groups of two or three, find out the answers to the following questions:

a) PC World is part of a larger group. Name the other two high-street chains that are part of the same organisation.

b) Which supermarket chain owns Safeway?

c) Name the five overseas countries in which The Body Shop has a franchise.

Scale of businesses

Whether you live in a city, a town or in the countryside, there is a network of business organisations to cater for all of your immediate wants and needs. Some of the businesses will be part of the public sector, such as refuse collection or healthcare. Public sector organisations are run and funded by local government or organisations acting for local government. Others will be provided by the private sector, such as supermarkets, chemists or newsagents. Private sector organisations are privately owned and are independent of the government.

Local businesses

Many local businesses are small, or small to medium-sized organisations. Local businesses aim to cater for the immediate needs of the local community. They therefore include convenience stores, takeaways, launderettes, public houses and restaurants.

activity
GROUP WORK
(1.8)

Identify the 10 nearest businesses to either your school or college. Are they local businesses or do they belong to larger organisations?

Regional businesses

Particularly in the countryside, where the population is far more spread out, it is not practical for businesses to establish themselves in every small community. Many organisations therefore try to identify an ideal location in a particular area that could serve a large community which is spread out in surrounding towns and villages. Many supermarkets have adopted this means of serving widespread communities.

You will also find that many county councils establish themselves in one of the larger towns or cities in a region. From here they organise and direct the council's operations throughout the region.

Some private sector organisations tend to establish their businesses in areas of the country that they know best. Some chains of retail stores can only be found in certain parts of the country and these can also be classed as regional businesses.

> ## activity
> **GROUP WORK (1.9)**
>
> Where is your local council based? Find a map of the area that it serves. Why do you think its headquarters is based in this particular location?

National businesses

There are a large number of private sector organisations that have stores or offices in virtually all the major towns and cities in the country. This is particularly true of supermarket chains, such as Sainsbury's, Tesco and Asda.

Banks and building societies are also examples of national organisations that have set themselves up in all of the main population centres in order to serve their customers.

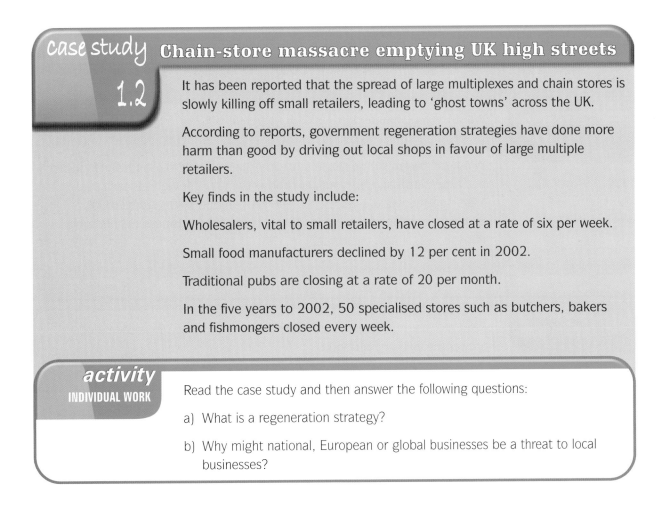

> ## case study 1.2 — Chain-store massacre emptying UK high streets
>
> It has been reported that the spread of large multiplexes and chain stores is slowly killing off small retailers, leading to 'ghost towns' across the UK.
>
> According to reports, government regeneration strategies have done more harm than good by driving out local shops in favour of large multiple retailers.
>
> Key finds in the study include:
>
> Wholesalers, vital to small retailers, have closed at a rate of six per week.
>
> Small food manufacturers declined by 12 per cent in 2002.
>
> Traditional pubs are closing at a rate of 20 per month.
>
> In the five years to 2002, 50 specialised stores such as butchers, bakers and fishmongers closed every week.

> ## activity
> **INDIVIDUAL WORK**
>
> Read the case study and then answer the following questions:
>
> a) What is a regeneration strategy?
>
> b) Why might national, European or global businesses be a threat to local businesses?

European businesses

The UK is one of the many countries in Europe that is part of the EU. Since joining the EU, it has become increasingly easier for British businesses to operate in the rest of Europe. It has also meant that European businesses have begun to establish themselves in the UK. In many major towns and cities in the UK, retail stores such as Lidl and Aldi, which are owned by European organisations, compete with UK chains. In turn, British businesses, such as The Body Shop, Marks & Spencer and Lush, have found markets in Europe for British products and services.

Global businesses

remember

Global businesses are also known as multinational businesses as they produce products and sell them in many different countries.

When we think about global businesses, we tend to think about huge organisations, such as Coca-Cola, Disney, Esso and Ford. All of these businesses are based in the US and there is barely a town or city in the UK, if not the world, where you cannot purchase some of their products or services.

Global businesses account for a huge amount of sales, profit and employment around the world. Increasingly these global businesses do not simply supply a country with their products or services, they set up their own factories, offices and even retail stores in markets around the world.

case study 1.3   Wal-Mart

Wal-Mart was founded in 1962. Its revenue is $244.5 billion per year (approximately £140 billion) and it employs 1.4 million people worldwide.

Wal-Mart began with a single store in Arkansas in 1962, and was founded by Sam Walton and his younger brother James. The Waltons built Wal-Mart into the world's largest retailer, with around 4700 stores today. Sam's descendants own about 38 per cent of the business. Sam's son Robson, 59, is now chairman.

Source: www.walmartstores.com

activity
INDIVIDUAL WORK

Read the case study 'Wal-Mart' and then visit the company website and answer the following questions:

a) What businesses does Wal-Mart own in the UK?

b) How many employees does Wal-Mart have in the UK?

c) How many stores does Wal-Mart have in the UK?

Classification of Business Activities

There are four different types of business activity:

- *Primary* business activities involve getting raw materials from the natural environment, e.g. mining, farming and fishing.
- *Secondary* business activities involve making things (manufacturing), e.g. making cars and steel.
- *Tertiary* business activities involve providing a service, e.g. teaching and nursing.
- *Quaternary* business activities involve research and development, e.g. IT.

The pie chart in Figure 1.1 below shows the employment structure in the UK – how the workforce is divided up between the three main employment sectors: primary, secondary and tertiary.

case study 1.4   The employment structure of the UK, Brazil and Ghana

The UK has a small proportion of people working in primary industry. Machinery has taken over many of the jobs in the primary sector. The tertiary sector is still growing.

Brazil is still developing its secondary sector, which means that a lot of people are still working in the primary sector. There are also many people working in the tertiary sector. In recent years there have been major improvements in healthcare, education and transport.

In Ghana the majority of people work in the primary sector. Lack of investment in machinery still means that most people work in farming, forestry and mining. Very few people work in the secondary sector owing to the lack of factories in Ghana.

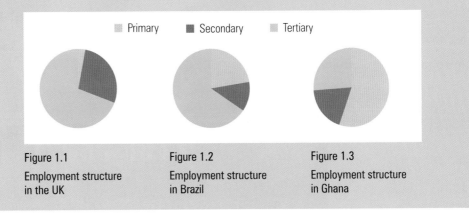

Primary   Secondary   Tertiary

Figure 1.1

Employment structure in the UK

Figure 1.2

Employment structure in Brazil

Figure 1.3

Employment structure in Ghana

Read the case study. Brazil has a larger population than the UK, while Ghana has the smallest population. Answer the following questions:

a) If the UK has so many people working in the tertiary sector, where do the primary and secondary sector products come from for these people if the UK does not produce them?

b) Why might Brazil gradually move towards the mix of sectors shown in the UK pie chart?

c) In time, will Ghana become like the UK or Brazil? Why?

The primary sector

The primary sector of industry generally involves the conversion of natural resources into primary products. Most products from this sector are raw materials for other industries. Major businesses in this sector include agriculture, fishing, forestry and all mining and quarrying industries.

Farming

Agriculture (or farming) is the process of producing food, feed, fibres and other products by cultivation of certain plants and the raising of domesticated animals.

case study

1.5

Farming in the UK

Intensive production systems, the increased use of machinery and the increasing use of pesticides and chemical fertilisers have resulted in huge drops in employment in the farming sector. There has also been a knock-on effect on employment in other rural services.

At the same time, the environment has suffered. Since 1945, the UK has lost 95 per cent of its wildflower meadows, 30–50 per cent of ancient woodlands, 50–60 per cent of lowland heath land, 140 000 miles of hedgerows and 50 per cent of lowland fens, valleys and basin mires.

Changes in agricultural practice are the main cause of these losses. In addition, contamination of rivers, groundwater and drinking water by artificial fertilisers and pesticides, and continued soil erosion have both become major issues.

activity

GROUP WORK

In groups of two or three, read the case study and answer the following questions:

a) What do you understand by 'a knock-on effect on employment in other rural services'?

b) What could be done to turn around the destruction of the natural landscape?

c) Why might the contamination of rivers be a problem?

keyword

Imported
– Goods or services that are produced or provided by an overseas country and brought into the UK.

keyword

Exported
– Goods or services that are produced or provided by a UK organisation and sold to an overseas country.

Forestry

Forestry is the art, science and practice of studying and managing forests and related natural resources. The production of wood has become an increasingly profitable industry in recent years.

Fishing

In 2003, some 631 000 tonnes of sea fish were landed into the UK and abroad by the UK fleet, with a value of £521 million. In addition, the UK **imported** some £1.44 billion worth of fish. The UK also **exported** fish and fish products to the value of £891 million.

The UK has a substantial fish processing industry of around 563 businesses, which employ some 18 480 people.

Extraction and mining

There are around 40 open-cast sites and 20 underground coal-mining sites in the UK. The majority of these are located in the Midlands, the north-east of England, south Wales and southern Scotland.

As well as coal mining, many businesses are involved in the extraction of chalk, limestone, clay, salt, sand, gravel and shale.

Several organisations are responsible for providing a healthy and plentiful water supply and for the treatment of sewerage. These organisations are involved in the management of rivers, canals, streams, lakes, reservoirs, wells, springs and underground waterways.

activity
**GROUP WORK
(1.10)**

In pairs, find out the name of the organisation that provides fresh water supplies to your area.

a) Who deals with the sewerage?

b) Where is the nearest sewage farm and where is the nearest reservoir?

remember

It is now believed that North Sea oil fields will remain active until at least 2020.

The UK was fortunate for many years to have significant gas reserves, particularly in the North Sea. In the mid 1980s it was predicted that North Sea oil would run out by 2000. But UK oil production continues to increase. Some oil fields, particularly those to the west of the Shetland Islands, have been discovered only recently and are at an early stage of their productive life.

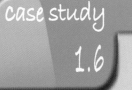

New gas pipeline

case study

1.6

By 2010 the UK will be importing around 50 per cent of its gas requirements. It is likely that in the future at least 20 per cent of the gas used by the UK will be imported from Norway. The gas will reach the UK via a 1200 km pipeline, which is being rolled out along the seabed across the North Sea from Norway to the UK. The pipeline is part of a Norwegian energy project that is due to be finished in 2007.

activity

INDIVIDUAL WORK

Read the case study and answer the following questions:

a) Using the Internet, find out where the pipeline will enter the UK.

b) Do you think the pipeline terminal will create many jobs in the UK?

c) What effect will this have on the local area?

The secondary sector

The secondary sector of industry is also known as the manufacturing sector. This sector of industry generally takes the output of the primary sector and manufactures finished goods or products to a point where they are suitable for use by other businesses, or for export or for sale to **domestic consumers**. This sector is often divided into light industry and heavy industry.

> **keyword**
>
> **Domestic consumers** – Household buyers rather than businesses.

Manufacturing

Manufacturing is the transformation of raw materials into finished goods for sale, or intermediate processes involving the production or finishing of goods. It is a large branch of industry and of secondary production.

Engineering

In 2000, the UK engineering industry had a turnover of almost £100 billion, 40 per cent of which was exported. Machinery and equipment had a turnover of £32 billion, with over 30 per cent being exported.

The engineering industry has a small number of large, successful businesses and a large number of small to medium-sized businesses, operating in areas as varied as **aerospace** and **telecommunications**. Many of the businesses produce highly profitable products and services that are at the forefront of engineering design and highly sought after by the rest of the world.

> **keyword**
>
> **Aerospace** – Manufacturing industry that produces parts and products for the aircraft industry, including rockets, engines and other equipment.

>
> **keyword**
>
> **Telecom-munications** – The manufacturing and service industries that produce or provide communications equipment.

Construction

The UK construction industry produces around 8 per cent of the country's wealth and employs two million people. The UK construction industry is the third largest in Europe and the fifth largest in the world.

The tertiary sector

The tertiary sector is involved in providing services, either at a personal or a commercial level. Personal services include professions such as doctors, solicitors, teachers and firefighters. Commercial services aim to assist businesses and include banking, accountancy, training and marketing services.

Private services

Private, or commercial, services are provided to individuals or businesses by specialist organisations. Many of these services have grown in size in recent years and collectively they provide an enormous amount of employment and income to the UK.

Tertiary private service
The quaternary sector

The quaternary sector is really a subset of the tertiary sector. It involves hi-tech industries, scientific research, consulting and some education. The sector can also include pure services such as the entertainment industry.

Some people believe there is a quinary sector, which includes health, education, culture and some forms of research.

Table 1.7 Tertiary private services

Tertiary private service	Description of service
Accountancy	Accountancy covers all forms of financial services, including investment and the provision of financial expertise to businesses. The UK is the world's leading international financial services centre employing more than 1 million people and with overseas earnings of £31.2 billion in 2000. The City of London is one of world's three leading financial centres and the largest centre for many international financial markets.
Administration	Many businesses choose to use a separate business to assist them with their administrative work. This can often take the form of a separate organisation dealing with their general office duties, personnel or legal and financial matters. This leaves the organisation free to concentrate on its own areas of expertise and to avoid having to take on additional staff to carry out these duties.
Banking	The UK has probably the most efficient banking system in the world. There are more foreign banks based in the UK than in any other country in the world – 481 in 2000 when London banks accounted for 19.1 per cent of global bank lending. The total wealth of the UK banks in August 2001 was £3441 billion, of which 55 per cent belonged to foreign banks.
Communications	In 2002, the UK communications sector still managed to grow by 1 per cent and was worth £30 billion in 2002. The sector increased by 4.6 per cent in 2003 to reach a value of £31 billion.
Consultancy	There are estimated to be between 30 000 and 35 000 management consultants in the UK, with a total worth of around £5.5 billion, of which exports account for £1 billion. The majority of international work carried out by UK firms is in Europe.
Design	The UK is considered to be the design workshop of the world. UK designers have an international reputation, particularly in the areas of retail interior/exterior, branding, advertising, corporate identity, product design and multimedia. UK design consultancies generated £1 billion in export earnings in 2000.
Distribution	Around 1.5 million people are employed either directly or indirectly by the distribution sector. This includes road haulage, warehousing and other forms of transportation.

Table 1.7 continued

Tertiary private service	Description of service
Energy supply	The UK electricity industry supplies electricity to over 26 million customers. Energy supply also includes oil and gas, and, more recently, wind farms are being constructed on the coasts around the UK to provide an all-year-round, clean energy source.
Entertainment	The UK entertainment industry includes musicians, actors and actresses, film, theatre, dance and a host of other entertainers. The UK entertainment industry is considered to be one of the best in the world and the West End theatres in London attract thousands of overseas visitors each year.
Healthcare	In 2005, the UK exported over £14 billion worth of healthcare goods and services in addition to providing services such as the diagnosis of illness and laboratory technology.
Hospitality and medical	The hospitality industry contributes some £21.5 billion annually. The industry employs more than 1.8 million people in the UK, working in around 300 000 establishments. By the end of 2005, a further 170 000 jobs will have been created. The private medical sector is also a major employer of medical staff. Health spending is due to rise considerably over the five years to 2010.
Publishing	There are approximately 50 000 publishers in the UK and Ireland, although only around 2500 of them are of any size. Over 130 000 new books are published each year, in addition to the many thousands of magazines and newspapers. UK book publishers export around £1.5 billion worth of books each year.
Repair and maintenance	The repair and maintenance industry includes garages that deal with vehicles and the innumerable repair services for domestic machines such as dishwashers, televisions and CD players.
Research	The term 'research' covers an enormous range of different activities, including the development of new products, ideas and processes, as well as investigations into particular markets. Research also includes scientific and medical development of drugs and equipment for other sectors such as healthcare, retailing, security and energy supply.
Retailing	Retailing is the UK's top service sector industry, employing around 2.4 million people in the UK. Its turnover has risen from just over £80 billion in 1984 to in excess of £175 billion.
Security	UK security companies and their services are world leaders, achieving success with equipment and services in overseas markets, particularly in the US, Europe, the Middle East and the Far East. The UK security industry was worth £4.37 billion in 2002, divided into electronic security £1.4 billion, physical security £331 million, police and public services £63 million and manned security £1.79 billion.
Tourism	Tourism is worth about £300 billion in the UK. It is one of the world's biggest industries and is growing fast, catering for both family holidays and business travellers. Tourism provides income for conservation and national heritage.
Transport	The UK exports a quarter of everything it makes each year. UK businesses have been involved in building much of the world's infrastructure (airports, railways, roads, bridges, ports, waterworks, power stations and electricity transmission lines).
Water supply and purification	The UK water industry (including the water utilities, contractors, consultants, equipment manufacturers, lawyers and financiers) is much in demand around the world. With the global water business worth up to $300 billion, the UK water supply and purification sector is the market leader in the world.

case study 1.7

UK entertainment

Videos, DVDs, CDs and games are an important part of the UK entertainment industry. With the exception of recorded music, all of these parts of the sector have grown and continue to grow year-on-year.

Table 1.8 Retail values in the UK entertainment industry (£ million)

	2000	2001	2002	2003	% Change 2002/03
Recorded music	2047	2111	2027	2007*	−7%
Video (excl. rental)	1200	1539	2050	2421	+18%
Games (excl. rental)	934	1057	1173	1259	+7%
Total	4181	4707	5250	5687	+8%

Source: Recorded Music: BPI figures for 2000–02. *Trade estimates for 2003. Video: BVA. Games: Chart Track/ELSPA.

activity
INDIVIDUAL WORK

Using the data in Table 1.8, create a bar chart using computer software. Your bar chart should include the three different sets of data as well as the total figures for each year.

remember

In every pound of public expenditure, central government spends 74p, local authorities spend 25p and public corporations spend 1p.

Local and national public services

The public sector employs approximately a quarter of the UK workforce and includes:

- Central civil government departments and agencies.
- The National Health Service (NHS) and its local trusts.
- The Ministry of Defence.
- The Northern Ireland Assembly, National Assembly for Wales and the Scottish Executive.
- Local authorities.
- Universities and colleges.
- Public non-financial corporations (e.g. the BBC).
- The Bank of England.

The main responsibilities of the government departments are shown in Table 1.9.

Main responsibilities of government departments

Table 1.9 The main responsibilities of government departments

Department	Responsibility
Social Security	Pensions and welfare benefits
Health	National Health Service
Defence	Navy, army and air force
Education and Science	Schools, universities, the arts
Home Office	Courts, police, prisons, fire service
Employment	Training schemes, job centres
Environment, Food and Rural Affairs	Agricultural policy, food, roads, housing, local authorities
Trade and Industry	Regional and industrial policy
Foreign Office	Embassies
Energy	Electricity, gas, oil, atomic energy

Education

Although the majority of teaching jobs are in state-funded secondary schools (more than 180 000 teachers work in secondary schools), there are a variety of other forms of employment in the sector – from university lecturers to nursery school and playgroup assistants.

activity
GROUP WORK
(1.11)

Using Figure 1.4 as a guide, identify at last one example of each of the different types of educational centres in your region.

Emergency services

There are 31 NHS ambulance service trusts in England (and three in Northern Ireland). They are the first and often the most important contact for around 5 million 999 callers every year. In 2002–03, the ambulance services received nearly 5.4 million 999 calls and provided over 4.8 million emergency responses.

Figure 1.4 The education sector

School education

→ There are 24000 schools in England wholly or mainly state funded. They are either:

→ community schools (the majority of mainstream schools)

→ foundation schools (more independent)

→ voluntary-aided schools (e.g. Church schools)

→ voluntary controlled schools (charitable foundations)

Further education

→ General further education colleges

→ Colleges of technology

→ Specialist colleges

→ Agricultural colleges

→ Community colleges

→ Sixth-form colleges

→ Tertiary colleges

Other teaching opportunities

→ Independent schools

→ Prison education

→ Pre-school (nurseries, playgroups)

→ Higher education (universities)

→ English as a foreign language

→ Sports education

→ Museum and environmental education

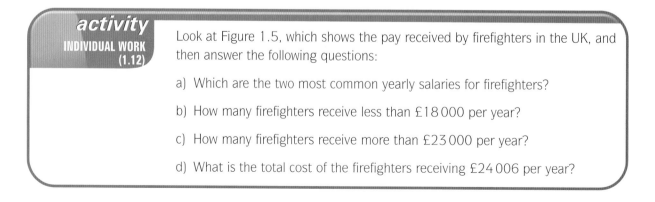

activity

INDIVIDUAL WORK (1.12)

Look at Figure 1.5, which shows the pay received by firefighters in the UK, and then answer the following questions:

a) Which are the two most common yearly salaries for firefighters?

b) How many firefighters receive less than £18 000 per year?

c) How many firefighters receive more than £23 000 per year?

d) What is the total cost of the firefighters receiving £24 006 per year?

Figure 1.5

The number of fire-fighters at each salary level

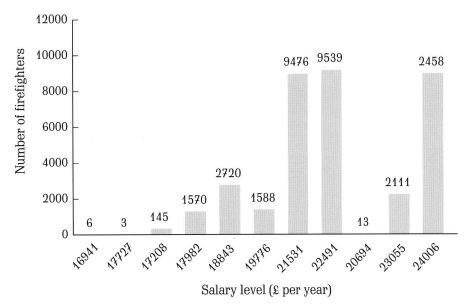

Healthcare

The NHS treats 1 million people every 36 hours. Approximately 1.3 million people were employed in the NHS in September 2003. This represented an increase of 60 000 since 2002 and an average increase of over 37 000 per year since 1997.

There were 633 375 professionally qualified clinical staff in the NHS including: 108 993 doctors; 386 359 qualified nursing, midwifery and health-visiting staff (including practice nurses); 122 066 qualified scientific, therapeutic and technical (ST&T) staff; and 15 857 qualified ambulance staff.

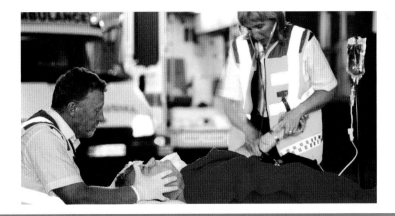

activity

INDIVIDUAL WORK (1.13)

After reading the information on the NHS, answer the following questions:

a) How many people work for the NHS according to the figures above?

b) Why do you think that the NHS is still growing in size?

c) Convert the pie chart in Figure 1.6 into a graph using Microsoft Excel or similar software.

Figure 1.6
Staff in the NHS in 2004.

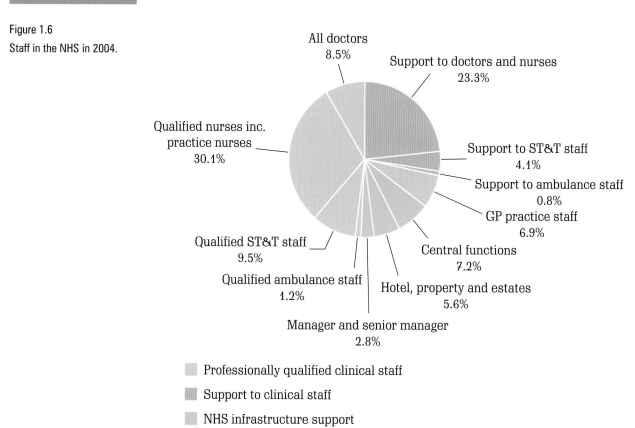

All doctors
8.5%

Support to doctors and nurses
23.3%

Qualified nurses inc.
practice nurses
30.1%

Support to ST&T staff
4.1%

Support to ambulance staff
0.8%

GP practice staff
6.9%

Central functions
7.2%

Hotel, property and estates
5.6%

Qualified ST&T staff
9.5%

Qualified ambulance staff
1.2%

Manager and senior manager
2.8%

▓ Professionally qualified clinical staff
▓ Support to clinical staff
▓ NHS infrastructure support

Housing

Public sector housing relates to council flats or council houses in England and Wales still provided by local authorities (district councils, unitary authorities and London borough councils). In recent years, many local authorities in England and Wales have handed over control of their housing to other organisations.

Law and order

The UK now has the highest ever number of police officers patrolling the streets. As of December 2003 there were:

- 138 155 police officers (an increase of more than 14 000 in 3.5 years).
- 3243 community support officers.

The military

The Ministry of Defence is responsible for the armed forces of the UK and for the defence of the country. In addition to the uniformed staff in each of the branches of the armed forces, the Ministry of Defence employs around 100 000 civilian staff.

Record number of police officers

Police numbers have reached a record high of 136 386 (in 2003), the Home Secretary announced.

The Home Secretary said: 'Police numbers are at an all time high. At the end of August 2003, there were 136 386 police officers in England and Wales, the highest number since records began in 1921, 9000 more than in 1997 and way ahead of our 2004 target.

It is vital that we make the best use of today's record number of police officers by continuing to take them out of the station and increase visibility, availability and accessibility.

By cutting bureaucracy in the police service as part of the police reform programme, the government is already freeing up officer time and bringing about a real difference to the everyday lives of officers on the front line.

Source: www.homeoffice.gov.uk

activity
INDIVIDUAL WORK

After reading the case study about the police, answer the following questions:

a) What does the Home Secretary mean by 'cutting bureaucracy'?

b) Why might it be important to 'increase visibility, availability and accessibility'?

Table 1.10 Number of defence personnel, 1 July 2001 (thousands)

Total UK-based personnel	**304.0**
Service	**205.7**
Civilian	**98.4**
Naval service	42.4
Officers	7.8
Other ranks	34.7
Army	109.5
Officers	13.9
Other ranks	95.6
Royal Air Force	53.7
Officers	11.0
Other ranks	42.7
UK-based civilians	98.4
Non-industrial	73.8
Industrial	24.5

Source: DASA (Civilian) and DASA (Tri-Service)

activity
INDIVIDUAL WORK
(1.14)

After reading Table 1.10, convert the figures into a graph using Excel.

Planning

Both local and central government prepare development plans which affect virtually every area of our lives, including building, use of land, industry, use of natural resources, technology, the military and the police, and numerous other concerns. Planning helps the government to control development.

Table 1.11 UK expenditure on defence 2001–01 (estimates £ billion)

	Expenditure	Percentage of total
Total expenditure	23.6	100
Split into:		
Expenditure on personnel: of the armed forces of civilian staff	8.8 6.5 2.3	38 28 10
Expenditure on equipment	9.8	41
Other expenditure: Works, buildings and land Miscellaneous, stores and services	5.0	21

Source: MOD Financial Controller (Corporate Financial Management)

Recreation

Local government is closely involved in the development and provision of recreational facilities across the country. The range of recreational facilities covers swimming pools, parks, museums, sports centres, libraries and the countryside.

Social services

Spending in England on social services is around £9 billion per year, and the average local social services authority spends £60 million to provide services for local people.

Voluntary/not-for-profit services

Even with the enormous range of private and public sector organisations, there is still a need for organisations to provide services, either by using volunteers or at a zero or reduced cost to users. Within the voluntary and not-for-profit sector, we can include a large number of different organisations, ranging from trusts to charities and groups that seek to promote particular interests.

Growth and decline of the sectors

After a period of time there is a tendency for countries to reduce the amount of work in the primary and secondary sectors and concentrate on the tertiary sector. This leaves the primary and secondary sectors open for other, less-developed countries to become involved in. Either as a result of natural resources running out or no longer being profitable, countries tend to look for overseas sources of primary sector resources, which they can exchange for manufactured goods or for tertiary sector services.

activity
**GROUP WORK
(1.15)**
Try to find out whether any primary or secondary sector industries used to operate in your immediate area. A visit to the local library to find a local history book or a visit to a local museum may reveal the type of industries that used to be major employers in your area. Why do you think these industries are no longer running?

remember

Developing countries rely on primary industries to begin with, or the immediate use of raw materials. Only later can they buy technology and machinery.

Decline of primary and secondary industries

There are many reasons for the reduction in the number of people employed in the primary and secondary sectors. Perhaps the two most important are the fact that machinery has gradually taken over many jobs that used to be done by hand and the fact that it is actually cheaper to buy raw materials and manufactured goods from abroad.

Most of the manufacturing in the world now takes place in less-developed countries where raw materials are cheaper and employees are paid a fraction of the wages that are paid to employees in more-developed countries.

Growth of tertiary service industries

As countries become more developed there is an increasing need for tertiary sector services. The UK has always had a strong reputation throughout the world for banking, finance and insurance services. These have always employed large numbers of UK workers.

> ## activity
> ### INDIVIDUAL WORK (1.16)
>
> Look at Figure 1.7.
>
> a) What was the overall percentage change in manufacturing between 1984 and 2000?
>
> b) What was the overall percentage change in finance and business services between 1984 and 2000?

Telesales
– Also known as telephone sales, involves calling customers, either at home or at their workplace, and attempting to sell them products and services.

Media
– The general term used to describe newspapers, television, radio, magazines and, increasingly, Internet news and information services. The media also includes marketing, public and community relations.

The UK also employs large numbers of people in the travel and tourism sector, **telesales** and marketing, the **media** and telecommunications. Many other businesses have taken on large numbers of workers to cope with the huge boom in retailing and in customer services.

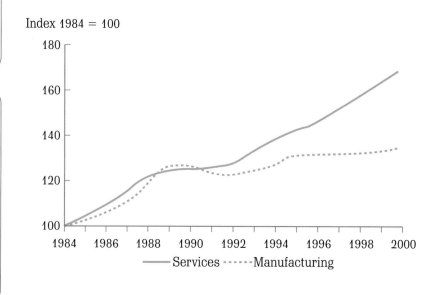

Index 1984 = 100

Business Aims and Objectives in Different Sectors

The aims and objectives of an organisation are closely linked to its available resources. As we will see, the aims and objectives of organisations tend to change over a period of time, largely as a result of their experiences and relative success or failure.

remember
Aims are often vague, whereas objectives are precise targets.

Aims

Depending upon the nature of the organisation itself, we can identify a number of key aims or objectives that are common to many different types of organisation.

Objectives

Objectives are meaningless if they cannot be measured or compared with actual progress or results. Aims can be seen as rather more vague targets, but objectives need to be very precise.

Organisations tend to identify the precise elements of their objectives by using what is known as the SMART technique.

SMART

The SMART technique is a way of setting, monitoring and measuring objectives so that it is clear to everyone that either progress has been made, action needs to be taken or the objective has been reached. Table 1.12 explains how a SMART technique could be used for a typical objective.

Table 1.12 How a SMART technique could be used for a typical objective

Meaning	Explanation	Example
S – Specific	Identifiable and measurable aspects of the objective	Increase sales by 20 per cent.
M – Measurable	Easy to calculate so the organisation knows if it has succeeded or failed	If sales were £1 million last year, they need to be £1.2 million this year.
A – Achievable	Can the organisation make the best use of its resources without setting the standards so high that it is impossible to reach them?	Last year the organisation increased sales from £800,000 to £1 million. Therefore it should be possible and achievable to make the same increase this year.
R – Recognisable	Can everyone in the organisation understand what is being measured?	Sales targets need to be shown in actual figures or percentages.
T – Time constrained (related)	Achieve target by a particular date and monitor the progress to that date	In order to be on target the business needs to achieve a 20 per cent sales increase in a year. They therefore know that to be on target they should have achieved a 10 per cent increase in the first six months.

case study 1.9 Adnams Books Ltd

Harry and Sylvia Adnams run a small book-publishing company. They have 20 staff and produce around 50 books each year. The company has recently applied for a large bank loan of £1.2 million to expand. The bank has asked them, among other things, to prepare a SMART statement to show how they will expand over the next five years.

Adnams intends to increase the number of books they produce by 25 each year for the next five years. It expects profits to increase by 25 per cent each year. Its current profits are £200 000 each year. It expects to have to take on an extra five members of staff each year.

activity

INDIVIDUAL WORK

Using the case study, state the SMART objectives of the business. Make sure that you make a comment against each of the five aspects of SMART related to their objectives.

For organisations to ensure that they make the best use of their resources in order to achieve their aims and objectives, they need to set in place a management system.

The management needs to ensure that the performance of each of the parts of the organisation is acceptable and that any targets that have been set are being reached or exceeded.

Purposes of a business's aims and objectives

The main purpose of a business's aims and objectives is to give the organisation focus. We will now look at these purposes in more detail.

Survival

Survival becomes important for organisations when they face difficult periods of trading. Many organisations will at some point face difficult times when they have to seriously consider closing down and giving up. In times when survival is the only aim, the organisation may have to lose members of staff, cut costs and ride out the bad period.

Break even

A business breaks even when its income is equal to its costs. In cases when its income exceeds its costs, the organisation has made a profit. But when its costs exceed its income, it is said to have made a loss.

Some costs are relatively easy to control. These are known as fixed costs. Typical fixed costs include rent or perhaps the wage bill, particularly if the staff are being paid salaries.

activity

INDIVIDUAL WORK (1.17)

Imagine that you run a small business. The costs of rent, rates, electricity and telephone bills are approximately £1000 per month. The goods you sell each month cost you around £1000. How much money would you need to make each month to break even?

Assume then that your business becomes more popular and that you to take on two members of staff that you pay £400 each per month. You also need to purchase another £1000 worth of stock each month. What does your income have to be now to break even?

Added to the fixed costs are variable costs, which change according to how busy a business finds itself. A busier business may need to take on additional staff or buy extra products. An organisation will then add its fixed costs and variable costs together in order to calculate their total costs. These total costs will then be compared with the organisation's income and if the income matches the total costs then the business has broken even.

Growth

For many businesses, growth is a gradual process, financed by profits or loans that allow them to take advantage of the current situation of success. Businesses need to be careful about growing too fast. While they do not want to be overwhelmed by customers that they cannot serve, they do not want to grow too fast and add huge costs to the running of the organisation without really knowing whether their income will increase.

Profit maximisation

Profit maximisation means selling a product or service with the largest possible difference between the cost of providing it and the price for which it is sold.

Profit maximisation relies on efficiency and making sure that time and money is not wasted on any single process in the production of a product or the providing of a service. It means making the best use of employees, premises and equipment.

Service provision

remember

Often, excellent customer service is the one thing that will make a customer choose one business instead of another.

Many businesses pride themselves on their responsiveness to customers. Indeed, customer service is seen as being one of the most important aspects of a successful business. An organisation will seek to ensure that all contact with customers is of the highest possible quality and that in the event of a problem or complaint the issue is dealt with promptly, efficiently and courteously.

Expansion of market share

Market share is the percentage of sales that is held by a particular organisation in the market. Market share can be measured either in terms of the income generated by sales or the number of products or service packages sold.

Businesses will obviously attempt to control as much of the market as possible and any increase in sales will mean that a competitor has suffered losses in sales.

---

activity

INDIVIDUAL WORK
(1.18)

R. L. Anderson Ltd manufactures silk flowers. It sells £750 000 worth on average each year. It has calculated that its eight competitors sell between them £6.25 million worth per year. Calculate Anderson's market share.

Anderson decides to buy one of their smaller competitors. The company sells £350 000 worth of silk flowers each year. Assuming that Anderson can continue this level of sales, what is its market share now, having bought the smaller company?

Relationship with other businesses

From the very beginning a business will be reliant upon other businesses. It will need products and services, ranging from office supplies, transportation, specialist advice and skills, and supplies of products.

The larger the business, the more relationships it builds up over a period of time. Many businesses operating across the world will have relationships with thousands of other businesses, both as customers and as suppliers to the business. Eventually, as the businesses develop, they will become reliant upon one another and will seek to continue their relationships and improve them as much as possible.

Stuart and Laura run a small café called Quick Bite. They have been operating the business for four years and have established themselves in the local high street.

Quick Bite supplies sandwiches to Canwell Construction, its local library and two local petrol stations. The café buys its bread from Beccles Mill and the rest of

their food and drink is ordered and delivered from the regional cash and carry, Savoy Stores. Tables and chairs are supplied by Brian Harwood Limited and kitchen equipment by Multi-Kitchen. Quick Bite uses Rodale Accountancy and Management for financial and business advice.

Draw a diagram showing the relationships between all of the businesses and Quick Bite.

Aims and objectives in different sectors

In this section we have not considered the different objectives of primary, secondary and tertiary sector organisations, but those of private, public, not-for-profit and voluntary organisations. The key differences between the four types of organisation are summarised in Table 1.13.

Table 1.13 Aims and objectives in different sectors

Aim or objective	Private	Public	Not-for-profit	Voluntary
Survival	Major objective in early years	This will be achieved if the organisation is providing a valuable service	Achievable if it works within budgets	Achievable if it works within budgets
Break-even	Target after around one year of trading	Must operate within budgets set by local or central government	Can only provide levels of service up to its income and not beyond	Can only provide levels of service up to its income and not beyond
Growth	Target once break-even has been achieved	If given additional tasks and responsibilities	Will grow provided there is a need for its services	Will grow provided there is a need for its services
Profit maximisation	Next target, often together with growth	Not applicable	Not applicable	Not applicable
Service provision	In relation to its customers in the form of customer service	Must provide good level of service to customers or clients	Can provide levels of service within its budgets	Can attempt to recruit more volunteers to provide additional levels of service
Market share	Gradually achieved through growth	Not applicable	Not applicable	Not applicable
Relationships	Will seek to establish lasting and profitable relationships with other businesses	Will rely on suppliers and relationships with other public corporations	Will seek to minimise costs while maintaining good relationships with other organisations	Will seek to minimise costs while maintaining good relationships with other organisations

Main Functional Areas that Support Business Organisations

Every organisation has its own way of structuring the functions, or tasks, that need to be carried out. Although the following section covers many common tasks or departments, not all organisations choose to divide their staff up into these particular areas.

remember

In many businesses networked computer systems have replaced distinct administration departments.

Administration

Many organisations have a central administration. The main function of an administration department is to control paperwork and to support all of the other departments, particularly by servicing their needs for secretarial work or administration duties such as filing, mailing and data handling.

activity
GROUP WORK (1.20

In groups of two or three, think of at least five routine tasks carried out by a member of an administration department.

Customer service

Employees become involved in customer service if they have any direct contact with the customer. Dealing with customers requires effective systems to handle enquiries and problems efficiently. Businesses wish to learn from any interaction they have with their customers and increasingly businesses keep records of dealings they have had with customers.

> **remember**
>
> Large organisations have very sophisticated distribution systems, with networks of warehouses and transport centres.

Distribution

Distribution deals with the transferring of products from the supplier to the customer. There needs to be an accurate and efficient system in place to monitor the location and the status of all of these movements. Businesses try to keep their distribution costs down and constantly look for more efficient ways of moving products from warehouses to retail outlets or from retail outlets to their customers.

Finance

Businesses need to keep records of all money coming into and leaving the business. These records allow the business to track its finances and assist it in controlling its spending and income levels and, ultimately, calculate whether the business is breaking even, operating at a loss or making a profit.

Human resources

The personnel, or human resource, department deals with the hiring and firing of employees, training, staff welfare, leave and pay. The human resource department maintains records on all members of the workforce, both those working full time and part time. The human resource department has links with all other departments within an organisation and is closely involved in making sure that the workforce is working efficiently and effectively.

IT

Many larger businesses need a dedicated information technology (IT) or computer service department. Responsibilities include hardware, software, and the maintenance of databases, telecommunications and other computer-related equipment within the business.

> **remember**
>
> Marketing is closely linked with research and development and production, but it must always provide support for sales.

Marketing and sales

The main function of the marketing and sales department is to try to identify customer requirements. It also needs to try to predict customer needs in the future. This department may carry out extensive research on a particular market to try to find out exactly what customers want, where they want it, how much they want to pay for it and the best ways in which customers can be told about it.

The sales section ultimately has responsibility for convincing customers to buy the organisation's products and services. The sales section employs experienced members that can answer many of the questions and queries posed and deal with any doubts the customers may have.

Production

The production department is involved in all of the functions related to producing goods or services for the customer. The production department monitors levels of waste to ensure the most efficient use of resources and checks the cost of raw materials and parts purchased to make sure the profit margins are maintained. The production department will also ensure that necessary machinery and equipment are purchased in order to produce products.

Research and development

The main function of the department is not only to design new products and services, but also to work out the most efficient method of producing or offering them.

The department will also randomly test products being manufactured to make sure that they meet quality standards and it will test competitors' products to see whether the organisation's products compare favourably with them. It will also keep a close eye on technological advances to see if design and production processes can be improved.

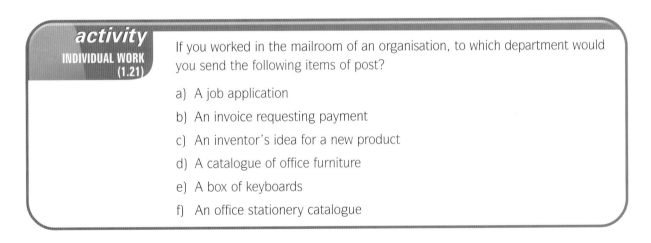

activity
INDIVIDUAL WORK
(1.21)

If you worked in the mailroom of an organisation, to which department would you send the following items of post?

a) A job application

b) An invoice requesting payment

c) An inventor's idea for a new product

d) A catalogue of office furniture

e) A box of keyboards

f) An office stationery catalogue

Relationships between functional areas

Although each part of an organisation has its distinct series of tasks and responsibilities, none of them could function without the support of other parts of the organisation.

An administration department would have little work if there were not other parts of the organisation generating work for it.

Customer services would not have a role had sales not sold products and services to customers.

Sales would often not be able to fulfil the needs of customers if the distribution department could not send out products and information.

All departments rely on production, which makes the products and ensures that there are stocks of the products ready for distribution to customers. But production would not be able to work if research and development had not created new products for it to make.

All parts of the organisation have to work within budgets and need to ensure that they can purchase products and services as they need to, and have a system that logs and monitors any money they have generated for the business. The finance department fulfils this.

The whole organisation is also dependent upon human resources, which will attempt to find ideal candidates for job positions in the departments.

The information flows from one department to another, as well as databases of information, are controlled, maintained and serviced by the IT department.

progress check

1. Give three advantages and three disadvantages of a partnership.
2. What is the difference between being a plc and being Ltd?
3. What is an SME?
4. Give three examples of business activities in each of the following sectors: primary, secondary and tertiary.
5. Give three examples of public sector organisations.
6. Why are less-developed countries more likely to have manufacturing industries?
7. What does expanding market share mean?
8. Why is it important for businesses to establish and maintain relationships with other businesses?
9. What is the role of an administration department in a business?
10. Give three examples of work carried out by human resources.

UNIT 2

Developing Customer Relations

This unit covers:

- how customer service is provided in business
- applying appropriate presentation and interpersonal skills in customer service situations
- how consistent and reliable customer service contributes to customer satisfaction
- how to monitor and evaluate customer service within an organisation

Customer service is the key to successful business. Every business has to deal with customers directly or indirectly. This unit aims to develop your understanding of customer service in different businesses.

Customers have various needs and expectations of the business and these will have to be met. In addition to external customers, businesses also provide a service to other parts of their own business.

Individuals working in customer service must always present themselves professionally and have good communication and interpersonal skills. Customers will expect a reliable and consistent level of service and this unit looks at how to develop those key skills. The unit also looks at how a business will monitor its levels of customer service in order to improve its overall provision.

grading criteria	To achieve a **Pass** grade the evidence must show that the learner is able to:	To achieve a **Merit** grade the evidence must show that the learner is able to:	To achieve a **Distinction** grade the evidence must show that the learner is able to:
	P1 describe three different types of customers and their needs and expectations	**M1** display a confident approach when delivering customer service to customers	**D1** anticipate and meet the needs of three different customers in a range of situations
	P2 demonstrate presentation and interpersonal skills in three different customer service situations	**M2** explain why effective presentation, interpersonal communication skills are important to customer service	**D2** analyse, using examples, how effective customer service benefits the customer, the organisation and the employee

▶

To achieve a **Pass** grade the evidence must show that the learner is able to:	To achieve a **Merit** grade the evidence must show that the learner is able to:	To achieve a **Distinction** grade the evidence must show that the learner is able to:
P3 describe how consistent and reliable customer service contributes to customer satisfaction	**M3** explain how monitoring and evaluating can improve customer service for the customer, the organisation and the employee	
P4 describe how customer service can be monitored and evaluated		

grading criteria

Providing Customer Service in Business

remember

High-quality customer service is now demanded by most customers.

Customer relations have three main parts. The first task is to identify customers; the second is to develop a relationship with those customers. Finally the business organisation must try to hold onto those customers in order to sell them products and services over a long period of time.

More broadly, we can see that customer relations involves a number of different aspects:

- Identifying customers that could be interested in the business's products or services.
- Giving customers good service.
- Allowing customers to buy products in ways that suit them (online or using credit or instalments).
- Making sure customers have all the information they need.
- Supporting the customer and reassuring them that any objections or queries they may have are answered.
- Closing sales efficiently and effectively.
- Following up sales with service and support.
- Contacting existing customers to achieve additional sales.

Customer needs and expectations

Customers need reliable products and services that they can trust, at the price they want to pay and these must be available when and where they want them. These are the basic demands of customers. However, customers require far more than just this, and the business needs to be aware of what else it can offer.

Customer expectations revolve around what is known as customer satisfaction. This means that the business needs to be aware of a customer's needs and expectations and provide products and services in such a way as to meet these demands.

Figure 2.1

What consumers would do to improve their health

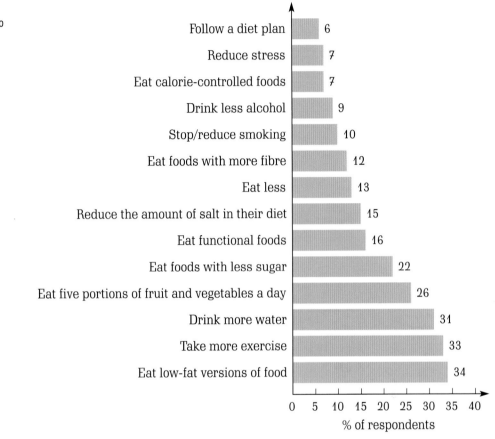

	% of respondents
Follow a diet plan	6
Reduce stress	7
Eat calorie-controlled foods	7
Drink less alcohol	9
Stop/reduce smoking	10
Eat foods with more fibre	12
Eat less	13
Reduce the amount of salt in their diet	15
Eat functional foods	16
Eat foods with less sugar	22
Eat five portions of fruit and vegetables a day	26
Drink more water	31
Take more exercise	33
Eat low-fat versions of food	34

case study

2.1

Good choice – Iceland

In over 600 face-to-face interviews during 2002, consumers were asked what they would do to improve their health.

The challenge for Iceland was to develop a healthy eating range that followed government nutrition guidelines, met customer demand and was still competitive within the marketplace.

The 'Good Choice' range was developed following a carefully written technical policy. In addition to the overall brand policy of allowing no genetically modified (GM) ingredients, artificial colours or flavours, the policy takes into account government advice on nutrition content, nutrition labelling etc. and customer feedback derived from research.

To ensure that nutrition labelling was clear and informative, customer research was carried out to identify what information customers wanted to see and how it should be displayed.

The resulting 'Good Choice' range was launched into stores in January 2002 as Iceland's healthy eating offering. The entire range has been specially developed to be lower in fat and with controlled salt levels. The 'Good Choice' range is the most successful Iceland sub-brand sold to date. The range has doubled in size, and was redeveloped and relaunched in January 2003 to ensure enthusiasm and awareness of the need for healthy eating is maintained.

activity
INDIVIDUAL WORK

Read the case study and answer the following questions:

a) Where would you find information on the government nutrition guidelines?

b) What is meant by 'brand policy'?

c) Why might customers be especially interested in the labelling?

d) What is a 'relaunch design brief'?

Customer service

Before even trying to define customer service, it is wise to define the word 'customer'. A customer is anyone who depends on a business for a product or service. This of course includes the internal customer and also covers long-term customer care.

There are many different definitions of customer service, such as a system organised to provide a continuous link between the time an order is placed and the goods are received with the objective of satisfying customer needs on a long-term basis. This is a little long-winded, but it means that thousands of little actions are performed by an organisation to keep the customer happy.

case study
2.2
Customer needs

AstraZeneca is one of the world's leading pharmaceutical companies. It is clear about its commitment to matching customer needs in this statement:

'Supply and manufacturing
We have around 15 000 people at 30 manufacturing sites in 20 countries dedicated to ensuring that we can deliver a reliable flow of all the products in our range worldwide.

Product strategy and licensing

Our product strategy and licensing organisation, working closely with our R&D community and major marketing companies, leads the commercial aspects of drug development and co-ordinates global product marketing strategy. This includes selecting the right products and projects for investment, developing cost-effective marketing platforms in time for new product launches and directing the creation and delivery of product marketing strategies that successfully align global and national plans.

Sales and marketing

We sell mostly through our own local marketing companies and our products are marketed mainly to physicians and other healthcare professionals. We also explain the economic as well as the therapeutic advantages of our products to governments and healthcare buying groups, such as managed care organisations in the USA.

In the marketing of our medicines, we are committed to ethical behaviour and aim to ensure we communicate information about our products effectively and in a proper manner.'

---

activity
INDIVIDUAL WORK

Read the case study and then answer the following questions:

a) What is meant by cost effective?

b) What is R&D?

c) Why might the way in which the business operates in the UK differ from a developing African country?

d) What is meant by, 'We also explain the economic as well as the therapeutic advantages of our products'?

Value for money

Customers are increasingly aware of the options they have in choosing a business from which to buy products and services. This means that businesses have to monitor the products, services, prices and customer care provided by their competitors. Customers, as we have seen, have become more discerning and more prepared to hunt for a bargain than they have been in the past.

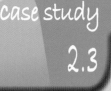

case study 2.3 — Plumbers 'worst value for money'

Plumbers are the worst value for money and provide the worst overall quality of service of any tradesmen, a survey claimed in June 2005.

Builders are seen to be the second-worst group at offering value for money and they are also regarded as the worst timekeepers, followed by plumbers, according to website www.propertyfinder.com.

Builders were rated as providing the second-worst overall service, after plumbers, with electricians in third place followed by painters and decorators.

At the other end of the scale locksmiths were seen as providing the best service, with 48 per cent of people rating them as good or excellent for all three categories, i.e. value for money, quality of service and timekeeping.

activity
INDIVIDUAL WORK

What could a local plumber do to explain to potential customers that the service offered is good value for money?

What other professions do you think offer poor value for money?

Information, assistance, special needs problem solving

In order for a customer to make an informed decision about a purchase, the business needs to provide accurate and reliable information and advice. Obviously, a business would not recommend to a customer that they purchase their products and services elsewhere, even if the products are superior to the ones they offer.

Increasingly, even the most basic products, such as food, have packaging that features important information and advice as to its use and consumption. Many businesses, particularly in the retail sector, provide extensive assistance and help to customers in order to persuade them to purchase products and services.

Although there is legislation to assist special needs or disabled customers to gain access to a business's premises, some businesses have also features such as baby-changing rooms, seating, ramps and even personal shoppers.

The vast majority of retail outlets and other businesses have dedicated customer service areas or departments, whose only role is to liaise with customers and assist them, not just in complaints, but with advice about products and services. This has become an important area of development in many businesses, as a high level of customer service can be seen as a huge advantage over competitors that do not value that aspect of their business to such a great extent.

Targets, health, safety and security

One of the greatest problems in providing customer service is to measure its effectiveness and gauge the impact it has on the profitability of the business. One of the first things that a business will do when setting up a customer service provision is to set a series of targets in dealing with customer complaints and problems. They will have a recommended maximum waiting time for customers; they may have clear instructions to their staff about the exchange of products or the refund of money paid.

With businesses increasingly using customer loyalty cards or store debit cards, a particular organisation is able to see whether a customer problem has led to a decrease in that customer's spending with the business. This would infer that they were not happy with the customer service. Or a business could detect whether the customer was happy with the provision and continued to shop with the organisation.

Although there is legislation to protect customers from hazards when they visit a business's premises, many businesses take this further than is legally required. Above all, customers want a safe and secure shopping environment, and cameras, security staff and special training for shop-floor staff are all designed to assist this, in addition to stopping shoplifting and theft.

---

activity

INDIVIDUAL WORK (2.1)

Visit one of your favourite stores and comment on that store's provision of the following:

a) Information and advice to customers.

b) Facilities for those with special needs.

c) Location and amount of staff on customer service desks.

d) Level of health and safety.

e) Whether there are any hazards in the store.

Internal customers

Not all people work directly with the organisation's external customers. Instead they deal with colleagues, who are their internal customers. Internal customers depend on their colleagues' responsiveness and ability to deliver service to them at the same level as if they were external customers.

It is helpful to think of the customer service network as consisting of a series of inputs and outputs, with one employee at the centre.

Various things get passed to that person (such as information, work tasks and queries) and they in turn pass on work or communications to others in the chain, or straight to the external customer.

Figure 2.2 shows how an employee can list their internal customer network – and what it is that gets passed along the service chain.

Figure 2.2

Inputs and outputs

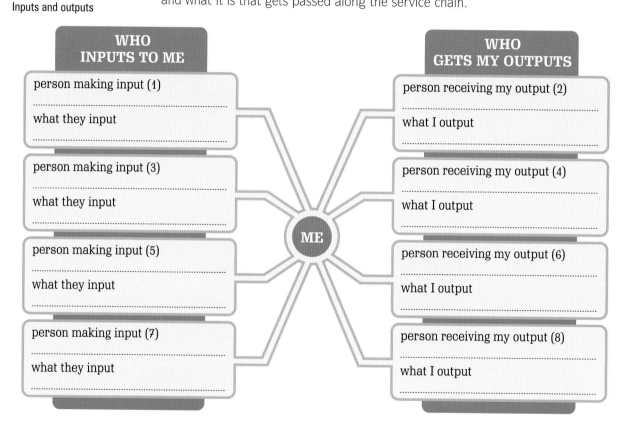

The internal customer chain works when everyone pulls in the same direction and there are no weak links. It all falls down when 'us and them' barriers start to develop, such as:

- Between the sections in a process chain
- Between head office and branches
- Between sales and marketing
- Between marketing and manufacturing.

External customers

A business will try to identify the type of person or business that is most likely to buy its products and services. It does this by attempting to identify the common features, or characteristics, of these customers. Some businesses will focus on age or **gender**, while others will focus on the frequency of the customer's purchases of products or services from the organisation. As we will see, each customer, an individual or a business, has certain attributes that the organisation attempts to identify to help increase sales.

For our purposes we need to identify three distinct sets of customers:

- Normally the term 'customer' can refer to an individual or a business.
- 'Consumers' are usually individual customers, such as people who purchase products from a supermarket.
- The term 'client' is also used to describe customers. It has several different meanings. For example, a professional, such as an accountant or solicitor, would refer to their customers as clients, whether they are other businesses or individuals.

In identifying the type of customer, the business seeks to match its products and services to their expectations as well as designing its advertising and publicity to suit the particular type of customer.

Developing Customer Relations

The terms 'customer', 'client' or 'consumer' are not just restricted to individuals or businesses outside the organisation. Indeed, any customer outside the organisation is referred to as an 'external market'. In other words, they do not have any close association with the business itself; they are merely customers of the business.

Particularly in larger organisations, such as the National Health Service, there is what is known as an 'internal market'. Parts of the organisation deal solely with customers within the organisation itself. An information technology department in a hospital, for example, would be responsible for installing and maintaining computer equipment for the rest of the hospital. It would not have external customers as it does not deal with consumers.

In the same way, other large organisations have specialist departments that just service the needs of other parts of the organisation. For example, administration would deal with routine and non-routine paperwork for the whole of the business. The personnel department would be responsible for recruiting and training all members of staff within an organisation.

For most high-street stores, their primary customer is the retail buyer. As we have seen, they are known as consumers as they are the end users of the products and services sold by the high-street shops.

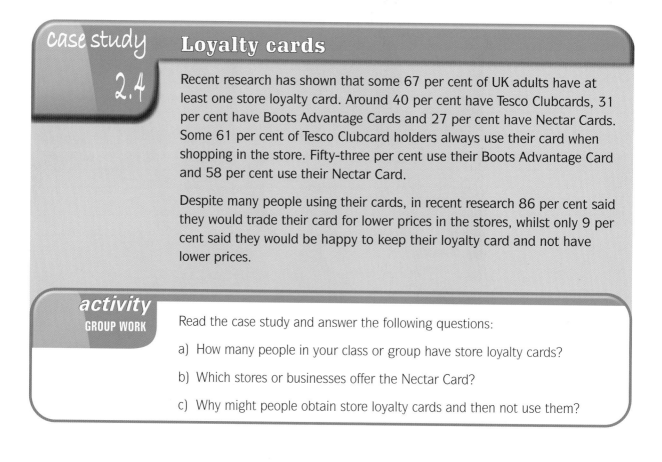

case study 2.4 — Loyalty cards

Recent research has shown that some 67 per cent of UK adults have at least one store loyalty card. Around 40 per cent have Tesco Clubcards, 31 per cent have Boots Advantage Cards and 27 per cent have Nectar Cards. Some 61 per cent of Tesco Clubcard holders always use their card when shopping in the store. Fifty-three per cent use their Boots Advantage Card and 58 per cent use their Nectar Card.

Despite many people using their cards, in recent research 86 per cent said they would trade their card for lower prices in the stores, whilst only 9 per cent said they would be happy to keep their loyalty card and not have lower prices.

activity — GROUP WORK

Read the case study and answer the following questions:

a) How many people in your class or group have store loyalty cards?

b) Which stores or businesses offer the Nectar Card?

c) Why might people obtain store loyalty cards and then not use them?

Customer attributes

An organisation cannot hope to satisfy the needs and wants of all consumers. Organisations segment, or break up, the market into sections which display similar characteristics or behaviour. There are a number of segmentation characteristics that allow an organisation to divide its market into recognisable groups. We will look at market segmentation in much more detail later, but the main segmentation characteristics are described below.

Age

Age is linked to an individual's purchasing power, that is, an individual's ability to independently make a choice and purchase a product or service.

Many products and services are specifically aimed at particular age groups. During children's television on independent networks (not the BBC, which does not carry advertising), the majority of the advertisements are for toys, games, music and food and drink.

The birth rate in the UK has remained relatively stable since the mid 1980s and women tend to live longer than men. Its population of around 60 million gives the UK an average age for men of 35 years and for women 38 years.

> **remember**
>
> Different age groups have different buying needs and available spending.

In pairs, discuss the implications for the following types of business in the following circumstances:

a) Assuming that people are living longer but are still encountering health problems, what might be the problems faced by a private health insurer?

b) If there were fewer teenagers in the country, what would be the implications for further and higher education and the music industry?

Buying patterns

Businesses can rate their customers in terms of the frequency of their purchases of products and services from the business. Regular customers could be described as heavy users of products and services. Customers who purchase fairly regularly could be described as medium users. Customers who are less frequent are often described as light users.

Businesses are also interested in occasional customers and, of course, potential customers who used to buy from the business but no longer do so, or potential customers who have never purchased from the business.

A business will tend to concentrate initially on ensuring that its heavy, medium and light users are retained as loyal customers and, if possible, that the frequency of buying is increased. They will also make attempts to persuade occasional users, or lost customers, to start buying from the business once more.

Most TV advertising is aimed at the broadest possible range of existing or potential customers. As there is so much competition for customers, even loyal customers have to be continually reminded that they are better-off dealing with a business with which they already have a relationship.

Think about TV advertising and why businesses choose to advertise their products and services at such a high cost. Are they advertising to:

a) Attract new customers?

b) Remind existing customers that the products and services they offer are still available?

Family status

Many organisations take the family status of their customers extremely seriously, particularly in the case of consumers as customers. Aside from the fact that around 30 per cent of all births are outside marriage, businesses use what is known as a 'family lifecycle' to describe the characteristics of their customers:

- The lifecycle usually begins when we leave our parents' home and become independent for the first time. Businesses will specifically target these groups, which are interested in fashion, recreation and holidays.

- Once we are married or with a partner, possibly with two incomes but no children, setting up a home is the most important concern and these types of customer are interested in buying household items.

- Once children become part of the family, we tend to borrow more money on credit, purchasing necessities rather than luxuries.

- As the children grow older, parents tend to go back to work and, as there is more money in the household, holidays and luxuries become affordable.

- When the children have left the family home, parents may become interested in travel, recreation and home improvements.

- When one of the partners is left alone, hobbies become important, as do health matters.

Gender

There are huge differences between the buying patterns of women and men.

Some businesses and organisations specifically target their products and services to appeal to a particular gender. Some products are specifically designed for a single gender, such as clothes, shoes and cosmetics. Other products could equally be used, and indeed are used, by both genders, but they have been advertised to appeal to one sex or the other. For example, some cars can be considered to be women's cars and their advertising is designed to reflect this.

activity
GROUP WORK
(2.4)

a) Try to think of at least five products or services that could be used by either gender but are specifically aimed at appealing to just one gender.

b) Think of five products that are specifically aimed at females and five others that are specifically aimed at males.

Customers with special needs

As we saw when we looked at different types of customers, some may have special needs, including people who have:

- A disability or who use a wheelchair
- A visual or hearing impairment
- Literacy or numeracy difficulties
- Small children
- A first language which is not English.

Many larger stores deal with all of these different types of customer with special needs, but others have to deal with the situation as and when it arises.

Benefits to the customer, organisation and employee

As we have seen, businesses want to respond to customer needs. They also want to encourage new customers. It is vital that the business has a good image as far as existing customers and potential customers are concerned. Obviously, businesses do not just have customer services for the benefit of their customers. They know that good customer service will be beneficial to themselves.

The first key benefit to good customer service is increased sales. Businesses need to generate enough money to pay their staff (which is obviously a benefit to the employees), they need to buy equipment and stock (which will be a benefit to the business, employees and customers), and make a profit (which will benefit the owners of the organisation).

Another key benefit to an organisation of having effective customer service provision is that customers will be happy. If they are happy they will continue to use the business and buy products and services from it. This is known as repeat business. The organisation wants the customers to keep coming back and to recommend them to their friends and family.

Many businesses spend a huge amount of money on advertising in order not only to tell customers about their products and services, but also to put across a positive and strong public image. They want customers to believe that their products and services are reliable, are value for money, and are safe and healthy, as well as providing a host of other features.

activity
GROUP WORK
(2.5)

Can you think of any businesses, either national or local, which have a bad reputation for having poor customer service? Do you have personal experience or is this something you have heard about from friends or family? Does it affect your decision whether to buy products or services from that business?

Appropriate Presentation and Interpersonal Skills in Customer Service Situations

For all organisations whose employees have direct contact with their customers, it is important that the staff look presentable. If they wish to represent a company in the best way, employees must think about the following:

- The way they dress for work.
- Their personal hygiene.
- The way they behave when they are at work.

- Their personality – whether they are often grumpy or sometimes a bit too loud.

- Their general attitude when they are at work – whether they look as if they are approachable and how they treat other people.

activity

INDIVIDUAL WORK (2.6)

Look at the list above. Why do you think all of these considerations are important? Give reasons for your answers.

Presentation

Some people are fortunate enough to be issued with a uniform that they have to wear for work. This may not seem very fortunate to you, but once you start work you will realise just how important it is that you dress in the right way.

Uniforms are issued by some organisations for a number of reasons:

- They form part of the company image, in that the uniforms may have the company logo printed on them.

- Employees will always be easy for the customer to find because they will all be wearing the same clothes.

- It means that companies do not have to pay their employees an allowance for their work clothing.
- All employees will turn up for work in the appropriate clothes and, hopefully, they will all look smart and well presented.

If an individual does not work for an organisation that issues a uniform then they will be expected to dress in clothes appropriate for the job. This means as smartly and as tidily as possible. Very often organisations insist on certain dress codes. These are rules about what can or cannot be worn for work. Some of them are based on health and safety factors:

- Long hair needs to be tied back if the job involves working with food.
- No nail varnish can be worn when food is being handled or prepared.
- Dangling jewellery should not be worn in case it gets tangled in equipment or machinery.
- Those who use certain machinery have to wear safety equipment like hard hats, goggles or waterproof clothing.

As well as health and safety clothing, sometimes organisations insist that their employees wear name tags on their clothing or wear their pass. These name tags and passes are worn for security reasons in an attempt to ensure that only authorised people enter certain areas of the organisation.

What is chosen to wear for work very much depends on the job being done. For instance:

- Some organisations insist that male employees wear a collar and tie to work.
- Some organisations do not allow their female employees to wear trousers.

---

activity
INDIVIDUAL WORK
(2.7)

Visit two or three local organisations. Note what the staff at each of these organisations is wearing. Do you think they are issued with a uniform? Is it easy to recognise who the employees of the organisation are?

Now write down what you think are the advantages and disadvantages to an individual who has to wear a uniform for work. Perhaps a member of your family or a friend has to wear a uniform. If so, ask them what they think the advantages and disadvantages are.

Whatever clothes are worn for work, they should always be clean. It would be useless for an organisation to give its employees a uniform to wear if they arrived for work with stains on their trousers or tops.

Presentation skills

There are a number of important things to consider when having a face-to-face conversation or talking on the telephone (both are forms of verbal communication). You need to consider:

- The way you speak, for example whether you make yourself clear or whether you use slang during your conversation.
- The pitch and tone of your voice.
- The way you listen and pay attention to what is being said.
- When not to speak or interrupt.
- What questions to ask.
- Body language – this can give someone who can see you an idea of what you are thinking. Body language can also help you to explain something.

Body language is very important in face-to-face communication. When having face-to-face communication with people, a mixture of verbal (spoken) and non-verbal (body language) communication is used. There are two considerations:

- Being able to read other people's body language.
- Being aware that the other person can read your body language.

Listening is important in both face-to-face communication and for telephone calls. It is a good idea to take notes during a conversation with a customer. This helps you to remember what has been said.

activity
**GROUP WORK
(2.8)**

How good are you at reading body language? Sit opposite a partner and see if you can show different feelings just by the expression on your face. Try showing each other the following expressions, but do not use any words:

- Anger
- Annoyance
- Shock
- Boredom
- Happiness
- Polite smiling
- Disapproval
- Fear
- Irritation

Non-verbal communication is body language. The key points of body language are:

- Facial expressions – these are the most common form of body language and we should always be aware of what our face is telling someone else.
- Gestures – we use our head and hands a lot when we agree or disagree with something.
- Posture (the way we sit or stand) – this can also tell others a lot about what we are thinking or how we are reacting to someone else.
- How close you get to other people – apart from shaking hands, we do not often get close to people we meet at work. Most people have an invisible circle around them that they prefer others not to enter. This means that they may feel uncomfortable if others get too close to them. Getting too close to someone else's face can be a sign of aggression.

- Whether you are sitting or standing – someone who is seated and having a conversation with a person who is standing up can often feel 'lower' in importance than the person standing.

- Eye contact – it is important to have eye contact with the person you are talking to. Eye contact shows the other person that you are giving them your fell attention and often helps them to understand what is being said. Sometimes it is possible to get a better idea of how someone is going to react by looking into their eyes. Be careful not to 'stare' into someone's eyes as this can be a sign of aggression.

activity
GROUP WORK (2.9)

In pairs, take it in turns to sit on your hands and describe to your partner the shape of a spiral staircase. How hard was it to describe without the use of your hands? What happened to your head?

remember

An employee's contact with a customer is often the only personal impression a customer will have of the business.

Interpersonal skills

Interpersonal skills refer to your ability to interact with other people. Some situations will require you to behave in a particular way. You may need to be formal and professional, you may need to be helpful or you may need to show your understanding of a situation, so that you give another person confidence.

Many employers look for employees that fit into their particular way of working. You will need to have good interpersonal skills if you are expected to work as a member of a team or have daily contact with customers or visitors to the organisation. Businesses lay down the kind of way in which they expect you to behave in all of these types of situation. They will look for a person with a positive and helpful attitude towards work and they will expect you to behave in a professional manner while at work.

Just like meeting someone for the first time in your social life, at work you get an immediate impression of what a person may or may not be like. Customers can be won or lost by their first impressions of an employee in a business.

An important part of customer service is training employees to deal effectively and courteously with customers. The training programmes used tend to focus on the following:

- Greeting customers
- Courtesy
- Confidence
- Concern
- Interest
- Thoughtfulness.

There are, of course, many different types of customer, but businesses insist that all customers are of equal value, regardless of how much they are spending. You will also have to deal with customers whose behaviour can be somewhat challenging. There are a number of different types of challenging behaviour, including the following:

■ Aggressive or angry customers

■ Customers with language difficulties.

This means that in dealing with customers in a service situation you will often have to use tact and discretion. The customer needs to be assured that you know what you are doing and that you intend to deal with the situation and not simply to ignore them.

Most businesses have set procedures and these should be explained to the customer. Regardless of the attitude of the customer, you should always endeavour to be as efficient as possible and to keep any promises made.

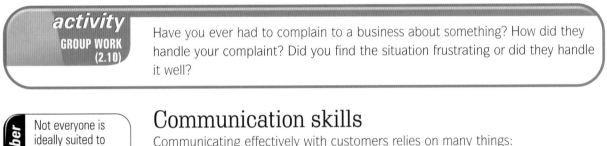

activity
**GROUP WORK
(2.10)**

Have you ever had to complain to a business about something? How did they handle your complaint? Did you find the situation frustrating or did they handle it well?

remember

Not everyone is ideally suited to face-to-face communication with customers.

Communication skills

Communicating effectively with customers relies on many things:

■ How promptly you deal with customers

■ The tone or manner with which you deal with customers

■ The message which you give to customers

■ Your non-verbal (body language) signals

■ Your listening skills

■ Your ability to understand the customers' body language

■ Your ability to deal with problems as they arise.

activity
**INDIVIDUAL WORK
(2.11)**

Your communicating skills can very much depend on how comfortable you feel dealing with people. Table 2.1 gives some examples of strengths and weaknesses that you may or may not have. Which are your strengths and which are your weaknesses? What can you do to improve on your strengths or deal with any weaknesses?

Developing Customer Relations

Table 2.1 Strengths and weaknesses

Strengths	Weaknesses
You like dealing with people	You are moody
You are patient	You do not like being interrupted
You can always find the right words	You are impatient
You are tactful	You are quite tactless
You are aware of others' feelings	You are rather shy
You are a good listener	You think customers are a nuisance and are often stupid
You like to help people	You think dealing with customers is simply hard work
You realise people have different views	You have never met a customer who is right

Just as each employee is different, so is each customer, and while there is no foolproof way of dealing with every customer, the following list suggests some ways of using your verbal and non-verbal communication skills to the best effect:

■ Always approach the customer with either a smile or a greeting, depending on whether you are face to face or on the telephone.

■ Try to build a good relationship with the customer from the beginning by looking at their body language or listening to them.

■ Make sure you have listened to and remembered what the customer has said.

■ When giving customers information, be confident and accurate.

■ Do not make promises that you cannot keep.

■ Be aware that the customer is getting a mental image of you from your voice and body language.

■ Find out what the customer actually wants rather than assuming you already know what they want.

■ If you need to take more time than usual in dealing with a customer, this is acceptable.

Body language can send various messages to the customer. You should always remember the following:

■ Turn your whole body towards the customer and not just your head when you are speaking to them. This shows you are interested in what they are saying.

■ Make eye contact with the customer. It shows that you are genuinely interested in what they are saying and are being honest with them.

■ Do not show signs that you are frustrated or bored, for example by fiddling with a pen or tapping your feet.

■ Stand, or sit up straight – it shows that you are confident.

■ Nod your head at appropriate points while the customer is talking to show that you are concentrating on what they are saying.

Communication situations

You create a huge impression on people whenever you communicate with them – from a memo to a colleague, to a phone call to or from a customer. There is a simple rule to follow: how would you feel if you had received the message?

In written communications always make sure your name and contact details (address, phone, fax, email) are included in any letter/fax/email. You should check them for content and accuracy. Once you have done this check the spelling and grammar. Now check the tone. Always remember that you should be concise but polite.

When you make a telephone call or talk to a person face to face, remember the following:

■ Always let the other person know who you are and where you are from.

■ Make sure you get through, or speak, to the right person.

■ It is reasonable to check if they have time to talk to you.

■ Make sure you repeat any important information you give or receive; this will help to avoid mistakes and confusion.

■ Always be polite.

Training programmes try to prepare employees for most situations, but not all situations can be predicted.

Situations when you are called on to deal with other people (whether they are colleagues, customers, supervisors or others) can be described as falling into one (or more) of the following categories:

- Urgent – a situation which needs to be dealt with immediately and you should stop what you are doing and get on with it.

- Non-urgent – something that will need to be remembered and done at a later date, but should not interfere with what you are doing at the moment.

- Difficult – a complex or awkward situation which may be urgent or non-urgent, it will need time and concentration and you may need help with it.

- Routine – a standard situation that you have coped with several times already, it may be urgent or non-urgent, but it will not present you with any particular problems.

Contributing to Customer Satisfaction

Customers usually need the desired products and services, in the quantity required, at the time they choose and at a competitive price.

Consistency and reliability

Most individuals working directly with customers will need to have a wide range of skills in order to handle the various aspects of customer service effectively. They will need to effectively handle customer requests, receive orders and identify and resolve problems. They will also need to meet the needs of customers in a courteous and professional manner. Typical duties, or the scope of a job role would include:

> **remember**
> Customers will expect a consistent, high standard of service.

- Effectively handling customer interactions by greeting the customer properly, evaluating inquiries, providing appropriate assistance, processing orders accurately, and following through to ensure customer needs are met in a complete, timely and effective manner.

- Identifying, recording and resolving customer complaints or problems and following up with the customer to ensure appropriate action was taken and that the issue is resolved to the customer's satisfaction.

- Managing customer communications efficiently, ensuring customer communications are recorded and processed in a timely and effective manner and are handled in accordance with company standards.

- Using selling opportunities through knowledge of the product line.

- Filing and recording all sales order transactions to maintain accurate customer records through completion of appropriate documentation and input to computer systems. Assisting customers as well as providing support for questions regarding products and services as required.

- Working with colleagues and other departments, keeping appropriate individuals informed to ensure positive customer relations are maintained.

- Successfully completing customer service training and attending required meetings.
- Maintain a good working relationship with suppliers, resolving issues as required.

activity
**INDIVIDUAL WORK
(2.12)**

Look on the back page of your local newspaper or in a national newspaper for advertisements for sales and customer service staff. Many of them will have website links with a fuller description of the required role. Draw up a shortlist of main duties of the various job roles.

Not all businesses have directly accessible customer service staff and prefer to provide their customer service help either online or via a freephone or low-cost telephone number. Businesses have realised that customers require assistance outside normal working hours and in many respects telephone services and online help provide 24-hour cover for customer service. The purpose of a reliable and consistent customer service provision is to provide accessible assistance to customers, regardless of when they need that help. This obviously has cost implications for the business and this is why frontline staff are primarily used for sales, and customer service assistance is usually off-site.

However, many businesses with high-volume customers do have customer service desks. As they will be required to provide information and help straightaway, these individuals need to be given sufficient training and possess a good level of understanding of the business's procedures as well as a good working knowledge of the products and services sold. They also need to be able to work under pressure, as it is difficult to judge how many customers will need help on a given day.

Whether the customer service is provided face to face, over the telephone or via the Internet, it needs to meet the specific needs of the customer. Any promises, such as the provision of follow-up information, or any other aspect of the query need to be confirmed with the customer. If a customer is promised something then it needs to be delivered when and how it was promised.

Businesses will monitor their customer service to ensure that it is always consistent and reliable. Some businesses use employees or outside agents to make calls to their customer service department in order to monitor the way in which their 'problem' has been handled.

link

Monitoring is dealt with in more detail on page 67.

Customer satisfaction

Research shows that a 5 per cent increase in customer loyalty can boost profits by 25 per cent to 85 per cent. Research has also revealed that satisfied clients lead to greater profitability and growth. To excel in today's competitive marketplace, organisations must create positive experiences for customers with each and every interaction.

remember

Most businesses make 80 per cent of their profit from 20 per cent of their best and most loyal customers.

There is a general acceptance in today's business environment that customer service and customer satisfaction are key elements for success. Customers are promised great service by advertising campaigns, so expectations are high.

I'm sorry, but I don't think there will be any left if you come back later

Confidence, expectations and value for money

As we have already seen, customer satisfaction has many key advantages, both to the business and to the customers. If a business can establish a reputation for high levels of customer service then it can hope to ensure that customers are not merely satisfied, but delighted and amazed at the level of service they receive from the business.

A business will always strive to exceed its customers' expectations of it, such as having a no-quibble refund policy (such as Marks & Spencer) or trying to source Fair Trade products from abroad as standard (such as the Co-Op).

activity
GROUP WORK
(2.13)

Can you suggest local businesses that are more expensive than others? What factors exist to allow them to charge more? Is their customer service better?

remember

It is difficult to build a good reputation, but it is even harder to rebuild a reputation that has been damaged.

Reputation

As a business builds up its customer base, the hope is that it will begin to achieve a reputation for high-quality products, services, staff and customer service. A business stands and falls on its reputation and the last thing that it wants is to be associated with poor-quality service. The worst examples of poor service can be seen on the BBC's consumer television programme *Watchdog*, but everyday customers have problems with organisations and report them to local Trading Standards (run by the local government to investigate customer complaints). As far as businesses are concerned, good news travels fast but bad news travels faster. They cannot afford for it to be known that they provide poor-quality service. If they fail to sort out a problem then their reputation will suffer.

activity

GROUP WORK
(2.14)

Is there a local business with a poor reputation? What do people think of the business and what should the business have done to improve their reputation?

Internal customer satisfaction

Internal customer satisfaction is the extent to which internal services meet the needs of employees within an organisation. Some organisations use satisfaction surveys to measure the importance of each service to internal customers, how well each service meets internal customers' needs, and what aspect of each service most needs to be improved.

One of the key problems in establishing and maintaining internal customer satisfaction is poor communication in the organisation. Here are some of the effects of poor communication:

- It decreases confidence and mutual trust in one another.
- It deters the staff from revealing important information.
- It causes significant employee distress.
- It leads to the employee not seeking further help.
- It leads to misunderstandings.
- It leads to the misinterpretation of advice.
- It underlies most employee complaints.

Codes of practice

Codes of practice and agreed levels of customer service provision are recommended, either in a specific business, an industry or, perhaps, a profession, such as dentistry. Codes of practice set down minimum standards of customer service to which all customers are entitled. These codes of practice have been agreed either by the business itself or by several businesses in a particular industry. They impose these codes of practice over and above what may be required of them by law.

Codes of practice may be detailed or sketchy, but they will seek to identify the ways in which the business and its employees deal with customers in every interaction they may have with them. Some businesses, particularly those related to health or professional services, will also have minimum ethical standards. This means that the quality of service must be true, fair and impartial and that customers should be given an opportunity to consider purchasing the products or services with the maximum amount of information and assistance.

Sample code of practice

Telephone contact
Before answering the phone ensure you are focussed on the call, you have pen and paper to hand and, where possible and/or appropriate, that you are logged into the customer record and product database systems.

Verbal handshake
Introduce yourself.

If it is not a convenient moment to take a call, e.g. you are in a meeting, take the caller's name and number and offer to ring them back stating the approximate time you intend to do so.

Getting the message
Control the call, establish who the caller is and where they are calling from (if they have not already told you), ascertain whether you can deal with their enquiry.

Correspondence
Letters/faxes from individuals:

Aim to reply within three working days.

If this is not possible acknowledge receipt of the letter within two days and notify the sender as to when they will receive a full reply to their enquiry.

Letters/faxes from other businesses:
As above, but aim to reply within five working days. If this is not possible acknowledge receipt within two days as above.

If you know in advance that you will be away from work for a period of more than five working days make appropriate arrangements for your post to be checked in your absence.

Emails
Aim to reply within three working days. If this is not possible acknowledge receipt of the message within two days and notify the sender as to when they will receive a full reply to their enquiry.

Personal contact
Ensure that you can give the person concerned your full attention.

Give a friendly greeting. A smile is always appreciated.

Remember to maintain eye contact. Speak clearly, this is especially important in the case of international customers. Be polite. Give a realistic timescale for any response requested.

activity

INDIVIDUAL WORK

What do you think of this customer care code of practice? What kind of organisation would need a code of practice like this? Try to convert the code of practice to suit a retail store.

Monitoring and Evaluating Customer Service Within an Organisation

Many organisations set up their customer service provision as a direct result of experiences they have had with customers. They can only base their systems on what they know and cater for the most common problems that customers may present to them.

They also need to make sure that the customer service provision not only maintains its high standards but is also adaptable and can be improved on a number of different levels as and when required.

Monitoring

The first aspect in ensuring that customer service remains efficient and effective is to set up monitoring systems. The purpose of the monitoring systems is to pick up problems as well as customer perceptions of the customer service provision.

The first and perhaps least efficient way of doing this is to rely on informal customer feedback. This means taking note of comments that customers make in relation to the customer service they receive. This is not a terribly good way of obtaining objective information about customer service as only the most vocal customers will comment.

keyword

Guarantees
– There are usually given free of charge by the manufacturer of a product, guaranteeing to the customer that the product will work for a set period of time.

keyword

Warranties
– These are similar to guarantees, but normally the customer pays for the extra protection. They are often known as extended warranties or insurance policies against repair and replacement costs.

A more structured way of collecting information is the use of customer questionnaires and comment cards. These are now widely used and certain customer service questions are even included on **guarantees** and **warranties**. They will ask customers various questions concerning customer services, such as the politeness of staff, their helpfulness and whether a situation was resolved to their satisfaction. The only problem with these types of questionnaire and comment card is the number of them completed by customers. They will need to be looked at in some detail and the results collated in order to be of any particular use to the business.

Staff can also provide useful feedback for monitoring and evaluating customer service. They can identify problem areas and most common complaints from customers. If taken together with customer feedback, questionnaires or comment cards, these can provide a good indication of how the customer service provision is working in practice.

As already mentioned, some businesses use 'mystery customers'. These are individuals unknown to the business and its employees. They will test the customer service provision by pretending to be a customer with a specific customer service problem. They will provide a report on how they were treated and whether they were satisfied with the level of help they received. This can prove to be a useful double check for the business, particularly if it has just changed the way in which it carries out customer services.

The final way of monitoring and evaluating customer service is to examine the number and nature of complaints or compliments received, either verbally or in writing from customers. Many businesses pin up their compliment letters, but hide those that contain complaints.

The complaints or compliments will probably contain detailed information about the transaction and use of customer service. How these were responded to can provide the business with useful case-study material with which to train its staff.

---

activity
GROUP WORK (2.15)

Have you ever completed a customer questionnaire or comment card? What kind of information did it ask for? How much importance do you think the business places on the information it receives in this way?

---

remember

New customers are always welcome as far as a business is concerned, but the business makes far more profit from repeat customers.

Evaluating

There are several different ways in which a business can evaluate its customer service provision. These are in addition to the regular feedback, comments and other information gained from actually carrying out customer service. A business can evaluate its customer service using some of the following methods:

- Level of sales – a steady or increasing level of sales would indicate that customers are happy overall with the customer service they are receiving from the business. Businesses would also take account of the number of products that have been returned faulty compared with the number of those products sold.

- Repeat customers – as we have already seen in this unit, repeat customers are of enormous importance to a business. Loyal customers provide the bulk of the profits for the business and retaining these customers not only increases sales, but also profitability.

- New customers – there are a number of different ways in which new customers could come to the organisation. Perhaps they are responding to advertising, but many purchase from the business for the first time as a result of recommendations. Once these customers have made their first purchase the business will want to ensure that they become repeat customers.

- Level of complaints/compliments – businesses want to minimise the number of complaints whilst increasing the number of compliments. It is rare for businesses to receive many written complaints or compliments, so for the most part these are not a great way of evaluating customer service.

■ Staff turnover – experienced and reliable staff are of great importance to any business. Continued problems with customers can force employees to look for work elsewhere. Staff become tired and frustrated if they are constantly dealing with problems and complaints from customers.

Draw up a list of 10 businesses in your local area. Ask at least 20 people whether they are regular or irregular customers of those businesses. Have they ever needed to complain? Have they ever complimented the business?

Improvements

By continually monitoring and evaluating customer service, a business will hope to make steady improvements. A business will try to ensure that its levels of service, products and services remain good value for money and that its overall package provides a reliable service to its customers.

If a business can achieve this then there are a number of key improvements that can be made to the business overall:

■ By improving customer service they will retain existing customers.

■ By improving customer service it will retain experienced, valuable members of staff.

■ As its customer service excellence becomes known the business will attract new customers.

■ This means that the business will sell more products and services, increasing its turnover.

■ The result of this is that the business will probably become more profitable and will almost certainly employ more staff.

■ If the business is doing well then it will be able to respond to its legal obligations quickly and exceed the requirements of law.

■ Finally, as the numbers of customers increase, staff numbers may increase, and as turnover increases, profitability will also increase. The opportunity to continually improve is therefore always in sight.

Try to identify a business in your local area that has gradually improved the overall look of its retail outlet. This may be a local business rather than a national chain as national chains tend to have a high level of investment when they first open.

Write a list of reasons why you think the overall look has improved for both staff and customers.

progress check

1. What are the three primary aspects of customer service?
2. What do you understand by the term 'value for money'?
3. Give three reasons why uniforms might be issued to employees.
4. Why might it be inappropriate to wear dangling jewellery at work?
5. How important would a non-urgent, routine task be? Give an example of such a task.
6. What are the alternatives to having in-store staff dealing with customer service?
7. How can customer loyalty increase profits?
8. Why is internal customer satisfaction important?
9. Why might profitable businesses be able to employ more staff?
10. If a business was suffering from a falling level of sales, what might be wrong with its customer service provision?

UNIT 3

Investigating Financial Control

This unit covers:

- the costs, revenue and profit for a business operation
- how businesses use break even analysis
- preparing a cash flow forecast
- how budgets are used for planning and monitoring business finances
- ways of recording financial transactions

Most but not all businesses are created to generate money. Businesses look for opportunities to expand into areas where they can make more money. In this unit we look at the ways in which businesses attempt to keep their costs as low as possible in order to generate the most profit.

This unit looks at costs and ways in which a business generates money, or revenue. The unit also looks at the concept of break even, which illustrates to the business what level of products or services need to be sold in order to cover all of their costs.

The unit looks at the use of budgets and how a business can try to control spending. Finally the unit looks at how the business monitors and records financial transactions and how this helps it to be alert to potential fraud.

grading criteria

To achieve a **Pass** grade the evidence must show that the learner is able to:	To achieve a **Merit** grade the evidence must show that the learner is able to:	To achieve a **Distinction** grade the evidence must show that the learner is able to:
P1 describe, using examples, the importance of costs, revenue and profit for a business organisation	**M1** demonstrate the impact of changing cost and revenue data on the break even point of a selected business	**D1** evaluate how cash flows and financial recording systems can contribute to managing business finances
P2 calculate break even using given data to show the level at which income equals expenditure	**M2** analyse the implications of regular and irregular cash inflows and outflows for a business organisation	

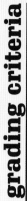

UNIT 3

grading criteria

Costs, Revenue and Profit

<table>
<tr><td>

keyword

Revenue – The income received by a business in exchange for selling its products and services.

</td></tr>
</table>

Profit is the difference between the selling price and the production cost. Product costs include not only the cost of manufacturing a product, but also all the other costs incurred in the process of producing or delivering a product or service.

A business reaches the break even point when its total **revenue** equals the total costs. Break even graphs are used to illustrate the total costs and the total revenue. At the point when the two lines cross, the business is said to have broken even. Businesses will use break even analysis to calculate the level of sales that are needed to break even. A business can use this information to work out the impact of a change in price or the level of sales needed to cover a new bank loan.

As we will see later in this unit, break even graphs are also used to work out what is known as the margin of safety. This is the amount by which demand can fall before the business starts to make a loss instead of a profit.

Business costs

<table>
<tr><td>

keyword

Opportunity cost – The true cost of something when measured in forms of what you have to forego (forfeit) in order to get it.

</td></tr>
</table>

There are two main ways of looking at costs, the most common being the accountant's view, which considers the value of the resources used by a business in order to operate. The alternative is known as **opportunity cost**. This can be a confusing term as it refers to the impact on a business if it chooses one alternative over another, meaning it cannot afford to do both. For example, the business might decide to go ahead with the purchase of replacement vans but will therefore 'forego' the advantages of being able to open a new store.

activity
INDIVIDUAL WORK (3.1)

Thould and Thornes Ltd estimates that its £34 products cost it £17, including all costs, and that its £35 products cost it £18. Which of the two types of product are more profitable for the business?

In order to work out the total cost to a business of supplying products and services, we need to investigate three key types of cost: fixed cost, variable cost and semi-variable cost. These different types of cost will be used below when we consider break even.

Fixed costs are costs that do not change, regardless of how many products or services the business is either producing or supplying. Typical fixed costs include rent or rates, both of which may have to be paid either monthly or yearly.

activity
INDIVIDUAL WORK (3.2)

Thould and Thornes Ltd pays £42 000 in rent per year and its rates are £12 000 per year. What is their monthly fixed cost for these two items?

Obviously, as the costs for these items are fixed they do not increase or decrease. This means that if the business makes better use of their facilities and either produce more products or provide more services, then the importance of these fixed costs is reduced. The same is true if the business is not as busy; they still have to cover the fixed costs.

Although we have said that fixed costs do not change, they do over a period of time. Rent and rates may increase each year, but since the business is only interested in the costs in the year in question, they are classed as being fixed as far as calculations are concerned.

activity
INDIVIDUAL WORK (3.3)

In Activity 3.2 you calculated Thould and Thornes' total fixed costs. If they sell 5000 units at £34 and 5000 units at £35, how much of the fixed costs are applied to each unit sold?

> **Output**
> – The total number of products or services produced or offered by a business in a given period of time.

keyword

Variable costs change directly in response to the **output** of a business. These costs include labour, fuel and raw materials. The more the business is producing, the greater these costs will be. Any change that increases output would increase variable costs, whereas any decrease in output would reduce variable costs.

If a business estimated that the costs to produce a particular product were £8 per unit and it produces 100 000 units in a year, then the variable costs associated with that level of output would be £800 000. If it doubled production and the costs remained the same per unit, then its variable costs would also double to £1.6 million per year.

The variable costs are not like the fixed costs because they can also be described as being direct costs. Direct costs are costs to the business that are closely associated with the production of a product itself. It is also usually the case that if a business is able to increase its output, its variable costs per unit reduce.

Before a business can work out its potential savings as a result of increasing output, it will usually assume that a 20 per cent increase in output would cost it, at least in the short term, a 20 per cent increase in their variable costs. Working things out on this basis is a far safer way to plan ahead than assuming that savings will be made.

activity

INDIVIDUAL WORK (3.4)

Thould and Thornes Ltd produces its own range of perfumes, which it sells at £34 each. Currently it produces around 2000 bottles per year. It has been told by its supplier that if it were to produce 3000 bottles per year, the current price of £9 per unit, which they pay the supplier, would be reduced by 20 per cent.

Calculate the current variable cost paid to the supplier based on 2000 bottles and the new variable cost based on the 20 per cent discount. What is the individual unit variable cost and what is the total variable cost in both cases?

remember

Semi-variable costs are dependent on how much something is used.

Not all costs fit into the fixed or variable categories. A business that offers home deliveries can class the cost of a van as a fixed cost. No matter how much the van is used by the business, it will still have to insure it and pay for its road tax. If the van is used more often, then it will be serviced more often, have more wear and tear, and use more fuel. In this situation the van can actually be classed as a semi-variable cost, as its exact cost is dependent on how much it is used.

Now that we have considered the main types of cost, it is possible to calculate total costs. Remember that total costs have enormous implications for the business in terms of its profits.

activity

INDIVIDUAL WORK (3.5)

Table 3.1 details the fixed and variable costs of a business producing springs at various levels of output. Make a copy of the table. In each case, work out the total cost and the cost per spring at different levels of output.

Table 3.1 Fixed and variable costs of Bert Sringer Springs Ltd at various levels of output

Level of output	Fixed costs (£)	Variable costs (£)	Total costs (£)	Costs per spring (£)
100 000	50 000	5 000		
150 000	50 000	7 000		
200 000	50 000	9 000		
250 000	50 000	11 000		
300 000	50 000	13 000		
350 000	50 000	15 000		
400 000	50 000	17 000		
450 000	50 000	19 000		
500 000	50 000	21 000		

Revenue

The revenue of a business is, basically, the income from its operations. It is important for the business to make the gap between costs and revenue as wide as possible as the greater the difference, the greater the level of profit.

In order to estimate the sales revenue, the business will estimate the number of products and services it might sell in the coming year. It can then work out the average selling price of its products and services and then multiply the estimated number of sales by this figure. The total revenue estimate uses the following formula:

Sales revenue = Estimated number of products and services sold × average selling price of the products and services

If a business estimates that it will sell 10 000 products in the coming year and that the average selling price is £19.99, then the calculation is:

Sales revenue = 10,000 × £19.99 = £199 990

> **remember**
> Sales revenue is equal to the number of products sold multiplied by the average selling price.

activity
INDIVIDUAL WORK (3.6)

Thould and Thornes Ltd sells high-price perfumes and aftershave lotions. In an average year it sells around 10 000 products at an average price of £34.50. What is its estimated sales revenue for the next financial year?

Even when the business is working out the true sales revenue for a year, the two key figures (costs and revenues) remain the same. For any business, the improvement in its sales revenue rests on these two factors. A business can either sell more products and services or it can sell its products and services at a higher price.

Thould and Thornes Ltd, as we have seen, sells around 10 000 products per year at an average price of £34.50. In actual fact, it sells 5000 products for £34 per year and 5000 for £35.

a) If it were to increase the price from £34 to £36 and from £35 to £38, what would be its new total revenue figure?

b) If it were to drop the prices from £34 to £32 and sell 6000 products, and from £35 to £33 and sell 6000 products, how would this affect its total revenue figure?

c) As an independent adviser, which of the two strategies would you recommend to the business?

Calculating gross and net profit

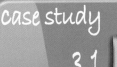

Profit is equal to the total revenue less the total costs.

Profit, for commercial businesses, is the most important consideration. It is relatively simple to calculate, as all that is needed is the total revenue (income) of the business and their total costs. The basic formula is:

Profit = Total revenue – Total costs

For example, if a business made £100 000 in sales this would be its total revenue. If the cost of running the business was £80 000, then this would represent the total costs. The profit would be calculated by subtracting the total costs from the total revenue, which would leave the business with a £20 000 profit.

Heritage sites fail to break even

In 2004, only nine of the 68 properties and historic buildings open to the public and staffed by the National Trust for Scotland were operating at a profit.

In 2001, the Trust began reforms to contain a cash crisis and stem falling visitor numbers, which had resulted in a deficit of some £2.5 million.

The reforms have already reduced the gap between operating costs and income from the low of £2.5 million to just over £500 000, with expectations that it will be out of the red by 2007.

A spokesperson for the Trust said: 'Of course, we have to remember that the trust is a charity and not a commercial organisation – clearly it would be unrealistic to expect all our properties to run at a surplus or even to break even. However, even a charity must operate in a financially prudent way.'

Read the case study about heritage sites and answer the following questions:

a) What do you understand by the term 'deficit'?

b) What do you understand by the term 'operating profit'?

c) What do you understand by the term 'surplus'?

d) What do you understand by the phrase 'financially prudent'?

We need to understand that there are several different types of profit. It is worth remembering that whatever the type of profit, the actual profit is always used in one of two ways:

■ To pay shareholders their dividends

■ To reinvest in the business.

Gross profit is the revenue earned by the business minus the cost of making that revenue. The formula looks like this:

Gross profit = Sales revenue – Cost of sales

This figure is often calculated to see how much profit the business is making compared with the actual direct costs involved in making that amount of revenue. In other words, how much the products, components, sales, employees and other directly related costs compare with the overall sales figures achieved by the business.

Percy's Unicycles have three stores. The first shop in Chichester has sales revenue of £66 000, the second shop in Bridport has sales revenue of £47 000 and the new shop in central London has sales revenue of £129 000.

Cost of sales for the first shop was £18 000, for the second shop it was £19 000 and for the London shop it was £47 000.

Calculate the gross profit for each of the shops individually and for the whole business.

Operating profit is another measure of profit and provides a better indication of the actual profit being made by the business. This time, the calculation takes into account all of the other overheads (costs) associated with doing business. The overheads include such necessary cost as rent and rates. The formula for calculating operating profit is:

Operating profit = Sales revenue – Cost of sales + Overheads

Operating profit provides a clearer indication of the profitability of a business as it takes into account all of the other necessary expenses of running the operation. Businesses cannot ignore the cost of rent, rates and other expenses and how this has an impact on the profitability.

Percy's Unicycles has three stores. The first shop in Chichester has sales revenue of £66 000, the second shop in Bridport has sales revenue of £47 000 and the new shop in central London has sales revenue of £129 000.

Cost of sales for the first shop was £18 000 and their overheads were £16 000, for the second shop sales cost £19 000 and the overheads were £22 000, and for the London shop sales cost £47 000 with overheads of £40 000.

Calculate the operating profit for each of the shops individually and for the whole business.

Businesses must also take account of the fact that they need to pay tax on their profits. In order to arrive at this figure, the business first has to calculate its pre-tax profits. The business begins with its operating profits and then subtracts what is known as 'one-off' items. Typical one-off costs can include the costs of restructuring the business and paying out redundancy. The pre-tax profits are calculated using the following formula:

Pre-tax profits = Operating profit + One-off items

> **activity**
> **INDIVIDUAL WORK**
> **(3.10)**
>
> You calculated the operating profit of Percy's Unicycles as a whole in Activity 3.9. The business restructured this year at a cost of £22 000. Calculate the pre-tax profits for the business as a whole.

A business must pay corporation tax. The current corporation tax main rate is 30 per cent. A small business will pay 19 per cent if they have taxable profits between £50 000 and £300 000. The starting rate is zero for companies with taxable profits of £10 000 or less.

> **activity**
> **INDIVIDUAL WORK**
> **(3.11)**
>
> You calculated the pre-tax profits for Percy's Unicycles in Activity 3.10. Now choose the appropriate level of corporation tax and work out the tax liability and the profit after tax for the business.

Table 3.2 shows how all of the calculations fit together and how this allows the business to make an accurate calculation of its expenses and its profits.

Table 3.2 Calculation of profit

Gross profit is the revenue minus the direct costs (cost of goods sold).	Sales revenue – Cost of sales = **Gross profit**
Operating (net) profit is the gross profit minus the indirect costs (overheads).	– Overheads = **Operating profit**
Pre-tax profit is the operating profit plus any one-off items, e.g. redundancy payments.	+ One-off items = **Pre-tax profit**
Profit after tax is the profit that is left after corporation tax has been paid.	– Corporation tax = **Profit after tax**

> **remember**
> In order to make a profit, a business' revenue must exceed its total costs.

> **keyword**
> **Asset** – An item that has a cash value. In the case of machinery, this asset used to produce products. Other assets could include land, buildings or patents.

Profitable operation

As we have seen, profit is found by comparing a business's revenues to its costs; the profit is equal to the total revenue of the business less its total costs. We have also seen that profits are used either to pay dividends to shareholders or they are reinvested in the business.

The fact that a business shows, in a given year, that it has made a profit does not actually reveal the whole picture. A business may have made a profit simply as a result of its normal trading operations. However, within the amount of profit being shown, the business may have obtained funds from a different source. Perhaps it has sold one of its **assets**.

Potential investors need to look very carefully at the source of the profits a business has made. If the business has genuinely made a profit from its trading operations, then investors will consider this to be a high-quality profit.

case study 3.2

Analysing costs, revenue and profit

A large number of businesses under-estimate their costs and over-estimate their potential revenues. If a business simply raises its prices, this does not mean that it will produce more revenue. It will instead inevitably lose customers, particularly if competitors do not raise their prices at the same time. Customers may choose to switch to cheaper products or services and so, in order to counteract this, the business that has raised its prices must stress the quality and availability of its products.

Cotter & Co. is a long-established family-run estate agency. It has an excellent reputation for reliability and quality of service. For many years it was the only estate agency in the area, but it chose not to take advantage of the situation by charging higher prices to property sellers. For the past five years the company has maintained its charges at 1.5 per cent of the selling price of the house. However, when a new estate agency opened in the area Cotter & Co. found it necessary to match the 1 per cent that this new competitor was charging. The drop in revenue was seen almost immediately and now the company feels it has only one option: to increase the charge back to 1.5 per cent.

activity
INDIVIDUAL WORK

Cotter & Co.'s profits have obviously suffered by matching the prices of its new competitor. What might be the implications to the business if it raised its price to 1.5 per cent?

Break Even Analysis

Although it is not always possible for new businesses, or businesses launching new products and services, to cover their costs with their sales revenue, ultimately this is their goal. The break even point occurs when the sales income from the products and services sold is equal to the total costs incurred by the business.

Break even

To calculate the break even point, three vital figures are required:

- The amount the product or service costs the consumer to buy
- The total fixed costs of the business
- The variable costs per unit.

remember

To work out break even you need to know the fixed costs, the selling price per unit and any variable costs per unit.

The simplest way to calculate the output level required to break even is to use the following formula:

$$\frac{Fixed\ costs}{Selling\ price\ per\ unit - Variable\ costs\ per\ unit}$$

If a business's fixed costs per month are £20 000, the selling price per unit is £1500 and the variable costs per unit are £500, then their calculations, applied to the formula, will look like this:

$$\frac{£20\,000}{£1500 - £500}$$

If the business subtracts its variable costs of £500 from the selling price of £1500, this leaves it with £1000. £20 000 divided by £1000 means that it must sell 20 units per month in order to break even.

The break even point is defined as being the point at which the level of sales is not great enough for the business to make a profit and yet not low enough for the business to make a loss. In other words, earnings from sales are just sufficient for the business to cover its total costs. This occurs when total revenue from sales exactly equals the total cost of production.

Break even point occurs when total costs = Total revenue

From this, it can be assumed that if total revenue from sales is greater than total costs, then the organisation concerned makes a profit. If the opposite is true and the total revenue is less than total costs, then the organisation can make a loss. As we have seen, the total cost of a unit of production is made up of two factors – the fixed and variable costs – where:

Total cost = Fixed costs + Variable costs

And the number of products sold multiplied by the selling price gives the total revenue.

Total revenue = Price × Quantity

If you sell five chocolate bars at 25p each, your total revenue is £1.25 (5 × 25p). How does a business determine its break even point? The easiest way to do this is by using of graphs. We have already examined the relationship between costs and output and now know that within a certain range of output, specific costs remain fixed regardless of the quantity of units produced.

Figure 3.1 shows how these fixed costs (FC) can be shown on a graph.

Figure 3.1
Fixed costs

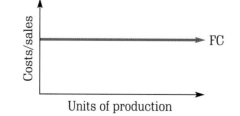

As we have seen, variable costs change in relation to the level of output. In other words, the higher the output, the higher the variable costs. Unlike the fixed costs, which remain constant, the variable costs (VC) mean that we need to add an upward, left-to-right sloping curve, known as the variable-cost curve, as can be seen in Figure 3.2.

Figure 3.2

Variable cost curve

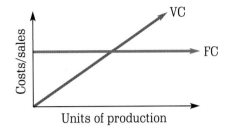

If we now add these two lines together we can put a total cost curve onto the diagram. Shifting the variable cost curve upwards, at all points, by the value of the fixed costs, represents this. In other words, we start where the fixed-cost line hits the costs/sales and then draw a line parallel to the variable-cost line. This gives us the total costs (TC), which is equal to the fixed costs plus the variable costs. This can be seen in Figure 3.3.

Figure 3.3

Total cost curve

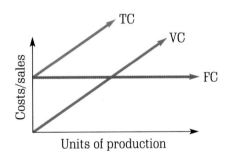

activity

INDIVIDUAL WORK
(3.12)

Himalaya Tents Ltd sells high-cost, professional tents to mountaineering expeditions. Total costs each month amount to £40 000. On average Himalaya's tents are sold for £2000 each.

a) How many tents would they have to sell each month in order to break even?

b) If total costs increased by 50 per cent, how many additional tents would the company have to sell in order still to break even?

activity

INDIVIDUAL WORK
(3.13)

A business has fixed costs of £30 000 per month. It has an average selling price of £600 per unit and variable costs per unit of £450. Calculate the number of units that must be sold in order to break even.

The next step is to add the total revenue line to the diagram. This line will also be left to right, upward sloping, as it follows that the more the business sells the greater the amount of revenue it receives. If, for example, the business were to sell five chocolate bars at 25p, then it would receive a total revenue of £1.25, whereas if it sold 10 chocolate bars it would receive total revenue of £2.50. The total revenue line (TR) starts from the same point as the variable-costs line and it should be remembered that if a business makes no products, then it receives no revenue. Figure 3.4 illustrates the addition of the total revenue line.

Figure 3.4
Total revenue line

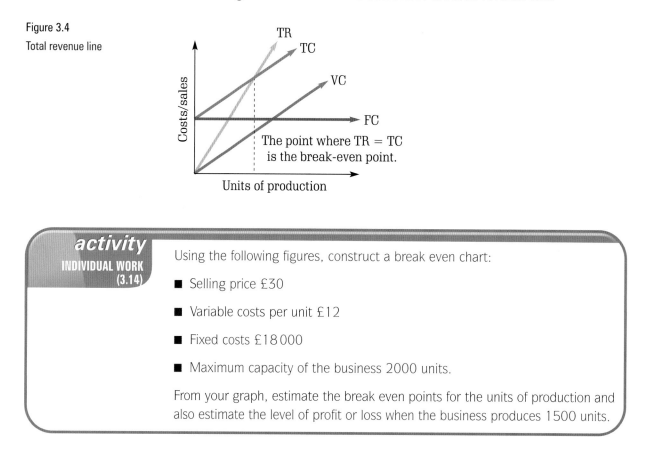

activity
INDIVIDUAL WORK
(3.14)

Using the following figures, construct a break even chart:

■ Selling price £30

■ Variable costs per unit £12

■ Fixed costs £18 000

■ Maximum capacity of the business 2000 units.

From your graph, estimate the break even points for the units of production and also estimate the level of profit or loss when the business produces 1500 units.

Balancing costs with revenues

Many businesses will have what is known as a selected operating profit, as featured in Figure 3.5. This is in excess of their break even point and provides them with a steady and reliable level of profit, capable of covering all of their costs.

The difference between the break even point and the selected operating profit is called the margin of safety. This is covered below, but for now we need to consider individual units of production.

The actual cost per unit is a total of the variable costs and the amount of the fixed costs that the business wishes to apply to each unit. If these two figures remain the same and the business increases the selling price of its products, then the profit margin per unit will increase.

A business sells on average 10 000 units at £34 per unit. It has fixed costs of £78 000, and based on the production of 10 000 units the variable costs are £89 000.

a) What is the profit margin per unit?

b) What would be the profit margin per unit if prices were increased by 10 per cent?

c) What would be the profit margin per unit if variable costs increased to £102 000, based on the original selling price of the unit?

Areas of profit and loss

Businesses will be concerned with establishing their exact break even point. At the very least they will try to adjust their output and consequently their total revenue in order to cover their total costs. Beyond this, they will seek to establish a sales level that provides the business, and consequently its owners or shareholders, with an acceptable level of profit.

Margin of safety

The margin of safety can be shown on a break even chart. It is the amount by which demand can fall before the business starts to make a loss. Essentially, it is the difference between sales and the break even point (BE), as shown in Figure 3.5.

Managing the break even point

Internal factors, such as recruiting additional employees, will cause fixed costs to rise, therefore the total costs will rise and the business's break even point will rise. If the business increases its prices then the total revenue figure should rise more steeply, meaning that the break even point falls. If the business decided to replace employees with machinery then, whilst its fixed costs will rise as a result of the investment in the machinery, its variable costs on direct labour would fall.

External factors may also have an impact on the break even chart. If there is a reduction in demand for the business's products or services, then a business will usually reduce its margin of safety, although of course the break even point will remain the same. If the business is forced to cut prices then the business will most likely see its total revenue line rise less steeply, which means that the break even point will also rise. If a business's variable costs increase then both the variable costs line and the total costs line will rise, pulling up the break even point.

Investigating Financial Control

Figure 3.5
The margin of safety

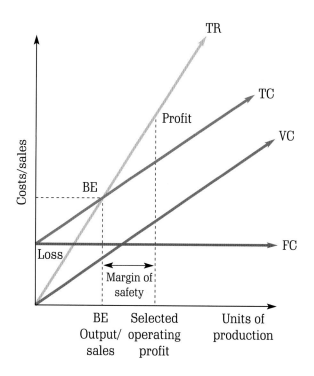

activity
INDIVIDUAL WORK
(3.16)

McGregor Enterprises produces 200 000 units per year, with an average selling price of £50. Its raw materials cost the company £5.70 per unit. Direct labour costs are split into two groups: £6 per unit for unskilled labour and £8 per unit for skilled labour. In addition to this, the company pays its management a total of £64 000 per year. Administration costs £112 500 per year and other salaries amount to £118 500 per year. Additional fixed costs amount to £98 000 per year.

Construct a break-even chart based on this information. State the amount of profit or loss made by the business at 100 000 units and 200 000 units.

Cash Flow Forecasts

Cash flow management is the process of monitoring, analysing and adjusting a business's cash flow. But what are cash flows? Simply, they are the day-to-day incomes and expenditure (costs and expenses) that a business experiences in the running of its operations. Obviously, the most important thing is for a business to avoid having cash shortages. These are caused by there being too much time gap between the point when money goes out of the business and when it comes into the business.

Using spreadsheets

The use of spreadsheet software, such as Microsoft Excel, allows the business to enter and store data in a grid format. It allows the business to perform numerical and statistical calculations. Once an appropriate formula has been entered, the program itself will make all the necessary calculations. Any entries on the spreadsheet can be changed, as can the formula. The effects of changes to the spreadsheet are automatic so there is no need to recalculate.

<table>
<tr><td>remember</td><td>Cash inflow includes all types of money received by the business.</td></tr>
</table>

Cash inflow

Cash inflow is money received and, as shown below, cash outflow is money that the business has spent. The main cash inflow headings include:

- Start-up capital – in the case of new businesses this includes all cash investments made by the owners. This investment will be used to pay any initial expenditure.

- Sales receipts – this is the income from any sales made by the business.

- Loan receipts – this is money that has come into the business in the form of a loan.

- Interest receipts – this is money received by the business in the form of interest from any other investment.

- VAT recoveries – if the business is of a sufficient size, it will be registered to pay Value Added Tax (VAT). Of course, if the business has received more VAT than it has paid out then this item would be transferred to the cash outflow.

Regular and irregular inflows

It is not always possible to predict or expect payments coming into a business. Regular inflows allow the business to have some degree of certainty as to the amount of cash that may be coming into the organisation over any given period.

Implications of varying the timing of inflows

A business may create its cash flow forecast on the basis of its known regular inflows of cash. As it cannot predict when or how much the irregular inflows will be, these cannot be incorporated into the cash flow with any degree of certainty.

Cash outflow

There are various cash outflow headings, which are essentially expenses. There are a number of headings that can be used under the cash outflow:

- Payments for assets – these are the costs of all machinery, office equipment and other items the business may have bought or purchased.

- Raw materials – these are all of the items that are used by the business to produce its products or provide its services.

- Wages and salaries – these are the total amounts of wages paid, including overtime payments.

- Rates and telephone bills – a business will have to pay water rates, sewerage rates and, of course, telephone bills.

- Other running costs – this category includes rent, rates and payment for power and other consumable items.

- Interest payments – these are payments made by the business as a result of having taken out hire purchase agreements or credit agreements to purchase assets.

- Loan repayments – if a business has a loan, it will have to repay the capital amount plus interest over an agreed number of months.

- VAT payments – if the business has collected more VAT than it has paid to other businesses, then it will owe HM Revenue & Customs the balance.

Regular and irregular outflows

The business cannot predict irregular outflows of cash.

A business will also try to make sure that it predicts additional payments that may fall due. An ideal example is an increase in business which means that employees are asked to do overtime.

Consequences of varying the timing of outflows

It is not always the case that an irregular outflow will be matched by an irregular inflow of cash. Normally a business will have negotiated payment terms with its suppliers so that it pays for the products after they have been sold.

activity
INDIVIDUAL WORK
(3.17)

A new business has start-up capital of £20 000. At present it does not have any loans. In its first month, its total sales revenue was also £20 000. It received no interest payments and it is not registered for VAT. In the first month the business bought £10 000 worth of assets. Raw materials cost it £2500. Wages and salaries cost £4000. Water rates and telephone bills amounted to £400 and the company estimated that its other running costs amounted to another £400. There were no interest or loan repayments.

Create a cash flow showing total cash inflows and total cash outflows for the month. What balance will the business begin with at the start of next month? Use Excel software to create your cash flow.

Cash balances

Although it is important to make sure that all of the figures in a cash flow forecast are correct, most people who will look at the cash flow forecast will only be interested in the cash balances.

The importance of the cash balance figures is explained below:

■ Opening balance – this is the amount of money available to the business at the beginning of the specified period, such as a week or a month.

■ Closing balance – this figure shows the difference between the income and expenditure during a period of time, such as a month or a week.

■ Income per period – this is the total amount of money that came into the business during the week or month.

■ Expenditure per period – this is the total amount of money spent by the business during the week or month.

It is important to note the relationship between the balances shown and the cash flow in the business. If a business spends more than it earns in a given month, the closing balance for that period will be a negative figure. This negative figure will be brought forward as the opening balance for the next month.

Interpreting the forecast

keyword

Invoice
– The document that gives full details of the products or services sold and the prices of those proudcts/services.

Regardless of the efforts made in selling products or services, a business is only assured of continued success and survival if it actually receives the money. Many businesses, particularly those that deal with other businesses as their customers, work on a credit basis. This means that the business provides the products or services and then produces an **invoice** or bill for those products and services. Every business will have its own particular terms for business. It is normal practice for businesses to be given at least 30 days to pay their bills. This is where credit control comes into the equation.

If payment has not been received by the end of the agreed period, then the supplying business's credit control will begin a series of contacts with the customer to find out what the problem is. Sometimes, if the customer is having difficulty in paying, the supplying business may accept part payment of the invoice, with the balance being paid at an agreed date in the future.

case study 3.3 — Credit control Australian style

The Australian telecommunications business is no different from many other types of business around the world. Recent figures suggest that credit control problems account for over 10 per cent of all customer complaint issues. This has risen from just over 7 per cent. In nearly 40 per cent of cases Australian telephone companies prevent customers with payment problems from making long-distance calls, thereby reducing their overall bills. Credit control problems rank fourth in terms of problems experienced by Australian telephone companies, after billing queries, faults and lack of service in particular areas.

activity
GROUP WORK

Assume you are a small business and two of your largest customers are actually the worst in terms of paying you for your products and services. After negotiations the two customers, have been allowed 60 days to pay you, but on average they both take 120 days each.

a) Using the ideas in the case study, what do you think would be the implications to your business if you threatened to charge them interest after 60 days?

b) What do you think the implications would be if you suggested to them that the payment period be reduced to 30 days?

Budgets for Planning and Monitoring Business Finances

Budgets are used to set targets in order to control costs and revenues. Budgets are a vital part of a business's planning strategy, as the budgets detail the business's intended expenditure as well as its income. Budgets allow a business to identify where costs and revenues will occur and also provide the basis upon which these can be monitored.

The purpose of breaking down the overall budget into smaller parts is to allow each manager of a department or an area of the business to monitor their own budget and contribute to the overall control of the budget.

activity
INDIVIDUAL WORK
(3.18)

Hamish McDonald runs the IT department for a medium-sized business. He has been asked to prepare his budget for the coming year. His guidelines are that he may spend 10 per cent more than he spent last year. Hamish's wage and salary bills were £98 000. Equipment purchases were £110 000, but £50 000 of this will not need to be spent in the coming year as the new network is now in place. His parts and components cost £14 000, consumables, such as disks and CDs, amounted to £4000. His other various costs amounted to £1200.

Initially Hamish has been asked to prepare a budget showing his proposed expenditure for the first six months of the coming year. He needs to break down the spending on a monthly basis and has been told to assume that he will spend the same amount of money each month.

Prepare Hamish's budget using an Excel spreadsheet.

Planning

Budgets are an essential part of the planning process. They help to control activities and aid communication and coordination within the organisation.

Budget periods

A budget period is usually 12 months. In any case it is a length of time during which an allocated amount of money or resources are available to be spent by the business or a department within an organisation.

Income and expenditure

The budget allocated to the business or one of its departments is very much linked to its income and expenditure. A business, for example, will know that it needs to spend a certain amount of money in order to generate a specific amount of sales.

Cash balances

It is the responsibility of a named individual, usually referred to as a budget holder, to ensure that their area of the organisation does not overspend their budget.

Forecasts for fixed periods

A new business would find it difficult to predict whether a budget is sufficient to cover costs. As the business becomes more experienced it will have a firmer understanding of how forecasts work and whether they can be relied upon to help fix and control budgets.

remember

Forecasts are important in order for a business to plan ahead and calculate whether or not their budget is sufficient.

Monitoring

Budgets are used by a business to control and monitor their costs. The senior management of a business will approve each department's budget and then, to a large extent, allow that department to manage its own budget.

The purpose of regularly checking budgets for variances is to allow the business to react and take action before the situation gets out of hand.

Eurocartridge Ltd recycles and refills ink cartridges for printers. It had budgeted to sell £300 000 worth of Hewlett Packard cartridges. In actual fact, by the end of the year it had sold £360 000 worth of these cartridges. The company also sells recycled Epson cartridges and had budgeted that they would sell £300 000 worth during the year. Actual figures were £260 000. At the beginning of the year Eurocartridge had found a new supplier of ink. It had originally budgeted £62 000 worth of spending to its ink suppliers. The new supplier had only invoiced for £58 000. The business had also worked out its spending on employees, which amounted to £89 000. Extra work had meant that overtime had to be paid and that the wage bill for the year was in fact £95 000.

Look at the sales revenue for the two main products, the cost of the ink and the labour costs. Which of the spending items were favourable variances and which were adverse variances?

Once it has become clear that there are variances in the budget, the management of the business needs to move quickly to adjust spending so that it falls back in line with the budget.

Smooth Air Systems installs air conditioning units into retail outlets. It budgeted to install 700 units at an average cost of £4800 each. Total variable costs were £280 000 and total fixed costs were £210 000. As it transpired, the actual sales figures were 650 units at an average price of £5200. Smooth Air's actual variable costs per unit were £450 and total fixed costs had risen to £220 000.

Using a spreadsheet, complete all of the figures for the budget and the actual figures, including number of units sold, total sales revenue, variable cost per unit, total variable costs, total fixed costs and profit.

Identify each variance from the budget and state whether it is favourable or adverse.

Recording Financial Transactions

Many businesses break down their operations so that each department or cost centre is responsible for recording and monitoring its financial activities. However, businesses need to know far more than their total sales and costs. They need to know which department or cost centre is the most profitable and which products or services are selling best.

activity
INDIVIDUAL WORK
(3.21)

Bernice runs a gift shop. She sold three items for £10 each, five items for £5.50 each, seven items for £2.50 each, 11 items for £1.20 each and 14 items for 75p each.

a) How much money should she have in the till at the end of the day according to those items noted in her sales logbook?

b) Bernice only noted down the value of the sales. What other information should she have recorded?

Manual or electronic recording

Not all businesses have sophisticated cash registers that record the date and time of the purchase and exactly what was sold at that time. Many smaller businesses rely on a simple cash register and use a book to note down what has been sold.

Daybooks

For our purposes we will look at two different kinds of daybook. One will cover sales and the other will cover purchases made by the business. Basically, a daybook records each and every invoice, sale or purchase that has been made by the business.

If a business makes a credit sale, then they will have created an invoice. The business will keep a copy of the invoice and will enter the details into the sales daybook. Some businesses call their sales daybooks 'journals'. Sales daybooks do not tend to include cash sales because these are entered into a cashbook. Normally a sales daybook is simply a list, in date order, of any sales that were made on credit. It will show: the date, the name of the customer, the invoice number and the final amount of the invoice.

The entries are collected, usually over a week or a month, before being transferred to the main accounts, and then a new series of entries are started.

In the same way that many businesses sell products on credit, they also make numerous purchases on credit. The purpose of a purchases daybook is to keep track of everything they have purchased but not yet paid for.

remember

The purchases daybook is used to keep track of everything the business has bought but has not yet paid for.

Once again, only credit purchases are entered into the purchases daybook. Cash purchases go straight into the cashbook. Again the purchases daybook is a list, in date order, this time including any purchases that have been made on credit by the business. It will show: the date, the name of the supplier, the invoice number and the final amount on the invoice.

The entries are usually kept for a period of a week or a month before being passed on to the accounts department. The total of the purchases made over the period is calculated before the entries are passed on.

The following transactions have occurred at Burywood Removals Ltd:

a) It has received an invoice for 100 cardboard boxes, but the boxes have not yet been delivered.

b) A delivery of computer stationery has arrived, along with an invoice.

c) An invoice has already been completed for a customer that is moving in five days' time. The normal procedure is to send the invoice out five days after the removal date.

What would you do with each of these transactions? Are any of them ready to be put into the sales or purchases daybooks? If so, which of the two daybooks are relevant in each case?

Petty-cash recording

Regardless of the size of the business, it will have a petty-cash book. This is used to keep a record of small cash payments. It could be used for a number of small purchases, including stationery, postage stamps, travel and expenses and refreshments.

Anyone who wishes to claim money from petty cash must complete a petty-cash voucher. This describes what the money was spent on and how much was spent, and it will have a signature from the person who is claiming the petty cash and an authorising signature from that person's budget controller.

Nollie is the petty cashier for a small business. She has £100 at the beginning of the month (a petty-cash system sometimes known as 'imprest'). The following petty-cash transactions take place and she pays out:

■ £3.44 for stamps on 1st
■ £2.25 for envelopes on 2nd
■ Cleaners' materials of £14 on 6th
■ A ream of photocopy paper for £3.99 on 12th
■ £7.34 on stamps on 15th
■ £12 to the window cleaner on 19th
■ Taxi fare to a visitor for £8.50 on 23rd
■ A set of felt-tip pens for £3.99 on 28th
■ Self-adhesive labels for £4.99 on 28th

a) How might Nollie organise these payments in columns according to the type of purchase?

b) What is her total spending for the month?

c) How much should she have left in her float at the end of the month?

Cash-register recording

Some other businesses use a simple system that relies on a cash register to record the type of product sold. In a gift shop, for example, the cashier may enter the price of the product and then hit a key to identify it as a specific type of product, such as a card, wedding gift or small teddy bear. This allows the business to see which particular types of product are selling best in its shops and it can then adjust where the products are placed in the shop and how much space is given to them. This system does not record the actual product itself, so it would be difficult to know whether a birthday card, an anniversary card or a wedding card had been sold.

activity
INDIVIDUAL WORK (3.24)

Bernice has bought herself a new cash register and she can now record the sales in four categories: cards, artificial flowers, ornaments and vases, and pictures and mirrors. On her first day using the new cash register, she sells five plastic tulips at £1 each, a pottery dog for £5.50, an oval mirror for £15, a framed poster of Britney Spears for £12, a box of Christmas cards for £4.99, a glass jug for £6.50, three silk lilies for £1.50 each, a vase of plastic ferns for £10 and a pack of wedding invitation cards for £7.95.

Organise her sales for the day into the four categories and calculate the totals for each category. Were there any problems in categorising any of the products she sold? If so, state which products caused problems.

Direct computer input via software products

Many retailers use what is known as Electronic Point of Sale (EPOS). This is a system that allows the bar-code on each product to be scanned at the cash till. The bar-code is a unique identifying code for each product sold in the retail outlet. The cash till relays the information straight to the store's computer and the computer in turn relays the price of the product to the cash till.

Document sequence of transactions

We already know that all organisations need to buy raw materials and services in order to produce or provide their own products and services. In order to obtain these materials or services, the business will have to complete documents requesting them. A business may want to purchase any of the following:

remember
It is important for a business to record their capital items as the costs can be offset against tax.

- Materials, which can take several different forms. They may be raw materials needed to produce products. They may, however, be headed paper to produce business letters or cleaning products used on the production line.
- Capital items, which could be office furniture, new computer equipment, new buildings, etc.
- Services. To purchase a service from an individual or another business it is necessary for the business to raise a contract.

Investigating Financial Control

A business's purchasing department will be responsible for buying materials or services for the organisation. This involves a series of processes and the completion of various documents. Once it has been decided which supplier will be used, the business will complete and send an order form.

Order forms

An order form is a firm commitment that the business requires the materials. An example of a blank order form is shown in Figure 3.6, from which we can identify the main information that the supplier requires from the business.

Essentially, the following information is included on the order:

- To – this is the address of the business buying the materials.
- Order number – each order placed will have a unique number. This information is vital to both the supplier and the purchasing department of the business.
- Date – every order placed must be dated.
- Delivery address – this may be different from the address of the purchasing business as the materials may be required at a branch of their operations.
- Special instructions – these may include, for example, the fact that the order had previously been telephoned to the supplier, or that delivery of the materials has been agreed by a certain date.
- Reference number – which may be the number of the item as stated in the supplier's catalogue.

Figure 3.6

An example of an order form

- Quantity – the number of each item required.
- Description – identifies the exact nature of the item required.
- Unit price – the price of each item required.
- Amount – the total amount when the quantity and unit price are multiplied together.
- Authorised by – the purchasing business would have an individual, or a number of individuals, that are authorised to sign on behalf of the business.

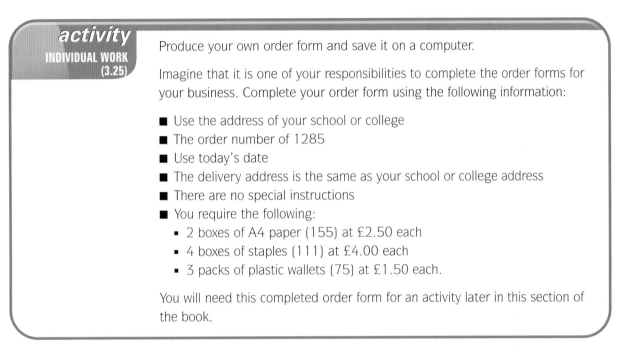

activity

INDIVIDUAL WORK (3.25)

Produce your own order form and save it on a computer.

Imagine that it is one of your responsibilities to complete the order forms for your business. Complete your order form using the following information:

- Use the address of your school or college
- The order number of 1285
- Use today's date
- The delivery address is the same as your school or college address
- There are no special instructions
- You require the following:
  - 2 boxes of A4 paper (155) at £2.50 each
  - 4 boxes of staples (111) at £4.00 each
  - 3 packs of plastic wallets (75) at £1.50 each.

You will need this completed order form for an activity later in this section of the book.

Delivery note

The supplying business will need to have a record of what has been prepared for despatch to the customer, but the customer will also need some documentation to check against their order. A despatch note, also known as a delivery advice note is sent to the customer when the goods are despatched and a copy will also be attached to the product's packaging or included inside the package.

The person receiving the products may not have a copy of the original order form, so all they will do is check that the delivery advice note states correctly what has actually been delivered. They will then complete a goods received note, which is used to update the stock records and to check against the original order before paying the supplier's invoice.

activity

INDIVIDUAL WORK (3.26)

Look at Figure 3.9. Consider each of the headings in turn and suggest your own reasons why these would appear on this document.

Figure 3.7
An example of a delivery advice note

DELIVERY ADVICE — No. ______

To: ______________________

______________________ Your order no. ______________________

______________________ Date: ______________________

The following items have been despatched today by rail/company van/post:

Quantity	Description	No. of packages
______	______________________	______________
______	______________________	______________
______	______________________	______________

I certify that the goods have been received today.

Signed: ______________________ On behalf of: ______________________

Date: ______________

Figure 3.8
An example of a goods received note

GOODS RECEIVED NOTE			No. ______
Date received		Order no.	Delivered by
Quantity	Description	No. of packages	Stores ref.
Received from ______________ Supplier	Entered in stock Date ________ Initials ________	Received by ______________________ Storekeeper	

remember Invoices should include any order number provided by the purchaser of the products or services.

Invoices

Once the products have been delivered to the purchasing business, the supplier will send its invoice. This will list the quantity and description of the goods sent, as well as the total amount owing. The invoice will also state a date by which a payment should be made, and will list any discounts made available to the purchasing business. The purchasing business will check that the:

- Order number is correct
- Goods listed match those delivered
- Quantity listed match those delivered
- Price listed matches that quoted
- Calculations are correct
- Discounts are as agreed.

The VAT will have to be calculated on the invoice:

- VAT is charged on the goods and the delivery charge.
- VAT is added to the total price of the goods less any discounts available.

Figure 3.9

An example of an invoice

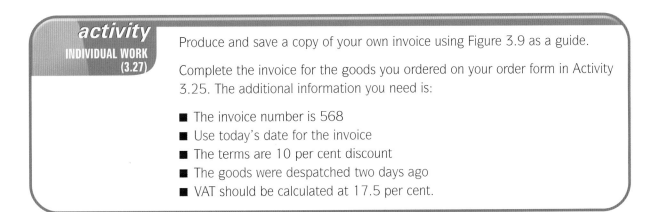

INVOICE

To: _____   Invoice no. _____
    _____   Date: _____
    _____   Terms: _____

Your order no. _____   Despatch date: _____

Quantity	Description	Unit price	Total price	VAT

Gross value
Less trade discount

Net value of goods

Plus VAT @ ____%

Invoice total

E&OE

---

activity

INDIVIDUAL WORK (3.27)

Produce and save a copy of your own invoice using Figure 3.9 as a guide.

Complete the invoice for the goods you ordered on your order form in Activity 3.25. The additional information you need is:

- The invoice number is 568
- Use today's date for the invoice
- The terms are 10 per cent discount
- The goods were despatched two days ago
- VAT should be calculated at 17.5 per cent.

Credit note

Should the supplier list items on the invoice by mistake, meaning that the invoice total is too high, it would have to send the purchasing organisation a credit note. This credit note would also be issued to the purchasing organisation if goods have been returned as being faulty.

Cash receipts and payments

A receipt is a document that confirms that a certain amount of money has been paid. This money could be paid from one individual to another, as when you go shopping and receive a till receipt, or from one organisation to another.

Receipts are normally quite simple to complete and usually include the following items:

- Name of the organisation issuing the receipt
- Date of the transaction
- Name of the person or business making the payment
- Amount of the payment
- Reason for the payment.

Payment advice

Once a month, often at the end of the month, the supplier will send a statement of account to each of its customers. This statement will list the transactions that have taken place between the two businesses. It will show the totals of each of the invoices sent to the customer, plus any payments made by the customer during the month. The balance shown at the end of the statement is the amount of money the customer owes the supplier.

> **remember**
>
> A statement of account details all the transactions carried out between a customer and a supplier.

activity

INDIVIDUAL WORK (3.28)

Consider your order form and invoice prepared in Activities 3.25 and 3.27. If you were transferring funds to the bank account of the supplier of this order, what information would you need to provide on the payment advice? Why do you think it is necessary to provide this information?

Fraud

No one knows the exact extent of employee fraud in UK businesses. Around 24 per cent, amounting to 900 000 small and medium-sized businesses, have suffered from employee fraud in recent years.

Many businesses are switching over to chip and pin and the deadline to adopt the new technology was 14 February 2006. A large number of businesses, however, are not ready and it seems that for a few months fraudsters will still be able to use a signature to obtain products.

Closed circuit television (CCTV) is often used to prevent what is known as 'internal shrinkage'. This entails watching point-of-sale areas in retail stores to see if cashiers are involved in fraud or theft. The monitoring systems can watch what cashiers do and provide the proof of what was sold, to whom, at what price and when. Given that crime as a whole cost the UK retail industry £1 billion in 2004, businesses are keen to develop any form of security that will protect them. CCTV is used in a large number of retail stores and in shopping centres.

case study 3.4 — Retail CCTV

In 1999, UK retailers spent £612 million on crime prevention methods, including CCTV. At the Legal and General's St. George's Shopping Centre in Preston, where there are around 200 shops, a large number of cameras cover all public areas, including escalators and the outside of shops. They can operate in daylight and in very low light, they are waterproof and have motorised zone lenses. In the same year, the British Rail Consortium worked out that customer theft accounted for £740 million, which was up 23 per cent from the previous year.

activity
GROUP WORK

Are you aware of the security measures in force at your local shopping centre? Are you even aware that you are being watched, both inside and outside the shops? Try to find out how significant theft from retail stores is in your area. A visit to your local police force's website, or perhaps a local Chamber of Commerce website, will reveal this information.

progress check

1. How would you calculate sales revenue?
2. What two items should you deduct from sales revenue to calculate operating profit?
3. What are the three figures required to calculate the break-even point?
4. If a business's variable costs increase, what happens to the break-even point?
5. Give five examples of cash outflows.
6. What is a cost centre?
7. What is the basic purpose of a budget?
8. What is a daybook?
9. What is a credit note?
10. What is 'internal shrinkage'?

Business Communication

This unit covers:

- the purpose of communications in business contexts
- using oral communication effectively
- using written business communication effectively
- the importance of interpersonal and non-verbal business communication skills

This unit looks at how to improve your overall communication skills. You will learn to understand the purpose of business communications and the types of situation in which communication takes place. You will learn about the importance of listening and understanding instructions in order to help you carry out tasks as required. In this way you will learn how to improve your oral communication skills, both to a single person and to a group. This unit also requires you to understand and practise your written communications so that you can pass on messages in a clear way. Above all, you will learn how to improve your interpersonal skills so that you can communicate with colleagues and customers and provide a valuable service to a business.

grading criteria

To achieve a **Pass** grade the evidence must show that the learner is able to:	To achieve a **Merit** grade the evidence must show that the learner is able to:	To achieve a **Distinction** grade the evidence must show that the learner is able to:
P1 describe, using examples, the purpose of business communications in different business contexts	**M1** explain how oral communications can be used in business situations	**D1** analyse the effectiveness of oral and written communications in a given business context
P2 respond to oral instructions, conveying a series of routine business tasks	**M2** give reasons for selecting appropriate documents and layouts for business purposes	**D2** evaluate the importance of effective interpersonal and non-verbal communication skills in a given business context

grading criteria

To achieve a **Pass** grade the evidence must show that the learner is able to:	To achieve a **Merit** grade the evidence must show that the learner is able to:	To achieve a **Distinction** grade the evidence must show that the learner is able to:
P3 make an individual contribution to a group discussion relating to business tasks and record the outcomes of the discussion	**M3** explain the interpersonal and non-verbal communication skills used to support effective communication	
P4 produce three documents to support straightforward business tasks		
P5 demonstrate interpersonal and non-verbal communication skills when demonstrating business communications		

The Purpose of Communications in Business

Business communications, both written (including electronic) and oral, are created to distribute information within and outside the organisation. Examples of business communications include reports, letters, memoranda, electronic mail and conversations.

Purpose

As we have seen, business communications are valuable to an organisation providing that it succeeds in achieving the three basic rules of being concise, accurate and clear.

Business contexts

Communications take place in all kinds of different situations. It is useful to think about communications as being either formal or informal. Formal communications take place normally when dealing with customers and in certain cases between colleagues and supervisors, particularly at meetings. Formal communications mean having to present information in the most professional manner possible.

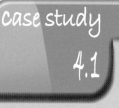

case study 4.1   Tom Watson

Tom has just joined Norwich and Coleman as their business communications manager. He has an enormous pile of work in his in tray and several emails to deal with. His immediate work is:

a) To produce a poster explaining to employees the consequences of arriving late for work.

b) To prepare for next month's shareholders' meeting.

c) To deal with a request from the sales department for training.

d) To place an advertisement in the local newspaper.

e) To draft a letter to a longstanding customer that is upset with the level of service.

activity
INDIVIDUAL WORK

Look at the five jobs in Tom's in-tray and try to identify the type of business communication he should use to deal with each.

A more informal approach takes place when communicating with colleagues on a daily basis. The types of communication used in particular circumstances are shown in Table 4.1

remember

Formal communications should always be used when dealing with customers from outside the business.

Table 4.1 Communications used in particular circumstances

Situation	Formal	Informal	Explanation
Telephone contacts	Yes	Yes	Formal if dealing with individuals outside the organisation or more senior employees.
Meetings	Yes	No	Meetings have set, formal procedures.
Technical enquiries	Yes	No	There is a need to be clear and specific.
Supervisors	Yes	Yes	Depends on situation.
Colleagues	No	Yes	Usually informal but professional.
Customers	Yes	No	Usually formal as they expect a professional attitude.
Complaints	Yes	No	Specific procedures would need to be followed.
Presentations	Yes	No	Professional and formal approach is required.
Confidentiality	Yes	No	A professional approach is expected.

Oral Communication

Day after day information will flow in and out of the business. This all has to be checked, read, understood and communicated to someone else or another department in the business. There are several advantages and disadvantages in using verbal or spoken communication as opposed to written communication. These are shown in Table 4.2

Table 4.2 Advantages and disadvantages of verbal communication

Advantages	Disadvantages
Communication is quick.	Speech has to be clear.
Communication is cheap.	The person passing on the message has to be clear about what they are saying.
The voice can be used to emphasise points.	It is not ideal for long or complicated messages.
Immediate feedback can be obtained from the recipient (person being communicated with).	The recipient could be distracted by, for example, a telephone ringing or a noisy office.
Confirmation can be obtained that the recipient has understood the message.	A conflict of opinion could cause an argument or disagreement.
Body language and facial expressions can be used to be help explain things.	There is no written confirmation that the conversation has taken place.

Face-to-face communication and telephone conversations are two of the most important ways in which we communicate verbally every day. In any organisation there may be different forms of face-to-face communication, including:

- Conversations that take place in the office or at a person's desk.
- Brief chats in the corridors or at lunch breaks.
- Informal meetings, when two or three employees talk about something.
- Formal meetings, when groups of employees are called together to make decisions.
- When one member of staff is giving instructions to another.
- Talking to customers, either in person or on the telephone.

Listening skills

People speak at a rate of 100 to 175 words per minute (wpm). It is very easy to let your mind drift and think about other things when people are talking. In order to ensure this does not happen you will need to actively listen or listen with a purpose. If you find it difficult to concentrate, try repeating their words (in your head) to reinforce the message. Listening is an important verbal communication

remember

News on the TV is read at approximately 140wpm. A good shorthand writer would be able to cope with 100wpm.

Business Communication

skill. We all listen to a number of people every day, but not many of us can remember what was said in these conversations. As a useful back-up, it is always a good idea to try to take notes, particularly of important conversations or instructions. This will help you to remember what has been said.

Listening to and understanding instructions

Throughout the course of any working day, most people could receive instructions from a number of different people. Being able to listen effectively is even more important if the person giving instructions is unsure of a number of things, including:

- The exact details of what they need to tell the listener
- How interested or receptive the listener is
- How knowledgeable the listener is about the subject of the instructions.

In order for the listener to understand the instruction they have to:

- Hear the instructions clearly
- Interpret the instructions
- Evaluate their response to the instructions
- Act upon the instructions and make use of the information they have heard.

If we are to make good use of our listening skills it is important to:

- Concentrate on what is being said
- Avoid becoming distracted
- Repeat the words or phrases used in the conversation
- Look at the person speaking and respond
- Be ready for the other person to stop speaking
- Ask questions and comment on what has been said.

How good a listener are you?

In pairs, get your partner to tell you about a recent holiday or an outing they have taken. Let them talk to you for three minutes about their visit but do not interrupt them or ask them questions. Now recount everything that you have remembered about their visit. Did you remember most of it or did they have to remind you about some things?

Now swap roles and repeat the process.

Interpreting, confirming and clarifying instructions

remember
In order for instructions to be carried out fully, they should have an objective and be clearly understood.

Any task will have an objective, either for the individual, the team of people involved, or the business as a whole. In order to carry out the task properly and meet the objectives the listener will have to be clear about:

- Why the instructions have been given
- For whom the work is being done
- The outcome of the task involved
- When the task has to be completed.

Clarifying means making clear or dealing with any confusion that might arise out of the objectives. The clearer the objectives, the better chance the person instructed to carry out the task will have of achieving them.

Figure 4.1 shows the task cycle, which is the processes that involves receiving instructions through to reporting that the task has been completed.

If the instructions given or the explanation of the tasks is not clear, then the person receiving the instructions should always make sure that they fully understand what is involved. Sometimes this involves asking a series of questions in order to obtain more information or to clarify the set of instructions.

Figure 4.1
Task cycle

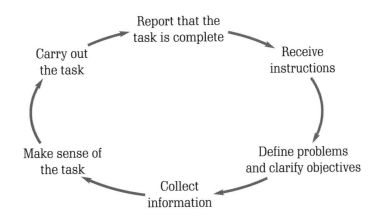

Report that the task is complete

Receive instructions

Carry out the task

Make sense of the task

Define problems and clarify objectives

Collect information

You will come across tasks that have different priorities. Broadly they can be broken down into four different categories:

- Urgent and important tasks
- Urgent but not important tasks
- Important but not urgent tasks
- Not urgent and not important tasks.

activity
INDIVIDUAL WORK
(4.2)

Using the four categories above, prioritise your workload at school or college at the moment. Which category would most of your tasks fall into? If many are urgent and important how do you prioritise them?

Making notes

Always be clear why you are making notes. This helps you to be selective and focused. The process of making notes is useful to:

- Provide a record of information for future use.
- Aid concentration.
- Improve understanding by choosing what is useful and discarding what's not needed.
- Help with the process of memorising.
- Stimulate your brain into thinking about material in critical and creative ways, prompting new ideas.
- Help with the process of planning and preparing work.

One-to-one communication

In a normal working day an individual will need to take part in oral communications with several different types of people. There are ways and shortcuts when communicating with colleagues who understand jargon and procedures. These shortcuts would not work if you were talking to someone from outside the organisation. Equally, technical information, which may be understood by those with particular knowledge, will leave others confused and unable to understand the conversation.

Conveying messages, use of language and expression

To be a good communicator takes practice and experience. There are many key things to remember when you are communicating. Remember that you will have to learn how to conduct yourself in a professional manner as this will be how colleagues, fellow employees, customers and others view you:

- Always try to speak clearly.

- Try not to speak too quickly or too slowly.

- Use the right words for the situation and do not be too complicated or too simplistic.

- You should be able to listen to what the other person is saying so you can respond properly.

- You should show confidence.

- Try to put the other person at ease.

- Think about what you say and try to make your responses logical .

- Try to use the right tone and not be too aggressive or passive.

- You should not allow your feelings to confuse the conversation.

- If you have a strong accent talk slightly more slowly so that people can understand you.

- If you think your voice is not pleasant to listen to, try to lower the pitch of your voice a little.

- Never interrupt until the other person has finished.

You will often be given information that does not have any direct relevance to you. You may be responsible for opening the mail and passing the letters and other information to others. In the case of oral communications, you may take telephone messages or meet individuals face to face, and again the content of the information may not have any direct relevance to you. You will have to pass on messages and often complex information or instructions to others. It is essential that this is done accurately.

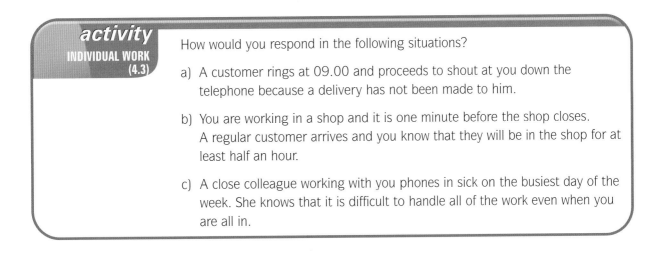

activity
INDIVIDUAL WORK (4.3)

How would you respond in the following situations?

a) A customer rings at 09.00 and proceeds to shout at you down the telephone because a delivery has not been made to him.

b) You are working in a shop and it is one minute before the shop closes. A regular customer arrives and you know that they will be in the shop for at least half an hour.

c) A close colleague working with you phones in sick on the busiest day of the week. She knows that it is difficult to handle all of the work even when you are all in.

Working in groups

In many businesses and organisations you will be expected to work as a member of a team. Teamwork is often vital. Provided each individual employee knows what they are supposed to do, how to do it, what they need to do it and by when it has to be done, then the purpose of their job role is helping the business to meet its set of objectives.

remember

Tasks can be carried out more quickly if the work is allocated to those in the group who have particular expertise.

Making relevant contributions to team tasks

Every team has its own mix of individuals. Some quietly work in the background and are happy for others to make the important decisions. Some teams are a combination of difficult characters, often competing with one another to make decisions and to appear to be in charge.

A team needs to be a good mix of individual members, each with their own skills, abilities and experience. They are there to support one another. Table 4.3 shows the different types of people you could find in a group.

Table 4.3 Characteristics of individuals

Task-based characteristics (those that get the job done)		Function-based characteristics (those that enable the work to be done)	
Initiators	People that set goals and suggest ways in which things can be done and ways of dealing with team problems	Encouragers	People that accept others and are responsive and friendly towards them
Information or opinion givers	People that provide the team with figures, ideas and suggestions	Expressers	People that share their feelings with the team and help establish relationships
Information seekers	People that need facts and figures to get their work done	Compromisers	People that want the team to work and will give way on things if it helps the team to function
Elaborators	People that clear up confusion by giving examples and explanations	Harmonisers	People that try to deal with problems in the team and reduce tension
Summarisers	People that pull together various facts and ideas and keep the team informed of progress	Gatekeepers	People that encourage some of the team to get involved with a task but freeze out those that they do not want working on it
Agreement standards	People that check that everyone in the team agrees with them that the task should be done	Standard-setters	People that try to set the minimum standards of work and try to get everyone in the team to stick to them

Meetings and team briefings

Team planning is of vital importance. All of the tasks set for the team need to be broken down into manageable pieces. Team meetings and briefings exist to prioritise the work and to allocate parts of the tasks to each of the members of the team. By instigating a planning process the team and its individual members can help manage their workloads. This can take the pressure off individuals and the team leader.

Typically, a meeting or team briefing would cover the following matters:

- The general objectives for the team
- The major objectives for the team
- Steps needed to meet these objectives
- How the team intends to meet these objectives
- The role of each member of the team
- The deadlines for particular parts of the tasks or objectives.

Team briefings differ slightly from meetings as they usually involve simply informing the team about something, perhaps a change of procedures or a new set of priorities. Meetings are where work is prioritised and allocated, whilst team briefings provide necessary background information and instructions for the team.

Responding to others and moving discussions forward

In team meetings it is important to look at all of the information available, the tasks and objectives to be met and any other factors that may affect the way in which the team can operate in the near future. Normally, teams will consider the following points:

- They will look at where they are at the moment
- They will consider deadlines and whether they will be achieved
- They will prioritise deadlines and goals
- Each team member will have an opportunity to express their opinion
- Once opinions have been expressed the team will try to reach an agreement
- Individual team members will be given, or will volunteer to do, certain jobs
- The team will request any resources it needs to carry out their work.

Written Communication

The use of written communication as opposed to verbal communication is also common in all businesses and organisations. The key advantages and disadvantages of the written communication are shown in Table 4.4.

Table 4.4 The advantages and disadvantages of written communication

Advantages	Disadvantages
Written communications are more formal.	It can take a long time to get the communication right.
A record of the communication is created (which can be kept and filed).	It needs to be accurate and error free.
The communication can be re-read and referred to later.	It must not have spelling mistakes look messy because this gives a bad impression of the business.
The communication can be copied for others to read.	It needs to legible (the receiver must be able to read what the sender has written).
It is ideal for communications when the sender and the receiver are in different places.	
Written communication can use diagrams and instructions to back up the words.	

activity

INDIVIDUAL WORK (4.4)

What method of written internal communication do you think the managers of a business would use to inform their employees about the following issues:

a) To invite a manager from another branch of the business to join them for lunch after a meeting.

b) To provide the results of some research to all the managers of the business.

c) To inform all employees about a change to the car parking arrangements.

d) To tell someone they have a pay rise.

e) To tell all employees the details of the forthcoming Christmas party.

Documents

Businesses communicate with their customers, suppliers and with one another. This particular unit deals primarily with internal communications, although some are more widely used and sent to customers. We will look at the following types of written communication in this unit:

■ Letters – businesses tend to send these to customers.

■ Memoranda – these are in effect shortened versions of a letter.

- Reports – these are detailed investigations into a particular subject.
- Agendas – which are a list of subjects that will be discussed at a meeting.
- Minutes – these are a summary of a previous meeting and detail what was discussed, decisions made and who is responsible for carrying out further research or tasks.
- Purchase orders – these are documents that are sent by the business to a supplier, which officially authorise the purchase of products or services.
- Invoices – these are documents detailing products or services supplied to a customer.

Letters

Even the simplest letter must follow a particular format and set of conventions. These are rules that dictate how the document will look. Each different type of business communication, or document, has a different set of formats and conventions. By following these, you will give the person or people who see the communication a much better chance of understanding the information contained in it.

Business letters need to be neat, accurate and well-presented as businesses see their letters as being a reflection of their professionalism in all things that they do. They will tend to use headed paper (see Figure 4.2), which means that many of the details in the following list are printed on the paper and appear on every letter that leaves the organisation. This also means that the person preparing the letter does not have to type these details every time a letter is sent out.

activity

INDIVIDUAL WORK (4.5)

We have given you five reasons why a business might write a business letter. Can you think of any others? Write down your other reasons for an organisation writing a business letter. Remember that a business letter goes to someone outside the organisation.

Letters may be written for a number of different purposes, including:

- Contacting potential customers – people who are either buying or may buy the organisation's products or services.
- Communicating with suppliers – which are other businesses that may provide items such as products, stationery or office equipment to the organisation.
- In answer to a customer complaint.
- To tell existing customers about a new product the business might be about to make available.
- Contacting a future employee who has applied for a job with the organisation.

A business letter will be ordered in a certain way to make sure it contains all the necessary information. As well as the name and address of the business on the headed paper, it will contain:

- The name and address of the recipient (the person the letter is being sent to).

- The date the letter is being prepared or sent.

- Sometimes a reference – which can be the initials of the writer or a set of numbers. This will help the writer of the letter to know where to file it and also to keep all the paperwork together if there are lots of letters relating to the same subject.

- The word(s) 'URGENT' or 'CONFIDENTIAL', which also helps the recipient to recognise how important the letter is.

- A salutation – this is the start of the letter and could be 'Dear Mr Smith' or 'Dear Sir'. If the name of the recipient is known, then it is normal to use it and start with their name. If the name of the recipient is not known, then it is more appropriate to use 'Dear Sir' or 'Dear Madam'.

- A subject heading – which will help the recipient to see immediately what the letter is about.

- The paragraphs of text.

- The complimentary close – this is the way the letter ends. If 'Dear Sir' or 'Dear Madam' has been used in the salutation, then the letter is ended with 'Yours faithfully'. If the name has been used, for example 'Dear Mr Smith', then 'Yours sincerely' is used in the complimentary close.

- The name of the person sending the letter (and their job title), placed after the complimentary close, leaving enough room for their signature.

- If the letter includes any additional items (called enclosures), this is indicated at the end of the letter by 'Enc', or 'Encs' for more than one enclosure.

remember

Letters that start with Dear Sir or Dear Madam close with Yours faithfully; letters that start Dear Mr or Dear Mrs close with Yours sincerely.

Figure 4.2

An example of headed paper

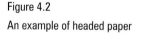

Nelson Thornes
a Wolters Kluwer business

Delta Place
27 Bath Road
Cheltenham GL53 7TH
United Kingdom

+44 (0)1242 267100 tel
+44 (0)1242 221914 fax
cservices@nelsonthornes.com
www.nelsonthornes.com

Businesses will have different rules about how their business letters are displayed. The most common way of displaying a business letter is the fully blocked method of display. This means that each part of the letter starts at the left-hand margin (see Figure 4.3). Fully blocked letters use 'open' punctuation – no commas at the end of lines in the address, salutation and complimentary close.

activity
INDIVIDUAL WORK (4.6)

You recently bought a toy for your little nephew's birthday. On the box it stated that batteries were included. On the day of his birthday, your nephew was in tears because he could not play with his toy there were no batteries in the box. You now want to write a letter of complaint to the toyshop.

Write your letter using the correct layout for a fully blocked letter. Use today's date. The address of the toyshop is:

Children's Toys The Precinct Swinfield Surrey

SW1 5BF

You should sign the letter yourself. Be careful about your spelling and punctuation and use an appropriate style and tone for your letter.

Figure 4.3

An example of a business letter using the fully blocked style

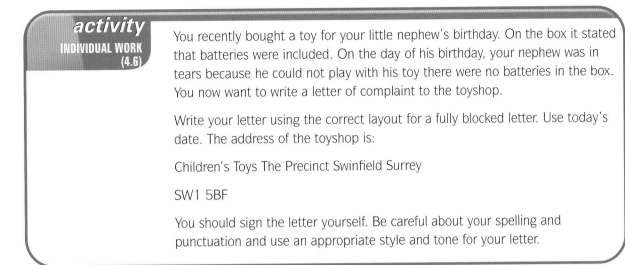

Figure 4.4

An example of a business letter using the indented style

```
  ⬤ .Nelson Thornes          Delta Place          +44 (0)1242 267100 tel
      a Wolters Kluwer business   27 Bath Road        +44 (0)1242 221914 fax
                                  Cheltenham GL53 7TH  cservices@nelsonthornes.com
                                  United Kingdom       www.nelsonthornes.com

  REF: DES/JDS/291003                                  29 OCTOBER 2---

  CONFIDENTIAL

  Laura Buchan,
  The Old Post Office,
  London,
  Norfolk
  NR31 6BJ

  Dear Ms Buchan,

               Your application for the post of administrator


  xxxxxxxxxxxxxxxxxxxxxxxxxxxxxxxxxxxxxxxxxxxxxxxxxxxxxxxxxxxxxxxxxxx
  xxxxxxxxxxx


  xxxxxxxxxxxxxxxxxxxxxxxxxxxxxxxxxxxxxxxxxxxxxxxxxxxxxxxxxxxxxxxxxxx
  xxxxxxxxxxxxxxxxxxxxxxxxxxxxxxxxxxxxxxxxxxxxxxxxxxxxxxxxxxxxxxxxxxx

  xxxxxxxxxxxxxx
                         Yours sincerely,

                        Jonathan Sutherland
                        Recruitment officer

  Enc
```

Memoranda

Internal memoranda are used as a form of communication between different departments of an organisation. They are usually shorter than a business letter and normally deal with a particular subject. When more than one point is being made it is normal to number the points. Increasingly people will sign memos, rather like a business letter, but usually a person's initials will do. Many organisations use printed memorandum paper, in much the same way as they would use a letterhead paper.

Memos have a very clear format. They always have the following:

TO: Names of those who will receive the memo.

FROM: Name of person sending the memo.

DATE: When the memo was sent.

REF: The subject of the memo.

activity
INDIVIDUAL WORK
(4.7)

Your employer has asked you to write a memo to all staff concerning the way A4 paper is being wasted. He or she is concerned that too many hard copies of documents are being printed and then not used. The stationery bill has increased by 20 per cent in the last three months and this is causing budget problems.

Reports

Report writing is not only vital to a business, is also carried out in order to achieve goals or objectives. Businesses can commission reports for many different reasons, including:

- To identify problems and find solutions to those problems
- To provide progress reports on particular projects
- To investigate particular areas of the business's activities
- To identify the need to change policies.

Although reports can be written as memos (a memo is an internal document) for fast responses to problems, a more formal and longer form of report can also be used.

There are many different ways in which these reports can be written, but generally they have the following sections:

- Title page – the subject of the report.
- Terms of reference – what you have been asked to do or research.
- Procedure – how you have gone about gathering the information which you have included in the report.
- Findings – what you have found out.
- Conclusion – here you conclude and sum up your findings.
- Recommendations – on the basis of your findings and conclusions, you make your recommendations.
- Appendices – documents, charts, diagrams, tables and other information which is referred to in the rest of the report. This is where the more extensive information is placed in the report.

You should also sign and date your report.

Agendas and minutes

Preparatory documents and circulating documents

The first document we need to consider when thinking about preparing for a meeting and circulating any appropriate documents is the notice of meeting. The notice of meeting is a form of communication that calls the relevant people to attend the meeting. It is possible to use any method for an informal meeting, but with a formal meeting the rules and regulations laid down in the business's procedures would be followed. Possible methods of preparing a notice of meeting may include:

- Written or typed advance notice
- Verbal notice
- Notice-board posting.

Whatever form of notice is used, the following basic information must be included:

- The venue (where the meeting is to be held)
- The day, date and time of the meeting
- Details of any special business to be discussed at the meeting
- The type of meeting (where appropriate)
- The name of the person calling the meeting (usually the chairperson)
- The date of the notice.

Figure 4.5

An example of a notice of a meeting

25 November 2---

NOTICE OF MEETING

There will be an Acquisitions Meeting for all editors involved in the Health and Social Care department of the publishing house on Friday, 3 December 2--- at 09.30. Current projects will be discussed as well as amendments to publishing deadlines.

Helen Scott

An agenda will contain the following information:

- The date, time and venue of the meeting.
- The title 'Agenda' will confirm the purpose of the document.
- Item one is always the apologies received from members not able to attend. Apologies are sent to the meeting via the chairperson. A record is kept for the minutes of the meeting so that all concerned will know that those unable to attend had been invited and that they had 'sent their apologies'.
- Item two is always checking for accuracy of the minutes of the previous meeting. Once this task has been accomplished, the minutes will be signed by the chairman of the meeting.
- Item three always deals with any matters that have arisen from the minutes of the previous meeting.
- The remaining items to be dealt with during the meeting are then listed, each with a separate number.
- 'Any other business' (AOB) gives members the opportunity to introduce any matters they wish to discuss that have not been included in the agenda.

Those attending the meeting will sign the attendance sheet so that their names can be listed on the minutes of the meeting. Any other papers that the chairperson has said are necessary will be distributed to each of the members of the meeting.

Figure 4.6

An example of an agenda

> ABC Ltd
> Meeting of all First-Aid Qualified Staff
>
> A meeting of all staff holding a current first-aid qualification will be held in the training centre on Friday, 25 January 2--- at 11.15
>
> AGENDA
>
> 1. Apologies for absence
> 2. Minutes of the last meeting
> 3. Matters arising from the minutes
> 4. Report from Brian Phillips on recent government legislation regarding first-aid requirements
> 5. Details of forthcoming training courses for qualified staff
> 6. Implications of cover required for staff absence
> 7. Any other business
> 8. Date of next meeting
>
> Helen Scott

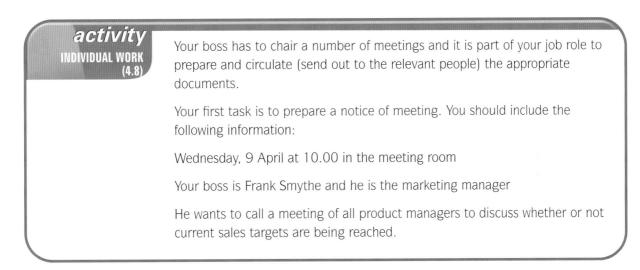

activity

INDIVIDUAL WORK (4.8)

Your boss has to chair a number of meetings and it is part of your job role to prepare and circulate (send out to the relevant people) the appropriate documents.

Your first task is to prepare a notice of meeting. You should include the following information:

Wednesday, 9 April at 10.00 in the meeting room

Your boss is Frank Smythe and he is the marketing manager

He wants to call a meeting of all product managers to discuss whether or not current sales targets are being reached.

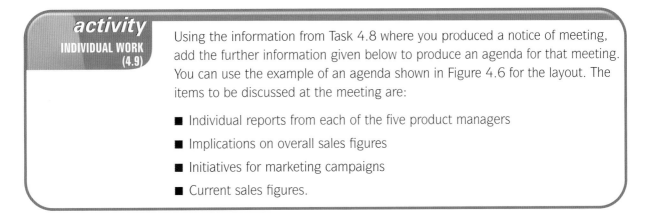

activity

INDIVIDUAL WORK (4.9)

Using the information from Task 4.8 where you produced a notice of meeting, add the further information given below to produce an agenda for that meeting. You can use the example of an agenda shown in Figure 4.6 for the layout. The items to be discussed at the meeting are:

- Individual reports from each of the five product managers
- Implications on overall sales figures
- Initiatives for marketing campaigns
- Current sales figures.

Compiling, circulating and checking minutes

During the meeting a series of notes have to be taken. These notes will later become the minutes of the meeting. These minutes are then distributed to all those who attended the meeting and a copy is filed. It is essential that an accurate written record of the meeting is provided for all those who attended and also for those who were unable to attend. At the next meeting, these minutes will be read under item two of the agenda and anything that needs reporting on as a result of the minutes will be dealt with under item three.

Minutes will be presented in the same order as the agenda and will include:

■ A list of those present at the meeting.

■ A list of those not present, but who sent their apologies.

■ A statement that confirms that the minutes of the previous meeting have been read and signed as being a true record.

■ An account of discussions that took place during the meeting.

■ A note of tasks that were allocated to individuals.

■ Reports that were received from individuals.

■ Actions to be taken in the future as a result of the meeting.

■ An account of any decisions that were made as a result of discussions.

■ Details of individuals to whom decisions taken may refer.

Minutes should be concise and precise, but they should not lose any accuracy in this process. The style of writing should be brief and to the point. Figure 4.7 shows an extract from a set of minutes.

Figure 4.7

An extract from a set of minutes

---

4. Report from the Chief Safety Officer

Mr Mills reported that the recent government legislation concerning health and safety at work procedures would require careful consideration. The new procedures would be copied and distributed to all concerned. Mr Mills stated that he would like a sub-committee to be formed to study the legislation and report back at the next meeting.

Mr Taylor, Mr Brenner and Ms Oliver volunteered to form the sub-committee and agreed to meet on Tuesday, 27 June 2-.

5. Implications of possible new extension to the office block

Ms Oliver reported that she had seen the plans for the new office block and is concerned that not enough space had been allocated to each member of staff using that block. After some discussion it was decided that Mr Mills would speak to the architects and report his findings to the next meeting.

---

activity

INDIVIDUAL WORK (4.11)

You now have to prepare your own set of minutes for the meeting you have recently held. Make sure that your minutes follow the same order as the items on the agenda. Did you arrange another meeting in the future? If so, put the date of the next meeting in the appropriate place. Present the agenda items as a numbered list in the minutes if this is appropriate.

Was your note-taking efficient enough for the preparation of the minutes to be quite straightforward?

Compare the content of your minutes with those of members of your group who attended the meeting.

Purchase order

A business may want to purchase any of the following:

- Materials – which can take several different forms. They may be raw materials needed to produce products. They may, however, be headed paper to produce business letters or cleaning products used on the production line.
- Capital items – which could be office furniture, new computer equipment, new buildings, etc.
- Services – to purchase a service from an individual or another business it is necessary for the business to raise a contract.

An order form is a firm commitment that the business requires the materials. An example of a blank order form is shown in Figure 4.8.

From Figure 4.8 we can identify the information that the supplier requires from the business. Essentially the following information is included on the order:

> **remember**
>
> Purchase orders should always be checked against invoices received from suppliers.

- To – this is the address of the business buying the materials.
- Order number – each order placed will have a unique number. This information is vital to both the supplier and the purchasing department of the business as we will see later.
- Date – every order placed must be dated.
- Delivery address – this may be different from the address of the purchasing business as the materials may be required at a branch of their operations.
- Special instructions – these may include items such as the fact that the order had previously been telephoned to the supplier.
- Reference number – which may be the number of the item as stated in the supplier's catalogue.
- Quantity – the number of each item required.
- Description – identifies the exact nature of the item required.
- Unit price – the price of each item required.
- Amount – the total amount when the quantity and unit price are multiplied.

■ Authorised by – the purchasing business would have an individual, or a number of individuals, that are authorised to sign on behalf of the business.

The order form is sent to the supplier's sales department, which has the main responsibility of creating orders for that business's products and services.

Figure 4.8

An example of an order form

ORDER FORM				
To: _____		Order no. _____		
_____		Date: _____		
_____				
Delivery address:		Special instructions:		
Ref. no.	Quantity	Description	Unit price £	Amount £
Authorised by: _____				

activity

**INDIVIDUAL WORK
(4.11)**

Produce your own order form and save it on a computer.

Imagine that it is one of your responsibilities to complete the order forms for your business. Complete your order form using the following information:

■ Use the address of your school or college

■ The order number is 3829

■ Use today's date

■ The delivery address is the same as the school or college address

■ There are no special instructions

■ You require the following:
   – Three boxes of A4 envelopes (182) at £11.20 each.
   – Five HP16 black cartidges (924) at £17.95 each.
   – One hundred CDRs (1104) at £0.55 each.

You will need this completed order for an activity later in this section of the book.

Invoices

Once the products have been delivered to the purchasing business, the supplier will send an invoice. This will list the quantity and description of the goods sent, as well as the total amount owing. The invoice will also state a date by which a payment should be made, and will list any discounts made available to the purchasing business.

---

activity

INDIVIDUAL WORK (4.12)

Produce and save a copy of your own invoice, using Figure 4.9 as a guide.

Complete the invoice for the goods you ordered on your order form in Activity 4.12. The additional information you need is:

- The invoice number is 489
- Use today's date for the invoice
- The terms are 20 per cent discount
- The goods were despatched two days ago
- VAT should be calculated at 17.5 per cent

Figure 4.9

An example of an invoice

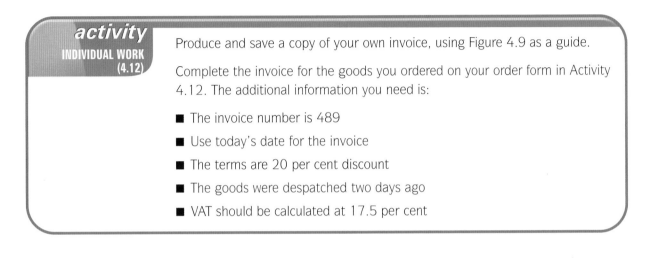

INVOICE					
To: _____ Invoice no. _____					
_____ Date: _____					
_____ Terms: _____					
Your order no. _____ Despatch date: _____					
Quantity	Description		Unit price	Total price	VAT
		Gross value			
		Less trade discount			
		Net value of goods			
		Plus VAT @ ____ %			
		Invoice total			
E&OE					

Appropriate layouts

Before we look at how organisations contact those outside the business, for example their customers, we should first consider the various ways that those inside the organisation present written communications to each other, including: memos, reports, newsletters, notices, agendas, minutes of meetings, company newspapers, notes and messages, and email messages.

---

activity
INDIVIDUAL WORK
(4.13)

What method of written internal communication do you think the managers of a business would use to inform their employees about the following issues?

a) To inform all employees that the business will change ownership next month.

b) To invite all supervisors to a meeting next week.

c) To tell all employees that the canteen opening hours will change next month.

d) To tell an employee that their statutory sick pay ends in a month.

e) To inform all sales people that new prices for all products will be effective on Thursday of next week.

---

remember

Many businesses have templates for their documents and require logos and addresses to be included.

Businesses communicate with their customers or suppliers using written forms of communication, including:

- Business letters – to the customer or a number of different customers.

- Compliment slips – which could be included instead of a letter, for example, with a copy of the organisation's brochure.

- Brochures or catalogues – which detail the products, services and other information about the business for the customers to browse through.

- Business cards – which would be left by one of the representatives of the business.

- Leaflets about the business.

- Advertisements about the business, including any special offers or discounts that may be available at the present time.

- Maps – which might be included in brochures or sent out with leaflets, showing customers how to reach the organisation.

Professional, appropriate expression

Whatever kind of written communication is used, whether it is to the employees of the business or to its customers or suppliers, it is important that a professional approach is maintained. Businesses will have what is known as a 'house style', i.e. a particular way of setting out standard items in each type of communication, and they will use the company's headed paper. They will also use a company logo to remind customers about who they are and what the business sells or stands for.

Look at the following types of communication style. One could be used in email, another in a formal business letter to a customer and the other in a telephone message for your manager. Identify which one is suitable in each case.

a) 'I regret, therefore, that under current company policies, we cannot refund your payment at this time.'

b) 'Toni, get me the figures for last month when you've got a chance. Cheers, Mike.'

c) 'When you were at lunch, Mr Sinclair called. He is keen to talk to you about an order, but wouldn't confirm his order until you have spoken to him. Can you call him back please between 3 and 4 this afternoon? His number is 07924443333.'

Writing documents for business

Remember that when you are writing documents for your business or your organisation, certain things will still need to be spelled out, even though the readers will be perfectly aware of technical language and procedures. This means that it is perfectly acceptable to use technical language or jargon, but an explanation will be necessary for those who do not understand.

Whenever you are preparing a document make sure that you put it together carefully. Documents often require more than one stage of writing. Begin with an initial draft and then ensure that it is correct and fits the purpose for which it has been written. Accuracy, consistency, legibility, fitness for purpose and its preparation by a particular deadline may be absolutely essential.

Appropriate use of occupationally relevant technical language

Technical style refers to written work where you need to use numbers, units, equations or technical jargon. There are a number of things to bear in mind regarding your technical style:

remember

It is always important to follow any standards or requirements set by the business.

- Clarity – you need to be clear so that there is no room for confusion. A reader or listener should not have to stop and work out what you mean.

- Clear purpose – there should be no misunderstanding about what you are saying or writing. Always remember that readers are usually busy people and will not have the patience to work their way through muddled or confused documents.

- Say it briefly – State your ideas clearly. Your important ideas should have subheadings and provide the structure of your document.

- Use appropriate words – you should always use the most appropriate words and support what you are saying with charts, tables, graphs, icons, illustrations or drawings.

- Be concise – a skilled writer will replace common key phrases with much shorter words or descriptions.

- Jargon – use words that everyone will understand (if you are writing for readers who will understand the jargon then it is acceptable to use it).

activity
INDIVIDUAL WORK
(4.15)

You probably know by now exactly what is involved in this unit. Have another look at the unit content for Unit 4. It is quite jargon-based. Translate the first assessment objectives into common language so that someone who does not know about the course would understand what is involved.

Recording and reporting
Note-taking

Note-taking is important. It is not always possible to remember what people have said and what decisions have been made; notes provide the user with their own record to use when required. Business notes are taken in a variety of situations at work, for example when telephone conversations occur, during meetings and when instructions are given.

There is no right or wrong way to take notes, but to be efficient and make sure they are understood, there are a number of skills that could be developed:

- Think before you write – remember that the words you write down may not be referred to for several days and you need to know what the sentences actually mean.

- Raise any questions at the time if there is something you do not understand.

- Try to develop your own way of standard note-taking – you may prefer to use plenty of sub-headings, or you may choose to underline important parts of your notes.

- Try to keep your notes in a notebook so that you always know where the notes are and they cannot be lost.

- Leave gaps between the main sections of your notes so you can add additional information later if it crops up again in the conversation or meeting. This will also make the notes easier to read.

- Concentrate on the main points and do not get lost in the detail, as some of the detail may not relate to the main point and not everything is of equal importance.

- Remember, the priority is to take good notes and helpful notes, rather than to save paper.

- Make sure that you can actually read what you have written – the faster you write, the less chance you have of being able to read your own writing later. If you abbreviate (shorten) words or put in initials for people, you will need to remember what these mean.

- If you are in a meeting, try to find a seat which gives you an uninterrupted view of those who are speaking – they may also show you diagrams or visual aids which you will need to look at. Bear in mind that you may not have to copy diagrams into your notes as these may be given to you as a hard copy later.

---

activity
INDIVIDUAL WORK
(4.16)

Practise your note-taking skills using the checklist above. Try taking notes from the TV news, from discussions in your group or from what your tutor's instructions are.

Reporting

Reporting back to those who have set work can be either formal or informal. Normally teams and departments have regular meetings at which the progress of work is discussed. However, reporting back also happens informally and an employee may be asked at any time by their team leader or supervisor to tell them how far they have progress with a task and whether they have had any difficulties.

Reporting back means giving a clear, concise and honest update on progress and it is an opportunity to alert others that help may be needed, or that a task may not be completed by the deadline given.

---

activity
INDIVIDUAL WORK
(4.17)

Design a questionnaire containing at least 10 questions about how at least five of your fellow students are progressing on their BTEC First course. Your questionnaire should obtain information about:

- Any outstanding work they have and the deadline for completion
- Any points that they know require immediate action
- Any points they would like to improve on, but not necessarily immediately
- What they intend to do about their outstanding work
- Their timescale for the completion of their action points.

Take notes while they are talking if you need more information than can be contained on the questionnaire.

Report back in written form to each of those interviewed, stating accurately and concisely what you have learned from their responses to your questionnaire.

Interpersonal and Non-Verbal Communication Skills

In any business or organisation it is important to ensure that you maintain a consistently high level of interpersonal and non-verbal communication skills. This means that you should always portray yourself in a professional manner.

Conveying a professional image

If it is important to a business to present the right image to its customers and the general public, then it should be equally important to the employees of that business. The way we dress, the image we present, the way we write or speak to customers, what we say and how we say it all affect the image of the business as a whole.

The organisation will also have set ways in which it wants its employees to deal with customers and with their fellow employees. These set ways are known as procedures and the employees should be made aware of these when they first start their job. Sometimes organisations issue booklets to their employees and these contain the procedures for dealing with customers. The procedures will be cover aspects of customer care.

Appropriate and confident manner

An employee's manner and degree of confidence can be important. There are several ways in which an employee could be described as being 'professional' in their behaviour at work. Their attitude is important, as is their personality, level of confidence and general behaviour in work situations.

An individual's personality will often determine their attitude at work and their behaviour while at work.

activity
INDIVIDUAL WORK
(4.18)

Do you have an appropriate and confident manner? Think about the following list and be honest in your answers. Are you:

- Conscientious?
- Neurotic?
- An extrovert?
- Agreeable?
- Open?

If you cannot decide for yourself, ask one of your fellow students or your tutor what they think.

Dress sense and industry conventions

For organisations whose employees have direct contact with their customers, it is important that the staff look presentable. To represent a company in the best way, an employee should think about:

- The way they dress for work.
- Their personal hygiene.
- The way they behave when they are at work.
- Their personality – whether or not they are often grumpy or sometimes a bit too loud.
- Their general attitude when they are at work – whether or not they look as if they are approachable and how they treat other people.

Some people are issued with a uniform that they have to wear for work.

If an individual does not work for an organisation that issues a uniform, then they will be expected to dress in clothes appropriate to the job. This means as smartly and as tidily as possible. Very often organisations insist on certain dress codes. These are rules about what can or cannot be worn for work.

Workwear very much depends on the job being done. For instance, some organisations insist that male employees wear a collar and tie to work, and some do not allow their female employees to wear trousers.

activity
GROUP WORK
(4.19)

In pairs, consider whether you know someone who is issued with a uniform for work. Or maybe you have to wear one for a part-time job you do. What do you think are the advantages and disadvantages of wearing a uniform for work?

Greeting and leaving business contacts

A business contact may be calling a business for any one of a wide range of reasons, from attending a meeting to enquiring about products, delivering parcels or repairing faulty machinery. Some of these visits may be prearranged by appointment, such as a meeting with a specific member of staff, whereas others may involve people arriving unannounced, such as a delivery driver or salespeople.

The business's reception area provides a visitor with their first impression of the organisation and it is important that this image is as good as possible. In order to achieve this, the area needs to be kept clean and tidy and the staff employed to cover reception duties should have a confident and friendly manner towards the visitors. The reception area should be manned at all times. Cover should be arranged for lunch and coffee breaks and for holiday and sickness periods. Some organisations employ gatekeepers who ensure any visitors are announced.

When meeting business contacts, the employee should try to do the following:

- Greet the contact courteously and use their name in the greeting, for example: 'Good morning Mr Smith', or, 'Good morning Brian' if the contact is a regular visitor to the employee and they are on first-name terms. In business situations it is usual for the two to shake hands.

■ Smile when the contact is met so that they feel welcome.

■ If the contact is well known to the employee, then some personal chat can take place, for example, 'How was your holiday?' or, 'Did you have a good weekend with your son after I last saw you?'

■ Offer them refreshments (if appropriate) and let them get settled before starting to talk about the purpose of the visit.

■ Concentrate while the meeting is taking place and make notes of important points, so that the contact can see the level of concentration and the intention to do a good job.

■ Give the contact positive feedback and promise that the matter will be dealt with positively.

When the contact is ready to leave, the employee should:

■ Shake hands once more.

■ Tell the contact it was nice to see them again.

■ Promise them that the matter will receive the employee's full attention.

■ Make sure they have full details of who they may need to contact or the employee's telephone number/email address.

■ Give them details of the next step to be taken (either what the contact has to do or what the business will be doing).

■ Wish them a safe journey (if appropriate).

■ Leave them with confidence that the meeting was a success and that they would be welcome again.

---

activity
INDIVIDUAL WORK
(4.20)

We have detailed the ways in which an employee can successfully deal with a visitor to the business's premises.

Write down how you think an employee should take a telephone call from one of the business's contacts. How should the employee greet the caller and reassure them that the employee is competent to take a message? How should the telephone call end?

Devon Holiday Cottages

The following telephone conversation took place at Devon Holiday Cottages one morning.

'Good morning, Devon Holiday Cottages.'

'Hello, this is Clive, is that Sarah?'

'Yes it is.'

'I don't know if you remember me Sarah, but I work for Framlingham Stationery and I visited you with the sales rep last month.'

'Yes I do Clive, hello, what can I do for you?'

'I was wondering if you could sort me out a cottage for August to fit six people?'

'Yes, I don't think that will be a problem. Do you want me to send you a brochure?'

'Yes that would be useful, but I wanted to talk to you about prices. I talked to Simon, the sales rep, on the way back from your office and he told me that you had sorted him out a 20 per cent discount for a holiday next July.'

'Did he really?'

'Yes and I wondered if you could do me the same deal?'

'I'll have to check on that Clive.'

'Thanks. Oh and one other thing, you know Florrie in your office? She's not got a boyfriend has she? I want to send her a bunch of flowers. Could you give me her home address?'

'I can't really say and I can't give you the address. It's against company policy.'

'Go on, I only want to send her a bunch of flowers.'

'Alright then, she is single and she lives at 42 Nelson Drive, Taunton. But don't tell her it was me that told you.'

'Thanks, that's lovely. I'll look forward to getting the brochure and hearing from you about the discount.'

activity
INDIVIDUAL WORK

Read the case study and answer the following questions:

a) What information should Sarah have had to hand to tell Clive?

b) What information should she not have told Clive?

c) How could she have withheld the information about Florrie without offending Clive?

d) What might be the likely result of Sarah having given Clive confidential information?

Conveying business information

All information passed on to either a colleague or a customer should be as accurate and as complete as possible. It is not always possible for an employee to give a customer all the information they require as the information may not be to hand or they may not be confident enough to convey it. In such cases, it is a good idea to check with another person to ensure the facts are right. In such cases, the employer should either assure the customer that they will call back with the information or ask them to wait while they find out the answer to their query.

Some information can be obtained easily, but the more complex the customer's query, the more difficult it may be for the employee to find the correct information immediately and to be confident that it is correct.

If a customer is asking a specific question there is little point in telling them about other things that they might be interested in or giving them more information than they really need. It is often a case of deciding what to say and what not to say, what to put in and what to leave out. The more complex the information is, the more chance there is that they will not understand it fully or will be confused by it.

It is vital that business information is accurate. This may sound obvious, but one incorrect figure or a decimal point in the wrong place could cause enormous problems, not only for the business itself but also for the customer. The same would apply to the address on an envelope. It can cause unnecessary delay and inconvenience if a document goes astray in the post because of an inaccurate address. Some businesses design their documents in duplicate or triplicate so that such inaccuracies can be spotted easily.

> **remember**
>
> It is important not to guess the answer to questions posed by a customer, but to give them accurate information.

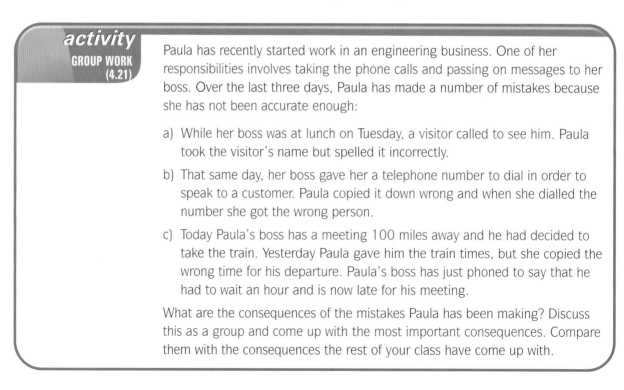

activity
GROUP WORK (4.21)

Paula has recently started work in an engineering business. One of her responsibilities involves taking the phone calls and passing on messages to her boss. Over the last three days, Paula has made a number of mistakes because she has not been accurate enough:

a) While her boss was at lunch on Tuesday, a visitor called to see him. Paula took the visitor's name but spelled it incorrectly.

b) That same day, her boss gave her a telephone number to dial in order to speak to a customer. Paula copied it down wrong and when she dialled the number she got the wrong person.

c) Today Paula's boss has a meeting 100 miles away and he had decided to take the train. Yesterday Paula gave him the train times, but she copied the wrong time for his departure. Paula's boss has just phoned to say that he had to wait an hour and is now late for his meeting.

What are the consequences of the mistakes Paula has been making? Discuss this as a group and come up with the most important consequences. Compare them with the consequences the rest of your class have come up with.

All documents and information given by the business should be checked thoroughly before being passed on or issued. The person completing the documents should do this, although this is not always as easy as it sounds. Sometimes you simply cannot see your own mistakes and it is more efficient either to get someone else to check the document or to read it to them and they can check the figures and data.

Dealing with confidential matters

As with confidentiality of information, it is also important for any employee to observe what is known as discretion. This section explains why an employee would have to be discreet about the business's activities.

Confidentiality, competitors and product development

Confidential information is also known as 'sensitive information'. As we already know, any employee who has to deal with confidential information will ensure that only those that are authorised are able to see it.

Much confidential information is kept on computer. Customer records, for example, would be held on computer by many businesses and they would not want to let their competitors know any of their customer details. Another reason for confidentiality of customer information is the Data Protection Act 1998. This is the legislation (law) governing how organisations keep information about customers on computer.

If sensitive information is kept on computer, businesses can make sure it remains confidential in a number of ways, including:

- Ensuring its employees have to use a password to use the computer system.
- Ensuring its staff have **screen-savers** so that they do not leave confidential material on their computer screen when they are away from their desks.
- Ensuring that computers are not situated in public areas of the business, for example the reception area, where the general public can see the screen.

keyword

Screen-saver – A moving image on the computer screen that appears if the computer is not used for a few minutes.

Potential internal problems and negative publicity

A business would want their employees to keep sensitive information safe and use discretion if the business is experiencing difficulties.

Confidentiality regarding the work carried out by an employee's business, its plans or its customers is essential at all times. If there is ever any doubt about whether information could prove to be embarrassing, even in the most innocent of conversations, it should not be mentioned. Employers expect a degree of confidentiality with regard to information leaking out, but this is equally as important in dealing with issues when discussing them inside the organisation. Discussing matters that could affect other departments or employees can cause unnecessary friction and problems and perhaps even **disciplinary procedures**.

activity

GROUP WORK
(4.23)

What might be the consequences if the minutes of a meeting discussing job losses within a business were passed to a local newspaper?

progress check

1. Give five purposes of business communication.
2. State three situations where formal communication is necessary.
3. Give four disadvantages of verbal communication.
4. What is the task cycle?
5. When are agendas and minutes used?
6. What is the difference between a purchase order and an invoice?
7. Why is it important to draft and redraft business documents?
8. Why is it important to convey a professional image?
9. Why is it important to keep accurate and complete records?
10. What might be the consequence of not keeping a conversation confidential?

People in Organisations

This units covers:

- how to prepare for employment
- the rights and responsibilities of employees and employers
- how effective working practices are developed
- planning career development

This unit looks at the contribution that individuals and groups make to an organisation. It looks at the skills of employees and how organisations select suitable employees to match particular roles in the business. Organisations also need to ensure that the overall skill base of their employees is constantly improving.

This unit also looks at your existing skills, knowledge, qualifications and interests, and how these can help you to choose a suitable job. You will also learn how to develop your knowledge and understanding of both the employer and employee rights and responsibilities.

The unit also looks at how employees can make an effective contribution to work and to the organisation, how to be a good team member and how performance reviews can assist the employer and the employee.

grading criteria

To achieve a **Pass** grade the evidence must show that the learner is able to:	To achieve a **Merit** grade the evidence must show that the learner is able to:	To achieve a **Distinction** grade the evidence must show that the learner is able to:
P1 match current knowledge and skills to possible job opportunities using appropriate sources of information and advice	**M1** explain the importance of terms and conditions of employment	**D1** analyse, using examples, the implications of terms and conditions of employment
P2 complete an application for a selected job opportunity	**M2** compare and contrast the organisational structures and job roles within two business organisations	**D2** evaluate how personal attributes and team working contribute to working practices
P3 describe the terms and conditions of employment in a selected organisation	**M3** explain the importance of team working and personal attributes within two business organisations	

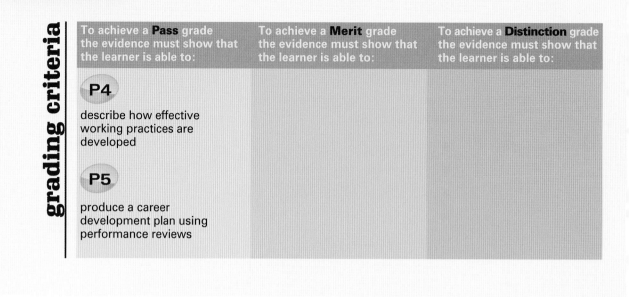

To achieve a **Pass** grade the evidence must show that the learner is able to:	To achieve a **Merit** grade the evidence must show that the learner is able to:	To achieve a **Distinction** grade the evidence must show that the learner is able to:
P4 describe how effective working practices are developed **P5** produce a career development plan using performance reviews		

Preparing for Employment

You may not necessarily know exactly what you want to do in terms of work after you have finished this course. You will probably have already done some part-time work or have had work experience. If you have, no doubt you will have found these experiences very useful.

The trick is to find suitable work which will interest you but that matches your skills and knowledge. We will look at the qualities that employers look for and how you can best attract employers' interest.

Personal audit

> **remember**
>
> A personal audit is a way of assessing your current skills and knowledge and how these can be matched against possible job opportunities.

A personal audit involves looking at your knowledge and skills and how these can be matched to job opportunities. This course will provide you with good background knowledge business as you will be looking at various aspects of work and how organisations operate. As you complete various units, you will find that you will be more or less interested in certain aspects of business. Perhaps you will find you have an aptitude for numbers, or you prefer working with people.

Types of employment

For the purposes of this unit we need to consider paid employment rather than self-employment. This still includes an enormous variety of different work types and styles.

Full-time employment

Full-time employment, as it suggests, means that the employee is working a full week and does this every week apart from the time they have allocated for holidays.

activity
**INDIVIDUAL WORK
(5.1)**

Answer YES or NO to the following statements:

- I enjoy working with others
- I am good at organising my time
- I am good at planning my work
- I set myself targets
- I review what I have done and what needs to be done
- I am confident at making decisions
- I am good at problem solving
- I am good at researching information
- Once I have found information I know how to use it
- I have good communication skills
- I feel at ease dealing with people
- I am confident in interviews
- I am happy dealing with mathematical problems
- I have skills in ICT.

This should identify your key strengths and weaknesses. These are the base skills that many employers are looking for. This should help you to identify which types of job opportunity would suit you best.

keyword

Shifts
– A period of non-standard working hours, such as starting at lunchtime and working through into the evening or beginning earlier in the day and finishing after lunch.

Typical full-time jobs include teachers, local government officers and office workers. Usually, full-time employees are paid on a monthly basis, but others such as factory workers might be paid on a weekly basis.

The contract of employment for full-time workers will state the number of hours that they are expected to work, the availability and pay (or time off in lieu) for working overtime, and their holiday entitlements. Around 60 per cent of those in work have full-time jobs, but not all of them work standard 9 a.m. to 5 p.m. and may work **shifts**, at home, at night, or even three or four 12-hour days each week.

Part-time employment

Part-time employment is common in the UK and it very much ties in with employees' needs to have flexible working arrangements.

Normally part-time work is no more than 25 hours per week. The majority of part-time workers are women, accounting for well over 50 per cent of the total number of employees in part-time work. Part-time workers have the same rights as full-time employees.

Temporary and permanent employment

When an employee begins work for an employer, the contract of employment will state whether the job is a temporary or permanent one. If the job is temporary, the contract will state that the employee has been taken on to work for a specified period of time, such as six months or a year. Temporary contracts are given to employees to cover long-term sickness, maternity leave or short-term needs of the employer to take on more staff.

The majority of jobs are classed as permanent as there is no definite period of time that the employee is expected to work for the employer. An employer may wish to terminate the contract because the job of the employee is no longer needed or perhaps the business is about to close.

---

activity

**INDIVIDUAL WORK
(5.2)**

Visit the labour market page on the National Statistics website, then answer the following questions:

a) What is the total number of people employed in the UK?

b) What is the total number of hours worked by employees per week?

c) What is the average number of hours worked per week?

National Statistics
www.statistics.gov.uk

Sources of information and advice

In this section of the unit we will look at the sources of information about job opportunities and advice on getting a job.

There are various sections of the media, including newspapers, TV, radio and the Internet, where you can find information about jobs or applying for work. The Teletext services on digital TV have printed details of employment prospects and job vacancies around the country.

remember

A vast amount of information is available on the Internet to help you discover job opportunities.

Newspapers and magazines provide the majority of printed advertisements for job opportunities and many of the national and regional newspapers have particular days on which they advertise jobs in particular areas.

Specialist magazines will have useful information about particular occupations. Larger cities have free newspapers and magazines that are distributed at tube, train and bus stations. There are also thousands of recruitment agencies that advertise vacancies.

Locally, free newspapers or low-cost local newspapers contain local job opportunities and vacancy details.

By the end of 2006, the old-fashioned Job Centres will have been replaced by Jobcentre Plus offices. These are a useful source of information to help people find work. They also run a website where you can search by job type or title. Jobcentre Plus offers vacancies for full-time, part-time, temporary or permanent work.

Jobcentre Plus
www.jobcentreplus.gov.uk

The government also runs a website in conjunction with the job centres, called Work Train. At any one time they may have as many as 400 000 jobs. The site also includes training courses and voluntary work. Useful occupational profiles help you to match your own skills and interests with particular types of work.

activity
INDIVIDUAL WORK
(5.3)

Visit www.direct.gov.uk/employment and click on 'Jobseekers'. This will open a new window containing information on Jobcentre Plus, New Deal, interviews and the direct services offered either online or via the telephone.

Directgov
www.direct.gov.uk

Your school, college, government agencies and private employment agencies are only one batch of potential sources of information and advice. You may already have some work experience, either in part-time or seasonal work. Previous employers can be useful sources of information as they may know about vacancies that currently exist or will come up in the near future. Friends and family are also a useful source of information. Those that are in work will know whether their employers are looking for a new member of staff.

keyword

Job description
– A statement prepared by the business that identifies the nature of the job, including the tasks and responsibilities involved.

keyword

Person specification
– This is also sometimes known as a job specification. It identifies the characteristics of the successful individual needed to carry out the job.

keyword

Applications
– A written response to an advertisement, asking to be considered for a named vacancy.

keyword

Shortlist
– When the top candidates are identified and invited to attend for an interview.

keyword

References
– Statements made by independent individuals that comment on the character and/or abilities of the candidate.

keyword

Candidate
– A potential employee who has applied and been selected to attend for interview.

Recruitment process

There are a number of stages that a business needs to follow when recruiting a new employee:

- Deciding that there is a need to find a new member of staff.
- Designing a **job description** (see below) that explains what the job is all about.
- Designing a **person specification** (see below) that explains what sort of person is needed.
- Deciding where to advertise the job.
- Designing the advertisement for the job.
- Looking at the different **applications** for the job.
- Deciding on a **shortlist** of those who have applied.
- Interviewing those on the shortlist.
- Taking up **references** for the successful **candidate**.
- Writing to inform the successful applicant and then the unsuccessful applicants.

Job specification

A job specification details the duties of the person who will hold the post. It includes the following:

- The job title
- Where the post fits into the organisation
- The tasks and activities that the person will need to carry out
- The roles and responsibilities.

Job description

Typically, the job description will include the following:

- Job title
- Department, function or section
- Wage or salary range
- Main purpose of the job
- Duties and responsibilities
- Responsible to and for.

activity
**INDIVIDUAL WORK
(5.4)**
Find a suitable advertisement in your local newspaper, preferably one with plenty of information. Try to write a rough job specification based on the information you have.

Person specification

A person specification describes the qualities that a person should have to carry out the job satisfactorily. A business will use a person specification as a checklist so that they can compare the skills, experience and other features of candidates with the ideal person they have set out in the specification.

This specification will be carefully put together and will attempt to match the ideal qualities sought by the department or by the business.

Application form

Many businesses use standard application forms. They often appear to be very daunting, but the business may give you guidelines to help you complete the form. There is various advice that you should consider when dealing with an application form, for example:

remember

It is often a good idea to photocopy an application form and fill this in first before you complete the original.

- Photocopy the original and fill in the copy first.
- Spend time thinking about tricky questions.
- Make sure everything is spelled correctly and that you have used the correct grammar.
- Make sure your handwriting is legible.
- Focus on the skills that you think match the information you have on the job.
- Mention any personal achievements.
- Give some thought to open-ended questions, like: 'Why have you applied for this post?'
- Choose your referees carefully and ask their permission before using their names.

Curriculum vitae

It is a good idea for everyone looking for a job to prepare their own curriculum vitae, otherwise known as a CV. This is a document that provides all of the information about you and is, in fact, a history of yourself. There are many different ways to prepare a CV, and an enormous amount of information can be included, although you should try to make the CV as short and as neat as possible.

The main information that is required is:

- Your full name
- Address
- Date of birth
- Your marital status
- Education and qualifications
- Employment and work experience
- Hobbies and interests
- A statement about your good personal qualities or achievements
- Details of at least two referees.

Once you have completed your CV you will be able to update it regularly and adapt it for different job applications. Try to make sure that you do not go over two pages of A4 paper.

Letters of application

Some job advertisements will simply ask for a letter of application. This can often be sent either with a CV or with a completed application form. Sometimes the business will ask for the letter of application to be handwritten. If this is required you should follow these instructions. A letter of application should include the following:

- An opening paragraph that states where you saw the advertisement, why it appeals to you and why you are applying for the job.
- Summarise your main strengths, stressing your suitability for the job.
- Be enthusiastic.
- State when you are available for interview.
- State when you could start the job.

remember

Letters of application should always be brief and to the point and highlight anything relevant on your CV.

■ Keep the letter of application short and use the same layout as a business letter.

activity

**INDIVIDUAL WORK
(5.5)**

Using the same advertisement that you used for Activity 5.4, write a sample letter of application. You should state your interest in the job and the skills and knowledge you have that match the requirements for the job. You should also prepare your CV using word-processing software.

Rights and Responsibilities of Employees and Employers

Terms and conditions of employment

The relationship between employers and employees is complex. Contracts, agreements, procedures, policies and law rule it. Employees and employers both have rights in terms of their relationship between one another. Just as they have these rights, they also have responsibilities to abide by what was agreed between them and to follow the letter of the law in various Acts and regulations relating to employment.

Rights of employees

In this section we will look at the rights of employees, which are specifically laid down, often in contracts of employment or in staff handbooks. Employers are required to provide contracts of employment and state terms and conditions of service. They need to comply with the basic minimum standards laid down by the law.

Contracts of employment

Many employees work without written employment contracts and there are several reasons for this, among which are the nature of the work itself (part-time or casual work), jobs with odd hours, flexible working and, of course, self-employment.

Many employees who do not have a written contract will have to rely on a verbal agreement between themselves and the employer. Verbal agreements are no less valid than written ones, but they are difficult to pin down if there are problems.

activity

**INDIVIDUAL WORK
(5.6)**

Look at the example contract in Figure 5.1 and answer the following questions:

a) What do you think is meant by a 'collective pay agreement'?

b) What is meant by 'duration of employment, working hours'?

c) What is meant by a 'probationary period'?

Figure 5.1

An example of a standard
contract of employment

Contract of Employment

| **1. Company** |
| Name |
| Address |
| Chief executive |

| **2. Employee** |
| Name |
| Address |

| **3. Place of work** |
| Address |

| **4. Job description** |
| |

| **5. Collective pay agreement, safety representative** |
| The following collective pay agreement(s) apply |
| Parties to collective wage agreements |
| Safety representative |
| Check that all of the following points comply with the collective pay agreement. |

6. Duration of employment, working hours	
First day of employment	Last day of employment (if applicable)
Weekly working hours	Daily working hours (from/to)
Breaks	Notice period
Holidays are to be decided according to the provisions of the Act relating to holidays.	

| **7. Probationary period (if applicable)** | |
| Duration of probationary period | Notice during probationary period |

8. Pay		
Hourly/monthly pay	Overtime supplement (minimum 40%)	Public holiday allowance, night
Other supplements		
Allowances/expenses		
Salary is paid		
Holiday pay is additional to pay		

| **9. Other information** | | |
| | | |

| **10. Signatures** | | |
| Date | Employer's signature | Employee's signature |

keyword

BACS
– The abbreviation for Bank Automated Clearing System – employees' wages are paid straight into the bank and they can have access to the money immediately.

Payment terms

The contract should clearly state the employee's salary or hourly rate and detail when their wages will be paid (monthly, weekly, etc.). In addition, the contract will need to state how their wages will be paid (**BACS**, cheque, etc.) and give details of any requirements from the employee to make payment possible (for example, a personal bank account).

Probation

Probation periods are designed to give the individual an opportunity to work towards their full potential. In effect, a probation period is a test period during which the employee can decide whether the job is ideal for them. The employer can also assess the skills, knowledge and capabilities of the employee. Probation periods can last from a month to six months. Three to six months are the most common.

activity

**INDIVIDUAL WORK
(5.7)**

Perry's contract of employment states that he will be paid 12 equal payments per year. His yearly pay is £12 000.

a) How often does he get paid?

b) What amount is he paid each time?

At the end of the probation period, assuming that the employee is still happy to work for the business and the business is content that the employee is ideal for the job, the employee will be taken on permanently for the post.

Disciplinary procedures

Disciplinary action occurs when, in the view of the employer, employees fail to maintain the level of standards demanded of them. Disciplinary procedures are there to ensure that the employer deals fairly with the employee.

Table 5.1 An example of a disciplinary procedure

	Guidance notes
1 Purpose of the procedure The Company's aim is to encourage improvement in individual conduct and performance. This procedure sets out the action that will be taken when Company rules are breached.	*1 The purpose should remind people that the procedure is designed not as a dismissal procedure but as a means of encouraging employees to conform to acceptable standards.*
2 Principles If you are subject to disciplinary action: • the procedure is designed to establish the facts quickly and to deal consistently with disciplinary issues. No disciplinary action will be taken until the matter has been fully investigated; • at every stage you will be advised of the nature of the complaint, be given the opportunity to state your case, and be represented or accompanied by a fellow employee of your choice;	*2 Employers often lose at Employment Tribunals because they did not comply with the procedure – so always follow the procedure.*

	Guidance notes
• you will not be dismissed for a first breach of discipline except in the case of gross misconduct, when the penalty will normally be dismissal without notice and without pay in lieu of notice; • you have a right to appeal against any disciplinary action taken against you; • the procedure may be implemented at any stage if your alleged misconduct warrants such action. If you request, you have the right to be accompanied at a disciplinary hearing by a fellow worker or trade union official.	
3 Informal discussions Before taking formal disciplinary action, your supervisor will make every effort to resolve the matter by informal discussions with you. Only where this fails to bring about the desired improvement should the formal disciplinary procedure be implemented.	*3 Make sure that employees and managers understand the difference between routine admonishments and action taken under the procedure.*
4 First warning If conduct or performance is unsatisfactory, the employee will be given a written warning or performance note. Such warnings will be recorded, but disregarded after ___ months of satisfactory service. The employee will also be informed that a final written warning may be considered if there is no sustained satisfactory improvement or change. (Where the first offence is sufficiently serious, for example because it is having, or is likely to have, a serious harmful effect on the organisation, it may be justifiable to move to a final directly written warning.)	*4 It can be unfair to keep details of warnings on an employee's file indefinitely. Unless a warning is for a very serious matter, it should be disregarded after, say, six months to a year. The written warning should accurately record the warning given at the disciplinary interview. Do not write the warning before the interview.*
5 Final written warning If the offence is serious, or there is no improvement in standards, or if a further offence of a similar kind occurs, a final written warning will be given which will include the reason for the warning and a note that if no improvement results within ___ months, action at Stage 6 will be taken.	*5 The warning should state clearly that dismissal would result from a failure to comply.*
Dismissal or action short of dismissal If the conduct or performance has failed to improve, the employee may suffer demotion, disciplinary transfer, loss or seniority (as allowed in the contract) or dismissal.	*Except in cases of gross misconduct, employees should receive notice or payment in lieu.*
6 Statutory discipline and dismissal procedure If an employee faces dismissal – or action short of dismissal such as loss of pay or demotion – the minimum statutory procedure will be followed. This involves: • Step 1: a written note to the employee setting out the allegation and the basis for it • Step 2: a meeting to consider and discuss the allegation • Step 3: a right of appeal including an appeal meeting. The employee will be reminded of their right to be accompanied.	
7 Gross misconduct If, after investigation, it is confirmed that an employee has committed an offence of the following nature (the list is not exhaustive), the normal consequence will be dismissal without notice or payment in lieu of notice: theft, damage to property, fraud, incapacity for work due to being under the influence of alcohol or illegal drugs, physical violence, bullying and gross insubordination. While the alleged gross misconduct is being investigated, the employee may be suspended, during which time he or she will be paid their normal pay rate. Any decision to dismiss will be taken by the employer only after full investigation.	
8 Appeals If you wish to appeal against any disciplinary decision, you must appeal in writing within five working days of the decision being communicated to you to _____ (name or job title). If possible a senior manager who was not involved in the original disciplinary action will hear the appeal and decide the case as impartially as possible.	

Source: www.acas.org.uk

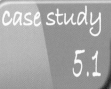

case study 5.1

Larking about

Norman had been in trouble before, but that was 13 months ago when Norman and Stan were playing about near the delivery area. Norman had pushed Stan and a reversing truck nearly crushed him.

Norman had been marched in to see the Personnel Manager who was terrified that Stan could have been killed and ranted on about insurance claims and how bad a death would be for the business. Norman had smiled (he regretted that later) and the Personnel Manager went mad. He scribbled out a written warning to Norman and sent him home for the day. His last words had been: 'Come back tomorrow young man and if your attitude is no better, don't even bother!'

Norman had come in the next day and had kept his head down. He had been a model employee ever since – that was until this morning, when he accidentally dropped a box on Stan's head and knocked him out. First there was the ambulance, then the safety officer and the police, and then the dreaded Personnel Manager.

'Right,' he had said. 'I've had to talk to you about messing around before, haven't I?'

'Yes, but ...' Norman had replied.

'Yes but nothing. This is your final warning. Collect it in writing from my office in an hour. The next time, you're out of here.'

activity
GROUP WORK

As a group, read the case study. Decide whether the Personnel Manager was fair to Norman. What should Norman have said and what should the Personnel Manager have done in the situation?

Once an organisation has written its disciplinary procedure, it is vital that all employees are either familiar with it or have access to a copy.

It is not always necessary to begin disciplinary procedures but, before this happens, it is usual for the following to take place:

- See if the matter can be resolved by informal discussions.
- The disciplinary matter has to be investigated fully.
- The employee involved in the disciplinary matter has to be told that they can be represented or accompanied by a person of their choice at all the meetings.

The disciplinary interview should ensure that the employee:

- Is made aware of any allegations against them.
- Is given the opportunity to put forward their side of the story.
- Is made aware of disciplinary action which can be taken against them if the allegations are proved to be true.

case study 5.2 — Allegations

Geraldine knew this was serious. The shop manager had called in the police and they were threatening to arrest her.

'You realise you can be sacked for this?' said the shop manager when she had told Geraldine to close her till and follow her to the office.

'Sacked for what?' she had asked.

'You know full well. I've got all the evidence I need,' she had told her.

Apparently a well-known shoplifter had been caught with three pairs of jeans from the shop in one of the shop's bags. She was asked where she had got the bag and she had told the store detective that her friend Geraldine had given it to her. Geraldine remembered the girl; she had caught her last month when she tried to steal a coat from the shop.

The police were sitting in the office taking notes and asked the shop manager whether she wanted them to arrest Geraldine. No one was listening to her. All the shop manager said was, 'No, I'll sack her and have done with it.'

With that she was given the balance of her pay in cash and told to leave.

activity
GROUP WORK

Did the shop manager deal with the situation in the correct manner? What should have happened?

Grievance procedures

The purpose of a grievance procedure is to enable individual employees to raise grievances (problems) with management about their employment, either by themselves or with a representative.

remember

Grievances should always be taken up with immediate supervisor or manager first.

Normally, the first step is for the employee to set out in writing the grievance which they have with the employer. The second step is for the employer to arrange a meeting to discuss the grievance. The employee has the right to be accompanied to this meeting by a colleague or perhaps a representative from the trade union. At the end of the meeting, the employer has to tell the employee about the decision made and that the employee has a right to appeal if they feel that the decision is unfair. Step three of the process allows the employee to make an appeal, which means that a second meeting is arranged, probably with a more senior member of the management.

Table 5.2 An example of a grievance procedure

	Guidance notes
1 Introduction It is the Company's policy to ensure that employees with a grievance relating to their employment can use a procedure which can help to resolve grievances as quickly and as fairly as possible.	*1 It is a good idea to set out company policy; it reminds managers of their role in dealing with grievances.*
2 Informal discussions If you have a grievance about your employment, you should discuss it informally with your immediate supervisor. We hope that the majority of concerns will be resolved at this stage.	*2 Informal discussions should resolve the vast majority of grievances.*
3 Stage 1 If you feel that the matter has not been resolved through informal discussions, you should put your grievance in writing to your immediate supervisor. The supervisor must give a response within five working days in an endeavour to resolve the matter.	*3 The first stage should allow supervisors to resolve the grievance without the involvement of any employee representative. The aim should be to resolve the grievance at the lowest relevant level.*
4 Stage 2 If the matter is not resolved, you may raise the matter, in writing, with the manager, who must give a response within five working days. You may be represented or accompanied at this meeting by a fellow worker of your choice or by a union official.	*4 The stages should reflect the levels of management in the organisation.*
5 Stage 3 If the matter is not resolved to your satisfaction, you should put your grievance in writing to the managing director or an authorised deputy. You will be entitled to have a meeting with the managing director or his/her authorised deputy to discuss the matter. The managing director or authorised deputy will give his/her decision within seven working days of the grievance being received. The managing director's decision is final.	*5 Time limits prevent issues running on and on, and encourage managers to deal with them promptly.*

Source: www.acas.org.uk

> **remember**
> Usually, the longer you have worked for a business or organisation, the longer your annual leave entitlement will be.

Annual leave

Every employee, whether part time or full time, is covered by the Working Time Regulations and is entitled to four weeks' paid annual leave. A week's leave should allow an employee to be away from work for a week. It should be the same amount of time as the working week: if a worker does a five-day week, they are entitled to 20 days' leave; if they do a three-day week, the entitlement is 12 days' leave.

The leave entitlement under the regulations is not additional to bank holidays. There is no statutory right to take bank holidays off. An employee who is not otherwise paid for bank holidays may take bank holidays as part of their annual leave entitlement in order to receive payment for these holidays.

case study

Trouble for Trudi

5.3

This was the second time that Trudi had walked into the office 10 minutes late this week. She was tired and angry about oversleeping, but her boss Frank had made her work until nearly 7 p.m. every day this week.

He had called her into his office and told her off and said that this was her first verbal warning and that next time she was late he would send her home and not pay her for the day. The time after that she had better start looking for another job.

Trudi had burst into tears. After all she had done for the department to catch up on the backlog of work, she thought he would understand that she was tired, was working late and not getting paid for it and that she had not deliberately been late.

After she had calmed down, she thought long and hard about it all and decided that Frank should not get away with treating her like that.

activity
INDIVIDUAL WORK

What should Trudi do? What should her first step be in beginning a grievance procedure about the way Frank has treated her?

activity
GROUP WORK
(5.8)

What types of business might have a Christmas or summer shutdown? What does this mean?

Maternity and paternity leave

Employees who are working parents have several key rights:

- They should receive paid and unpaid maternity leave
- They should receive paid paternity leave
- They are entitled to paid and unpaid adoption leave
- They can request flexible working hours
- They can ask for unpaid parental leave if they are parents of children under five
- They can ask to be granted unpaid time off to care for dependants.

Most female employees are entitled to 26 weeks' maternity leave, regardless of how long the employee has worked for the employer or the number of hours worked each week. Employees are either entitled to Statutory Maternity Pay or Contractual Maternity Pay. Some female employees, who have worked for their employer for 26 weeks by the beginning of the fifteenth week before the baby is due, may be entitled to a longer period of maternity leave (known as additional maternity leave).

activity
INDIVIDUAL WORK
(5.9)

a) What is meant by the phrase 'unpaid leave'?

b) How does the employer pay maternity pay?

c) Who actually pays for the maternity pay?

d) What is the length in weeks of the standard maternity leave and what is it for paternity leave?

(You will need to do some research.)

Jobcentre Plus
www.jobcentreplus.gov.uk
Citizens Advice Bureau
www.adviceguide.org.uk

Notice and termination

A typical contract of employment should refer to the following points with regard to notice and termination of contract:

- The amount of notice the employee has to give to the employer, usually expressed in weeks or months.

- Whether the employee will continue to be paid during their notice period and how much.

- Whether the employer can ask the employee to leave before the end of their notice period and whether they will pay the employee if this happens.

Normally, the employee is expected to work through the notice before leaving the company. However, in many cases, either the employee or their employer will want to cut short the notice period so that the employee can leave more quickly.

Redundancy

If the employer closes down the business, or a part of the business, he or she may no longer require the services of some or all of the employees. In cases of redundancy the employer must consult the employees and select fairly those to be made redundant. If possible the employer must offer them alternative employment in the business. This would be possible of the employer could manage to freeze the recruitment of new employees and give the jobs to the existing, redundant employees. An alternative is for the employer to reduce the number of hours that the employees work throughout the organisation.

Union membership

All employees have the right to join a trade union. They should not be dismissed, refused employment, harassed or made redundant on the basis that they are a member of a trade union.

remember

The number of people in trade unions has dropped significantly since the 1980s.

Just as employees have the right to be members of a trade union, they also have the right not be members. They should not suffer from harassment, dismissal or other unfair treatment on account of the fact that they have not joined a trade union.

Once an employee is a member of a trade union, they have the right to take part in normal trade union activities. These include recruiting other members, collecting trade union subscriptions and attending trade union meetings.

activity
INDIVIDUAL WORK
(5.10)

Using the Internet, find out the names of five leading UK trade unions. What types of employees are members of these trade unions?

Responsibilities of employees

The employee has a number of different responsibilities towards their employer. These could include:

- Acting in good faith towards their employer
- Accounting for any cash they may handle
- Ensuring that they keep the business's secrets confidential
- Following any orders or instructions, providing they are reasonable and legal
- Giving faithful service to the employer.

Specific responsibilities could include the following:

- Complying with company policies
- Representing the organisation
- Ethical behaviour
- Contract fulfilment.

activity
GROUP WORK
(5.11)

Discuss as a group what you understand by the terms 'act in good faith' and 'faithful service'.

Rights of employers

From the employee's point of view the laws and rights aim to protect them against dangerous practices, discrimination and unfair working practices. But these same agreements and laws protect employers against employees that refuse or constantly fail to carry out their responsibilities.

Specifically, the rights of employers are:

- Contracts of employment – to lay down the basic agreement between them and the employee.

■ Payment terms – which state how much, when and how an employee will be paid.

■ Notice and termination – should it become necessary to sack or ask an employee to leave, the number of weeks' notice involved and payments to be received.

■ Disciplinary and grievance procedures – these clearly lay down the grounds and procedures that must be followed in the event of the employer taking disciplinary action against an employee or the employee taking out a grievance against the employer.

■ Leave – beyond statutory minimum amounts of leave.

■ Union membership – the right to belong to a union and whether it is recognised by the employer.

■ Codes of behaviour – these are the way that the employer expects the employee to behave at work.

activity
GROUP WORK (5.12)

Draw up a code of behaviour for your class or group. What kinds of behaviour would be unacceptable? What would be the minimum standards required whilst in school or college?

Legal framework for employment

The British government has passed the laws that the word 'Act'. Some of contain them have been written as a result of Britain being a member of the European Union. The ones that contain the word 'Regulations' are direct copies of European Union law. All of the members of the European Union are expected to have the same absolute minimum standards in employment.

The Disability Discrimination Act 2005 (DDA 2005)

In April 2005 a new Disability Discrimination Act was passed by Parliament, which amends or extends existing provisions in the Disability Discrimination Act 1995, including:

■ Making it unlawful for operators of transport vehicles to discriminate against disabled people.

■ Making it easier for disabled people to rent property and for tenants to make disability-related adaptations.

■ Making sure that private clubs with 25 or more members cannot keep disabled people out just because they have a disability.

■ Extending protection to cover people who have HIV, cancer and multiple sclerosis from the moment they are diagnosed.

■ Ensuring that discrimination law covers all the activities of the public sector.

■ Requiring public bodies to promote equality of opportunity for disabled people.

Until 1995 the only law that dealt with the employment of disabled people was the Disabled Persons (Employment) Act 1944. The new Act makes it unlawful for an employer to discriminate against a disabled job applicant in the following ways:

- The selection for jobs
- The terms and conditions of employment
- Promotion or transfer to another area of work
- Training
- Employment benefits
- Dismissal.

Employment Act 2002

Many of the new arrangements relating to paternity and maternity leave mentioned above were part of this new law. Under the terms of the new Act, an employee can formally request a change to their working arrangements, particularly if they have parental responsibilities. An employee must have worked for the business or organisation for at least 26 weeks and have responsibility for a child under six years old. This is part of the gradual change towards employees being able to have flexible working hours.

The Act also included a new system that helps to resolve disputes between employers and employees, as the number of cases going to court had increased substantially. Finally, the Act helped employees on what is known as fixed-term contracts.

Employment Rights Act 2002

The Employment Rights Act 2002 covers the parents' right to apply to request for flexible working. This applies to those parents with children under the age of six or of disabled children under the age of 18, providing they have a qualifying length of service (currently 26 weeks' continuous service from the date of request). There is not an automatic right that an employer will be able to accommodate the employee's desired work pattern.

Equal Pay Act 1970

The Equal Pay Act 1970 (EPA) gives an individual the right to the same pay and benefits as a person of the opposite sex in the same employment, where the man and the woman are doing:

- Like work, or
- Work rated as equivalent under a job evaluation study, or
- Work that is proved to be of equal value.

The employer will not be required to provide the same pay and benefits if it can prove that the difference in pay or benefits is genuinely due to a reason other than one related to sex.

Health and Safety at Work Act 1974

The Health and Safety at Work Act 1974 (HASAWA) requires an employer to provide a number of levels of protection for their employees, including:

- It must protect the health, safety and welfare of all its employees.
- It must do this 'so far as is reasonably practicable', which means that employers can claim that the costs are too high to cover a particular risk.
- It allows the government to issue regulations, guidance and codes of practice that set out detailed responsibilities of the employer on health and safety matters.
- The Act set up the Health and Safety Commission and an inspecting authority known as the Health and Safety Executive.

The National Minimum Wage Act 1998

This states that most adult workers in the UK must be paid at least the national minimum wage, which is currently £5.05. This was first introduced on 1 April 1999 by the National Minimum Wage Act 1998 and the National Minimum Wage Regulations 1999.

The main rules of the minimum wage scheme are that:

- Adult workers aged 22 and over must be paid at least £5.05 an hour.
- Employers are required to pay a 'development rate' of £4.25 to 18–21-year olds.
- Employers must pay at least £3 per hour to young workers aged between 16 and 17.
- Employers must keep records to prove they are paying at least the minimum.

remember

Acts such as this are continually being amended to deal with new situations.

Race Relations Act 1976

The Race Relations Act 1976, as amended by the Race Relations (Amendment) Act 2000, makes it unlawful to discriminate against anyone on grounds of race, colour, nationality (including citizenship), or ethnic or national origin. The amended Act also requires public authorities to promote racial equality. The Act applies to jobs, training, housing, education and the sale of goods, facilities and services.

Race Relations (Amendment) Act 2000

The Race Relations Amendment Act 2000 places a duty on most public authorities to:

- Eliminate race discrimination
- Promote equality of opportunity
- Promote good relations between all racial groups.

The aim is to promote racial equality by helping public authorities to:

- Provide fair and accessible services
- Improve and provide equal employment opportunities for all racial groups (for existing employees and potential employees).

Sex Discrimination Act 1975

In terms of employment, the Sex Discrimination Act 1975 prohibits discrimination against men, women or children at work. The Act covers four main types of sex discrimination:

- Direct sex discrimination – when a person is treated less favourably than a person of the opposite sex, for example a woman being discriminated against because she is pregnant.
- Indirect sex discrimination – when an employer places a condition on work that could lead to discrimination against one gender.

remember

Many manual workers work longer hours than office or clerical staff.

- Discrimination on the grounds of gender reassignment – although not mentioned directly, employers must not discriminate against those that have chosen to change their gender.
- Discrimination on the grounds of sexual orientation – coupled with laws that came into effect in 2003, discrimination on the grounds of sexual orientation is now unlawful.

Working Time Regulations 1998

Workers cannot be forced to work for more than 48 hours a week on average. Young workers may not ordinarily work more than eight hours a day or 40 hours a week, although there are exceptions. Working time includes travelling where it is part of the job, working lunches and job-related training. It does not include travelling between home and work, lunch breaks, evening classes or day-release courses.

Effective Working Practices

This part of the unit looks at how businesses are organised and how job roles fit into that overall structure. We will look at how teamwork is of great importance to many businesses and how your own personal skills are important, both for your job role and for your work as a member of a team.

Organisational structures and job roles

It is important that we look at some of the different ways that an organisation will structure itself, as this has an impact on the way the owners can communicate with their employees. The structure of an organisation will vary depending on a number of factors.

Hierarchies

The best way to understand what a hierarchical structure looks like is to imagine a pyramid. At the top of the pyramid are the owners/directors, who make the decisions, but as you look further down, the pyramid widens. As it widens, more and more employees are involved, so the majority of the employees are at the base of the pyramid. The responsibility, power and authority are all much greater at the top of the pyramid and communication flows down from the top to the bottom.

Flat structures reduce the number of layers involved in a hierarchical structure. Each layer is able to communicate more easily with the other layers and this type of structure is often found in organisations that operate from a single site where all employees can meet with each other readily.

However large or small the business and whatever type of organisational structure is in place, it is important that the owners communicate their plans to those who will carry them through.

remember

Most organisations, if they were drawn as a diagram, would resemble a pyramid.

Figure 5.2

An example of hierarchical structure

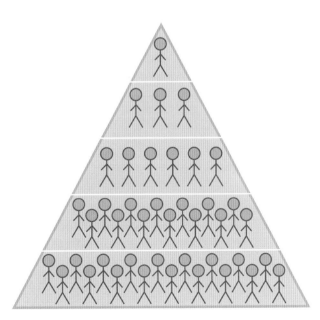

activity

**GROUP WORK
(5.13)**

Draw a pyramid like the one shown in Figure 5.2. Use the information below to draw the hierarchical structure of the business by placing the job roles in the correct section of the pyramid.

a) Harry, Clive and Sheila – shop assistants.

b) Judith and Kevin – trainee shop assistants.

c) Luke and Rachel – assistant managers.

d) Tracy, Malcolm and Dave – part-time shop assistants.

e) Heather – shop manager.

f) Reggie – regional manager.

We have seen the basic hierarchical structure of a business and now know that the majority of them look like a pyramid. The key decision makers are at the top of the pyramid and they filter instructions and orders through layers of management and supervisors to those that carry out the work at the bottom of the pyramid.

Not all organisations opt for a tall pyramid with several layers of management. There are other ways in which to organise the business.

■ A flat structure appears to be a squashed pyramid. There are fewer layers of management and the key decision makers are, perhaps, only one or two layers above those that do the day-to-day work. A flat structure is designed so that the key decision makers have close contact with those carrying out the work.

■ A matrix structure does not look at all like a pyramid. Imagine a number of small departments, responsible for specialised areas of the business such as accounts, human resources or marketing. Now imagine that the rest of the organisation is split up into other departments, perhaps one deals with customer service and another with sales or a third with distribution. All of these departments need the help of the specialised departments. So instead of employing their own accountant or human resource manager they use the services of the specialised departments. This means that the 'functional' departments, which are actually doing things, can concentrate on their tasks and leave the specialists to do the specialised work for them.

- A functional structure organises itself by identifying particular areas of the business and bringing all of those aspects together under one manager. A manufacturing business, for example, would have a purchasing department, a production department, sales and marketing department and a distribution department. Again they may have some elements of the matrix structure, or if they are big enough they will have their own specialists.

- A divisional structure can either be based on functional areas or, more likely, they are completely separate parts of a larger organisation. Separate divisions might exist in different countries or perhaps in different parts of a country. Many of the larger businesses in the world have separate divisions. For example Coca-Cola has separate divisions in each country in which it sells its drinks. Other businesses might have completely separate divisions that sell radically different products and services. Each division is in no way related but they might sell things to one another as well as customers.

Business structures and interdepartmental linkage

So far we have looked at particular types of organisational structure. It is also important to consider the fact that each business may have a number of different departments.

Every organisation has its own way of structuring the functions, or tasks, that need to be carried out. Although the following section covers many common tasks or departments, not all organisations choose to divide the staff up into these particular areas. Some organisations may put the administration together with their finance operations; others may put marketing and research and development together, while, just as commonly, sales and the customer service function may be carried out by the same people.

There are likely to be a number of different departments or sections with managers in charge of different aspects of the business activities, including:

remember
> Divisional structures are parts of larger organisations, and each division looks like a separate business.

- Human Resources Department – also known as the Personnel Department, deals with the recruitment, organisation and training of the employees of the business.
- Finance Department – in addition to paying the wages and salaries of the employees, it monitors the income and expenditure of the business.
- Production Department – involved in all functions related to producing the products or services for the customer to buy.
- Purchasing Department – involved in buying all of the materials required for the business to function.

- Distribution Department – responsible for ensuring the safe storage of the business's products and the transportation of them to the customers.

- Sales and Marketing Department – sometimes these are two separate departments, but their main responsibilities lie in making sure that the customer is aware of the products that the business offers and then selling them to the customer.

- Administration Department – controls all of the paperwork and supports the other departments by servicing their needs for secretarial work, e.g. filing, mailing, handling information, etc.

- Research and Development Department – works closely with the marketing department by keeping a constant check on the products being offered for sale by competitors. It also develops new products for the business to sell.

- Quality Control Department – often part of the production department, it tries to maintain a consistently high-quality product.

- Computer (IT) Services Department – responsible for the hardware and software that the business uses, as well as the maintenance of telecommunications and other technological office development. It will ensure that the employees are using the most appropriate equipment and that they are trained in any new technology that the business acquires.

> **remember**
>
> Quality control is essential to the business as it ensures that faulty or sub-standard products are not offered for sale.

Team working

If tasks are to be carried out to deadlines and the objectives of a business met, it is important that all employees know what is expected of them.

Businesses want their activities to run efficiently and they try to help employees realise where they fit into an organisation by providing them with procedures and policies that have to be followed. These procedures and policies mean that all the employees of the business are working in a similar way towards their own set of tasks and deadlines.

Knowing how one employee's job role links with other in their team, department, and ultimately with other departments within the organisation will help the individual to realise their position within the business and the importance of the tasks they do.

On the face of it, an employee should know what is part of their job role (or duties) from their job description. But this is not always the case as the job description is only a guide as to what is expected of an employee. Very often it is only after a little experience in the job role that it becomes clear exactly what the duties are. Perhaps more importantly, it also becomes clear how much one employee's job role affects the work of other people, teams or departments within the business.

We already know that businesses set up their operations by using a series of different functions, or departments, to carry out specific areas of their activities. Teamwork is also often vital to a business. Provided each individual employee knows what they are supposed to do, how to do it, what they need to do it and by when it has to be done, then the purpose of their job role is helping the business to meet its own set of objectives.

Understanding of team interdependence

In many businesses, employees are expected to work as part of a team and to contribute to the activities and success of that team. Teams are created for a variety of reasons, but they often have the following objectives:

- To help the business solve particular problems
- To help the business make particular improvements
- To help individual team members learn and develop
- To help encourage a feeling of team spirit within the business
- To encourage employees to be creative
- To encourage employees to exchange their ideas
- To encourage employees to work together in a constructive manner
- To develop the individual team members' skills
- To develop the skills of the team as a whole.

Teams can be created to carry out a variety of different tasks or for a specific series of short- or long-term jobs. A business's customer service provision is a good example of the way a business would use a team.

Teams have to organise themselves in the most effective way possible if they are to achieve their targets, complete tasks and meet deadlines. The classic way to approach target setting is to remember the word SMART, an acronym that stands for: Specific, Measurable, Achievable, Realistic, Timely.

Team planning is vitally important. All of the tasks set for the team should be broken down into manageable pieces, which are more manageable because they are under the direct control of the team members. The manageable pieces have to be prioritised and written down so that there is no confusion about them. By planning for the team as a whole, individual team members can also plan their own workload, which takes some of the pressure off individuals and the team leader.

Table 5.3 Characteristics of individuals

Task-based characteristics (those that get the job done)		Function-based characteristics (those that enable the work to be done)	
Initiators	People that set goals and suggest ways in which things can be done and ways of dealing with team problems	Encouragers	People that accept others and are responsive and friendly towards them
Information or opinion givers	People that provide the team with figures, ideas and suggestions	Expressers	People that share their feelings with the team and help establish relationships
Information seekers	People that need facts and figures to get their work done	Compromisers	People that want the team to work and will give way on things if it helps the team to function
Elaborators	People that clear up confusion by giving examples and explanations	Harmonisers	People that try to deal with problems in the team and reduce tension
Summarisers	People that pull together various facts and ideas and keep the team informed of progress	Gatekeepers	People that encourage some of the team to get involved with a task but freeze out those that they do not want working on it
Agreement standards	People that check that everyone in the team agrees that task should be done	Standard-setters	People that try to set the minimum standards of work and try to get everyone in the team to stick to them

activity

INDIVIDUAL WORK (5.14)

a) Do you recognise yourself in any of the categories listed in Table 5.3?

b) Do you have more than one of the characteristics listed?

c) What about other members in your group, perhaps those you have worked with in a team? Pick five other people and discuss with them whether or not the characteristics you consider them to have are the same ones that they think they have.

Personal attributes

Over the course of time in work you will be expected to develop your skills, experience and knowledge of the job. You will also need to develop your own personal skills and abilities in a number of different areas. Your employer will expect you to exceed minimum standards required, and provided you learn from your experiences and take advantage of the experience of others this should not be too difficult. The particular personal attributes that you will need to develop by working will include the following:

- Personal presentation – for example dress codes.

- Verbal and written communication skills – these will improve with practice. You will become more confident speaking to customers and suppliers and you will learn how to write formal business letters or internal communications following company policies.

- Following instructions – to begin with, you may not understand why you are being asked to do certain things. Different managers, supervisors and businesses have different ways of doing things. At least to begin with you should follow their instructions. In the future you may be able to suggest a better way of doing things.

- Punctuality and time planning – you will always be expected to arrive at work on time. In fact you should always try to arrive slightly early. On most days you will have to manage your own time and will have a number of tasks to complete before the day is finished. You will need to pace yourself and make sure that you complete as many tasks as possible, particularly those with deadlines.

- Courtesy – you should always behave in a polite and professional manner, both to colleagues and to those outside the organisation.

- Honesty – the term 'acting in good faith' covers this aspect. It means that you should not lie to your employer or colleagues or take any property that does not belong to you.

- Observe confidentiality – you will see and hear many things at work that should not be discussed outside the organisation. Some information is of a sensitive nature and could well be of use to the business's competitors.

---

activity

INDIVIDUAL WORK
(5.15)

Using the list of personal attributes above, write a short and honest opinion of your own personal attributes at the moment. Which of them are particularly strong and which could benefit from some development?

Planning Career Development

remember

It is always advisable to have a long-term view of your career so that you can plan the various steps towards your ideal job.

Career development does not necessarily mean that you need to know exactly what you are going to be doing in five or ten years' time. Career development means slowly moving forward, gaining skills, experience and qualifications, and taking note of areas of work that interest you and could form the basis of your career in the future.

This is best done by regularly reviewing your performance. This can include part-time work, activities in school or college and even reviews and reports from your teachers or tutors.

Reviewing performance

As we have said, you can review your own performance or ask others to review your performance and appraise the way in which you can currently carry out work. You can also set yourself targets so that you can gradually improve your overall skills.

A number of tables are included in this section which fall into the following categories:

- Professional
- Information handling
- Interpersonal
- Self-application.

Table 5.4 Professional reviewing performance

Skill	Current assessment	Improvement target
Appears smart and tidy		
Relaxed and confident in the company of others		
Enthusiastic and positive		
Gives the impression of being professional		
Gains and maintains attention and respect		
Learns and applies new information effectively		
Demonstrates knowledge of role		
Delivers work to an agreed level		
Able to adapt to change		
Willing to work to the satisfaction of others		
Keeps up to date in area of speciality or interest		

Table 5.5 Information handling reviewing performance

Skill	Current assessment	Improvement target
Understands meaning of written and verbal information		
Can see several points of view and weighs up alternatives		
Seeks out and uses facts where available		
Is unbiased and takes a rational approach		
Can use logical arguments and reasoning		
Can set priorities and targets		
Uses a system to keep track of work and deadlines		
Achieves tasks within required timescale		
Checks written work for errors before submitting		
Plans activities before starting them		
Can draw conclusions from a variety of information		

Together these provide you with a series of checklists that you can use yourself or get others to complete to comment on your performance.

Table 5.6 Interpersonal reviewing performance

Skill	Current assessment	Improvement target
Can speak clearly		
Can summarise		
Can retain the attention of others		
Can use words or diagrams with correct spelling, punctuation and grammar		
Can use a variety of questions to get answers		
Can actively show interest when other people are talking		
Can take notes and identify key information		
Allows time for others to understand and contribute		
Can ensure that everyone has a chance to contribute		
Willing to share information with others		
Is respected by others		

Table 5.7 Self-application reviewing performance

Skill	Current assessment	Improvement target
Can come up with solutions to problems		
Can take actions without being told to do so by others		
Can make decisions		
Can tackle problems		
Can identify problems and recommend solutions		
Does more than the minimum required		
Monitors and checks work to make sure tasks are completed		
Can respond to new information		
Works well under time pressures		
Can work well with figures		
Happy to accept tight deadlines		

activity
INDIVIDUAL WORK
(5.16)

Without referring to anyone else, complete the four tables on your own. Then ask a friend or your teacher or tutor to complete the tables about you. How do they compare? What have they noticed about you that you missed? How can you best fill in the gaps in your skills?

Career development

Career development is all about recognising and seizing on opportunities that could increase your employability, your general level of education, experience and skills. Opportunities arise at different times, both before you enter work and whilst you are in work. You should be looking for opportunities that will give you a chance to gain training, experience or qualifications whenever you can.

Typical types of career development include the following:

■ Induction – this is the initial period, just after you have started working for a business. The induction programme will tell you about the business, its procedures, policies and rules. It will explain to you how you are supposed to work and what the business expects of you.

■ Training needs – a good employer will carry out what is known as training needs analysis, both on its new employees and on a yearly basis with its existing employees. The business will use your job specification, person specification and your current abilities to help identify gaps between what you can do and what you are expected to do. The process should reveal any training that you require in order to get you up to scratch or to improve the way in which you carry out your job.

■ Development plans – in many ways these are similar to training needs analysis, but they usually take a slightly less formal approach. The idea is to identify your longer-term career plans and to match any training or qualifications that may be of assistance to you. These are normally carried out on an annual basis and have agreed targets.

■ Performance targets – these are minimum levels of work or output that you will be required to complete by your employer. Performance targets are difficult to set for some individual workers, so a departmental or section target may be set. These will require you to complete work by specified deadlines and very much depend on the type of work involved.

■ Certificated training – this is training that you may be offered, which leads to recognised qualifications, such as an NVQ. These types of training are extremely useful for personal development as they allow you to demonstrate your ability to work at a particular level.

■ Uncertificated training – these are normally in-house training programmes, designed specifically for the business, perhaps to update on policies and procedures. They are usually only relevant to the business in which you are working and may have no practical value if you switch jobs and move to another organisation.

■ Personal development – there are a number of different ways in which you can proceed with your personal development. Some may be formal and include, as we have seen, training-needs analysis, various types of training and development plans. Personal development is your own ideal improvement plan, which would have to be agreed with your employer.

■ Flexible working – this can simply be working odd hours, but more usefully it is your willingness to work in different areas of the business. This leads to what is known as multi-skilling, which is a measure of your ability to adapt to different types of work and your willingness to learn new skills so that you can be of greater use and value to your employer. You should seize chances to work in different areas of the business so you can get a better picture of what the business is all about and how particular tasks, carried out by different parts of the business, all fit together.

■ Progression opportunities – this means the opportunities that will present themselves for you to be promoted and to gain a higher-paid and more valued post at work. By gradually taking on training and opportunities to work in different areas of the business you will have developed yourself to such an extent that your employer recognises you should be rewarded for your efforts. As your skills and experience improve, progression opportunities will present themselves. With each step you will gain access to higher-level work and begin the process of improvement once again so that you can seize the next opportunity for progression.

progress check

1. What is a personal audit?
2. What is the difference between a job specification and a person specification?
3. Name five items that you may find in a contract of employment.
4. What is the purpose of a probation period?
5. Which law covers the right for parents to apply for flexible working?
6. What is a matrix structure?
7. What is the difference between a functional structure and a divisional structure?
8. State three key skills related to interpersonal abilities.
9. What is an induction period?
10. What is the difference between certificated and uncertificated training?

UNIT 6

Providing Business and Administration Support

This unit covers:

- the purpose of providing business and administration support
- how to operate office systems and equipment
- organising and providing administrative support for meetings
- the procedures needed to process, retrieve and archive information

Businesses need a variety of different forms of support in order to help them run in an efficient manner. This unit looks at both traditional administrative support, such as secretarial services, as well as more specialist support.

The unit looks at how different size organisations cope with their differing requirements. The unit also looks at other forms of business support, relating to managers, departments, knowledge, understanding, office systems, telephone networks and time management.

This unit aims to help you improve your administrative skills and prepare you to support meetings. As an important part of administrative support you will also learn about different types of filing systems, how to process, retrieve and archive information, as well as dealing with confidentiality issues.

grading criteria

To achieve a **Pass** grade the evidence must show that the learner is able to:	To achieve a **Merit** grade the evidence must show that the learner is able to:	To achieve a **Distinction** grade the evidence must show that the learner is able to:
P1 describe the purpose and types of business and administration support	**M1** compare and contrast paper and electronic diary systems	**D1** analyse the contribution that office systems and equipment make to the provision of business administration and support
P2 operate a diary system to support business purposes	**M2** explain the appropriate use of office equipment types, features and functions to suit different business purposes	**D2** analyse the organisation and administrative support provided for a meeting and recommend any improvements that could have been made

The Purpose of Providing Business and Administration Support

All organisations work in different ways and have different systems and procedures. A procedure is a set of rules or the business's preferred steps, which employees have to stick to when carrying out their tasks.

Administration procedures are important because an organisation's activities need to be coordinated and planned. If administration procedures are inadequate the organisation may not be efficient and its staff may not be effective as they may not have access to the information they need. Some administrative procedures are paper-based, whilst others are on computer systems.

Administrative procedures, or systems, are in fact a series of sub-systems which in turn are split into smaller sub-systems or steps. These procedures play an important role in helping the organisation to operate. All information has to be processed in some way and, perhaps, passed on to different parts of the organisation. Ultimately it will be stored in such a way that it can be retrieved when needed.

Purpose

A huge amount of information can come into a business. The administrative procedures are there to organise that information, pass it on to the right person and then store it so that it can be found if needed later.

Provided all of the business makes sure that they follow administrative procedures, they will have ensured the following:

- Consistency – every piece of information has been dealt with in the same manner.

- Effective use of time – although some administrative procedures may appear to be time consuming, they do save time in the longer term.

In other words, the overall purpose of providing business and administration support is to:

- Provide support for managers – so that information they need in order to make decisions is readily to hand.

- Support departments – so that individuals within the departments, which need particular information, can access it as and when they need it to carry out their work.

Types of support

As we will see in this unit, business and administration support covers a wide range of different areas of the business. Managers and departments need this support in order to ensure that they have up-to-date information and can carry out their work. Typical types of support include:

- Meetings – organising them, supporting the meeting whilst it is going on and providing after-meeting information and support.

- Documents – preparation of basic blank documents, including forms, letterheads and compliments slips, and a host of other documents used on a daily basis by different parts of the business.

- Arranging events, travel and accommodation – this is usually in response to managers requiring meetings or other activities.

- Managing diaries – each manager and many departments will have their own diaries detailing their commitments for example meetings, events and other activities.

- Handling data – this involves dealing with documents and other information from the point when it arrives at the organisation to its distribution around the organisation, its archiving or storage and then its accessibility if required.

Choose one of the following:

- Supporting meetings
- Producing documents
- Arranging events, travel and accommodation
- Managing diaries
- Handling data

Try to draw up a list of different aspects of the business's administration support that are required for each of these activities.

Operating Office Systems and Equipment

In this section of the unit we look at office equipment and three different types of office system that are used to help provide business and administration support. This is by no means a comprehensive list of the kind of systems or equipment that may be used in an organisation, but it serves as a series of useful examples to illustrate the breadth of business and administration support.

Diary systems

There are a number of different diary systems. Some are paper-based whilst others are electronic. We will begin by looking at the paper-based diary systems. Types of diaries could include the following:

remember

It is important that diaries are constantly kept up to date.

- A basic diary – perhaps one page per day or one page per week.
- Advanced diary – these have one or two pages per day, with times printed on the page so that details of meetings and appointments can be filled in.
- Loose-leaf binder systems – in effect these are rather like large filofax systems. You can choose whether to have one or two pages per day or indeed one page covering the week.
- Monthly view – these are basic loose-leaf or bound diaries, which allow you to organise your month's work and identify periods when you are not available.
- Weekly view – these allow you to organise your week and plot your appointments and priorities across the week.

Some diaries will also include other features, such as:

- A telephone list.
- Project sections, particularly in loose-leaf systems. These will have coloured tabs and you can put notes, perhaps from a meeting, in each project section.

The alternative to using paper-based diary systems is to opt for the increasingly large range of electronic diaries. As we will see, some are handheld whilst others are available through desktop or laptop computers.

Handheld organisers or PDAs provide all of the main advantages of having a detailed diary, with the advantage that some of them are also mobile phones and minicomputers. They can be hooked up to laptops or to desktop computers and information can be downloaded either onto the PDA or from the PDA onto the computer.

There are a number of different diary systems available for desktops and laptops. Some can be purchased and downloaded as software whilst other systems maintain the diary at a remote location and can only be accessed via the Internet. Many larger organisations have either adapted these systems or have had purpose-built diary systems created with access to the organisation's database.

Diaries are also used to record information. This is in addition to detailing when and where someone has to be for a meeting or an event. The information may include:

- The purpose of the entry – why the entry into the diary is necessary and to what it refers.
- People involved – when decisions need to be made, who needs to be there to help make that decision or solve that problem.
- Start and finish times – how much time an individual will be required for a particular purpose.
- Date and location – where an individual needs to be and on what day.
- Communicating – diaries can be compared, particularly if they are accessible on a networked computer system.

The most important aspect about a diary is that it needs to be up to date. The individual responsible for maintaining the diary needs to ensure that it is updated and that any changes have been made and any irrelevant information is removed. This is particularly easy with electronic diaries, but can be frustrating and confusing if paper-based diaries are used. If a diary entry has been changed then anyone involved (for example someone who is expecting to see that person) needs to be informed. There may be implications if a diary entry is changed and others may have to change their own diaries, particularly if a key individual has to be somewhere else and meeting cannot take place.

Telephone systems

Telephone systems, also known as PBXs (Private Branch Exchange) or switchboards, traditionally provided business with voice communications. Modern telephone systems allow users to enhance this with services such as messaging and call centres.

There are many different systems to suit the requirements of an organisation. A few examples of this are:

■ Voice telephone systems – these deal purely with voice but not data.

■ Converged voice and data systems – which are capable of dealing with both voice and data.

■ IP-based (internet protocol) solutions – more advanced systems that can deal with voice, data and video services.

Features of telephone systems can include:

■ A call-back facility which ensures that if a call is not answered, then when an operator becomes available the system will automatically call the person back.

■ Messaging systems, otherwise known as voicemail, which allows the user of each extension to leave a personalised message after which the caller can leave their own message.

■ Fax – a system that allows an original document to be copied and sent electronically to a remote fax machine where a hard copy can be printed.

■ Conference calls – a system that allows several people to contribute to a conversation on the telephone.

remember

Individual telephone numbers or extensions can be programmed to transfer the call to a mobile telephone.

There is an enormous range of different telephone systems. However, what remains the same is the way in which you should deal with telephone callers, take messages and then forward them. There are some basic rules that you should follow with regard to dealing with telephone callers, these are:

■ Not to let the phone ring longer than necessary.

■ If the call is an external one, make sure you answer the call with the name of the organisation.

■ Always pick up the telephone with the hand you do not write with.

■ Have a pen and pad near the telephone.

■ Take the caller's name and number and offer to ring back if you cannot answer the question straight away.

■ If the call is not for you and the person required is not available ask whether you can take a message.

■ Read back the message to the caller to make sure the details are correct.

Many businesses have telephone message forms or pads, which can be completed easily. These will include sections detailing who the call was from, the name of their company, their telephone number, the message and for whom it was left.

Forwarding messages is also important as you should pass on the messages quickly and accurately.

activity

GROUP WORK
(6.2)

Carry out the following in pairs, taking turns to be the person leaving the message and the person taking the message

Message 1

Can I leave a message for Miss Smith please? Can you tell her that I was supposed to be coming in to see her next Friday? I think that's the 12th. Well I'm afraid I won't be able to make it. Will you tell her I'll come in the following week at 11 if that's OK? My name is Claire Saunders from AGM Limited. My number is 01223 765100.

Message 2

Hello can you put me through to Miss Smith please. My name is Somersgill. I'm disappointed with the delivery we had today. One of the boxes has burst. We ordered them three weeks ago, order number 12345 and paid £700.
I need a replacement batch sent today. I'm very cross as this is the second time it has happened. Get her to ring me back as soon as possible. I'll be here until three. If it is after that she will have to speak to Brian. His extension number is 271 and mine is 248. The number is 0100 74 13 42.

Electronic communication systems

An increasingly important skill is the ability to communicate effectively using email. Email provides the opportunity to instantly reply to messages and queries and to attach documents, such as brochures, price lists and order forms.

The key functions of email are outlined in the Table 6.1.

Table 6.1 Key functions of email

Function	Description
Reply	By clicking on this button you are able to open a new window in which you can type an email directly to the sender.
Forward	By clicking on 'forward' you can then type in another email address and send an exact copy of the original email to another person.
Copy	'Copy' is email's version of a letter's cc (carbon copy). This means that you are sending an additional copy or copies of the email to other people.
Attachments	By clicking 'attachments' you can then browse your documents and pictures and select them to be attached to the email you are sending.

remember

Email address books are the modern equivalent of A–Z paper-based address books.

Email software is becoming increasingly sophisticated. You can choose to automatically store the email addresses of those who have sent emails to you and incorporate them into your contacts list. By clicking on the email address you can either send an email to that person or add details about the contact, such as their postal address, telephone number and full name.

You can organise your emails into folders so that all emails relating to a particular topic can be stored together.

There are, however, a number of risks related to email. Most businesses have virus-scanning software to prevent viruses attached to emails from causing damage to their computer system.

All email addresses receive mail from unknown senders. Some of these senders may be new customers, but others may just be sending **spam** emails, trying to convince you to purchase products or services you do not want. Great care should be exercised in opening any attachments from recognised sources. Some email attachments, once opened, automatically launch malicious programs onto the machine and may cause problems with the computer network.

It is also important to remember that although you can attach any documents from your computer to an email, individuals outside the business may not be allowed to see some of these documents. If you are ever in any doubt about attaching a document to an email, even though it may have been requested, you should check with someone with more authority or experience first.

keyword

Spam
– unsolicitied, unwanted, irrelevant or inappropriate messages, usually advertising, sent to large numbers of email addresses. Also known 'junk mail'.

Office equipment

The vast majority of copiers are now digital and have the following advantages:

- They combine the functions of copiers, network printers and fax machines
- Fewer moving parts mean fewer mechanical breakdowns
- Less noise makes for a quieter business environment
- They are better at reproducing fine lines and photographs.

Modern digital copiers are sometimes referred to as multifunctional as they can do more than just copy. They are capable of printing, faxing and scanning. A multifunctional copier connected to the internal network allows the business to print, copy or send faxes from computers. Users can also make collated or stapled sets of documents. Copier speed is measured in copies per minute (cpm), pages per minute (ppm) or outputs per minute (opm). This refers to the number of letter-sized pages the machine can produce in one minute when running at full speed.

The key features of modern copiers are:

- Printing – good speed, ability to produce stapled copies of documents.
- Faxing – send and receive faxes.
- Image editing – include automatic page numbering, can reduce and enlarge copies.
- Duplexing – can produce double-sided copies.

- Automatic sizing – can automatically reduce or enlarge to A4 or other sizes.
- Security coding – copier requires a code to be entered before beginning (this prevents unauthorised use).

Binding machines

There are a number of different types of binding machine, including:

- Wire binding machines – a double loop wire machine is easy to use. After punching the paper, you insert and close the wire. The wire closer is usually built into the machine.

- Comb binding machines – plastic comb binding is one of the most popular forms of binding. Plastic combs are not only durable, but they can be re-used. Plastic comb binders first punch the holes for the paper. After punching the holes, you place a binding comb on the machine. You then pull a handle that opens the combs up for you. While the comb is open, you place the comb through the holes and close the plastic comb.

- Thermal binding machines – the thermal binding machines use pre-glued spines. You apply the paper into the pre-glued spine and place it in the pre-heated holding tray on the machine. The machine heats the glue up. After the glue cools you have a well-bound document.

- Slide binding machines – after punching the holes, you put the binding strips through the holes. The machine will then cut the excess prongs off and seal everything with heat. This provides a very secure bind.

- Coil-binding machines – coil binding is a continuous PVC filament formed into the shape of a spring. You may recognise this type of binding. It is very similar to the spiral notebooks you may have used in school. As with plastic binding and double loop wire binding, you can purchase the coil-binding machine with a manual or electric punch.

Laminating

There are two basic types of laminating machines:

- Hot laminating machines – these are the most common types of laminators. They use heat to apply the lamination. Hot laminators provide a better-quality lamination that is more resistant to wear and tear. This is the preferred method of lamination for materials that are not affected by heat.

- Cold laminating machines – cold laminators use pressure-sensitive adhesives to bind the lamination film. Cold laminating machines are used when the material being laminated is sensitive to heat. For example, some inkjet printers use inks that can melt when heated. There are other types of printers that use heat-sensitive paper.

Laminating pouches are pockets of laminating material into which the item to be laminated is placed. A hot laminator is used to seal the pouch and bind the layers together. Excess material is trimmed off leaving the laminated item. Pouches come in a variety of sizes and thicknesses.

remember

Binding machines allow large documents to be presented professionally and the documents are more durable than if they are stapled together.

Laminating film also comes in a variety widths and thicknesses. As with pouches, the thicker the film, the stiffer and more durable the laminated item will be. Some laminating films are identified as being 'low melt' films. These films require less heat and are used when laminating materials that are sensitive to high temperatures, such as photographs.

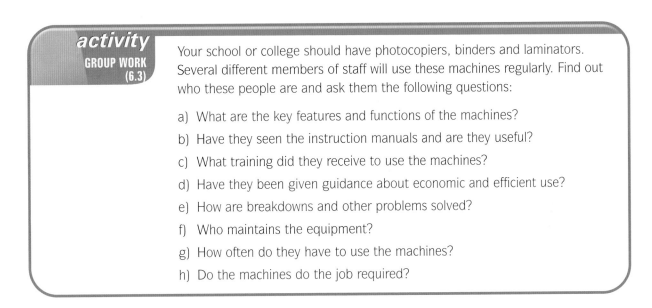

activity

GROUP WORK (6.3)

Your school or college should have photocopiers, binders and laminators. Several different members of staff will use these machines regularly. Find out who these people are and ask them the following questions:

a) What are the key features and functions of the machines?

b) Have they seen the instruction manuals and are they useful?

c) What training did they receive to use the machines?

d) Have they been given guidance about economic and efficient use?

e) How are breakdowns and other problems solved?

f) Who maintains the equipment?

g) How often do they have to use the machines?

h) Do the machines do the job required?

Organising and Providing Administrative Support for Meetings

Meetings are important and frequent events in any business. They are opportunities for decisions to be made once various matters have been discussed. The more complex the meeting, the more administrative support is required.

To begin with, people need to know what the meeting is about, and those who are invited to the meeting may need documents to help them prepare for it. The larger the meeting the more complex this process becomes and it may involve sending out paperwork, organising the room, arranging travel, accommodation and refreshments.

Organisation and support

Preparation for business meetings

Meetings are held in all organisations. They can be informal or formal, requiring a range of communication methods and administrative support. Formal meetings are often governed by the **consitution** of the business. This means that when the rules of the organisation were written, they included those relating to the procedure for formal meetings.

keyword

Constitution – The rules made when the business was first started up that state the procedures and policies of the organisation.

Types of formal meeting include:

■ Annual General Meeting (AGM) – these meetings are held once a year and are used to assess the trading or affairs of the business over the previous year. Officers are elected at the AGM for the coming year. AGMs are open to all shareholders of the business and 21 days' notice must be given prior to the meeting.

■ Board meetings – the directors of an organisation attend board meetings, which are chaired (headed) by the chairperson of the board of directors or that person's deputy.

■ Statutory meetings – after a report has been circulated to all members, a statutory meeting is called so that the directors of the business and its shareholders can communicate. It is a requirement of the law that these meetings take place.

Informal meetings, on the other hand, have no procedural rules. They might be set up for a number of reasons, for example so that a group of people working on a particular project can get together to share progress to date.

> **remember**
> All organisations have regular meetings in order for information to be exchanged.

Meetings can be either internal or external to the business. An internal meeting is attended by employees of the business, and held within the business's premises. An external meeting is held at alternative premises and may be attended by individuals who are not employed by the organisation, such as shareholders.

Meetings are held in order to allow verbal communication to take place. Usually meetings are held for one or more of the following reasons:

■ To share information.

■ To share new ideas or proposals.

■ So that employees feel involved in the day-to-day running of the business and their interest is maintained.

- So that assistance in certain areas can be sought by more than one individual.
- To report back on an activity that has been taking place.
- So that the activities of the organisation can be coordinated.
- So that any problems can be discussed and any rumours or anxieties quashed.

A meeting allows for several individuals to meet at an arranged time to discuss particular topics. Depending on the type and size of the business, a secretary or administrative assistant may be involved in a number of different types of meeting.

Ability to carry out appropriate preparatory organisation

The term 'tabling documents' means getting all the paperwork ready that is required for a meeting. Members attending the meeting will need their own individual copies of any relevant documents and the person arranging the meeting would put these papers at each person's place around the table.

Preparatory documents and circulating documents

The first document we need to consider when thinking about preparing for a meeting and circulating any appropriate documents is the notice of meeting. The notice of meeting is a form of communication that summon the relevant people to attend the meeting. If people from outside the business are to attend the meeting, the notice will be sent with a covering letter. If the meeting only involves those internal to the business, a memorandum will be attached. Possible methods of preparing a notice of meeting may include:

- Written or typed advance notice
- Verbal notice
- Noticeboard posting.

Whatever form of notice is used, the following basic information must be included:

- The venue (where the meeting is to be held)
- The day, date and time of the meeting
- Details of any special business to be discussed at the meeting
- The type of meeting (where appropriate)
- The name of the person calling the meeting (usually the chairperson)
- The date of the notice.

The document that is used to inform those people who are to attend a meeting about the nature of that meeting is known as an agenda. An agenda gives the date, time and venue of the meeting.

Specifically, the agenda will contain the following information:

- The date, time and venue of the meeting.
- The title 'Agenda' will confirm the purpose of the document.
- Item one is always the apologies received from members not able to attend. Apologies are sent to the meeting via the chairperson.
- Item two is always the checking for accuracy of the **minutes** of the previous meeting. Once this task has been accomplished, the minutes will be signed by the chairman of the meeting.
- Item three always deals with any matters that have arisen from the minutes of the previous meeting.
- The remaining items to be dealt with during the meeting are then listed, each with a separate number.
- 'Any other business' (AOB) gives members the opportunity to introduce any matters they wish to discuss that have not been included in the agenda.

During the course of the meeting, either the chairperson or the minutes secretary will distribute a series of documents that need to be completed by the members of the meeting. Those attending the meeting will sign the attendance sheet so that their names can be listed on the minutes of the meeting.

---

activity
INDIVIDUAL WORK (6.4)

Your boss has to chair a number of meetings and it is part of your job role to prepare and circulate (send out to the relevant people) the appropriate documents.

Your first task is to prepare a notice of meeting. You should include the following information:

Tuesday, 4 February – At 10.00

Your boss is Simon Brett and he is the Sales Manager

He wants to call the meeting in his office of all sales representatives to discuss whether or not current sales targets are being reached.

---

activity
INDIVIDUAL WORK (6.5)

Using the information from the previous task where you produced a notice of meeting, add the further information given below to produce an agenda for that meeting. You can use the example of an agenda shown in Figure 6.01 for the layout. The items to be discussed at the meeting are:

- Individual reports from regional sales representatives
- Implications on overall sales figures
- Initiatives for new sales representatives
- Current sales figures.

Figure 6.1

An example of an agenda

ABC Ltd
Meeting of all First-Aid Qualified Staff

A meeting of all staff holding a current first-aid qualification will be held in the training centre
on Friday, 25 January 2--- at 11.15

AGENDA

---

1. Apologies for absence
2. Minutes of the last meeting
3. Matters arising from the minutes
4. Report from Brian Phillips on recent government legislation regarding first-aid
   requirements
5. Details of forthcoming training courses for qualified staff
6. Implications of cover required for staff absence
7. Any other business
8. Date of next meeting

Helen Scott

Advance organisation

Meeting facilities, refreshment, accommodation

Arranging a meeting can be time-consuming, particularly if some of those
attending are involved in travel and overnight stays. Wherever possible, any
arrangements should be made in advance of the date of the meeting.

Matters that should be arranged ahead of time include:

- Finding out the travel and overnight accommodation requirements
- Booking the meeting room
- Ordering any refreshments that may be required during the meeting
- Booking car parking spaces.

The day before the meeting is scheduled to take place, the following activities
need to be carried out:

- Collect spare copies of the agenda for distribution at the meeting.
- Get the minutes of the previous meeting from the file as these will be
  required for the meeting.
- Gather any relevant papers and information documents concerning items that
  are to be discussed according to the agenda.
- Make a list of any people who have sent their apologies because they are
  unable to attend the meeting.
- Make sure adequate stationery is available for the meeting table.

remember

Unless meetings
are well planned
and resourced they
could be a waste of
time for the
participants.

On the day of the meeting, the following need to be arranged:

- Confirm the parking arrangements.
- Contact reception and notify staff of the names of the visitors expected.
- Arrange with the switchboard to re-route any calls (unless emergency calls) while the meeting is in progress.
- Make sure that the meeting room is ready.
- Place the writing paper, pens, copies of the agenda and other documentation at each seat around the table.
- Provide jugs or bottles of water glasses around the table.
- Place a 'Meeting in Progress' notice on the meeting room door.
- Place the list of apologies next to the chairperson's seat as this will be the first item on the agenda.
- Provide the chairperson with the minutes of the previous meeting as these will be read at the start of the meeting.

activity
**INDIVIDUAL WORK
(6.6)**

In preparation for the forthcoming meeting of sales representatives that Simon Brett is holding, write yourself a checklist of what has to be done. In this case nobody has to stay overnight, but all of the reps will be travelling from their own region to attend the meeting. Draw up your checklist under the headings 'One week before', 'The day before' and 'On the day'. Your checklist should start with your instruction to send out a notice of meeting and end when the meeting starts.

Assisting in the effective running of appropriate meetings

Once the meeting gets underway it is the role of the chairperson to take control. But obviously he or she will require some assistance and this is often the role of the minutes secretary. Usually the minutes secretary will sit beside the chairperson and sometimes, if the minutes of the last meeting were not circulated, the secretary will be asked to read them out to the meeting members.

A successful meeting relies on organisation and the following are guidelines for such a success:

- The minutes of the previous meeting must be signed by the chairperson to allow them to be regarded as a 'true and accurate record' of what took place.
- The minutes of the current meeting must be taken.
- Safety and security procedures should be followed at all times during the meeting.
- Confidentiality of information is vital to businesses.

Deputising in the event of emergencies

Named individuals in a business will be invited to attend particular meetings, but due to pressure of work, sickness and holidays, sometimes these individuals cannot attend. In these circumstances someone has to go to the meeting on their behalf and this is known as deputising.

This can cause problems for the person expected to deputise, particularly if they have not been given very much notice. They may not know what was discussed at the last meeting, what kind of decisions have to be made or which topics are to be discussed.

Appropriate advance clarification of meeting purposes

Agendas will list topics, issues and other matters that need decisions. If those attending the meeting need additional information, then it is usual for any other useful documents to be attached to the agenda when it is circulated.

Sometimes the items on the agenda require an individual to explain a particular situation or report on progress since the last meeting. Knowing what will be discussed or decided upon at the next meeting gives those attending a chance to research particular areas, discuss the matter with colleagues and to decide what they think is the best course of action.

Time allocation and focused guidance of discussion

It the chairperson's responsibility to make sure that not only the decisions that need to be made are actually made, and information that needs to be passed on is passed on, but also that the meeting does not overrun.

remember

Most meetings are allocated a certain amount of time and it is important for the chairperson to ensure that everything is discussed and all items on the agenda are considered.

The chairperson must make sure that discussions or arguments do not stray away from the topic being discussed. If other matters arise from discussions, then these can be added to a future agenda. The chairperson must always remind those at the meeting that particular decisions will need to be made and that the meeting cannot finish until they have been decided. All points and conversations must take place through the chairperson, who will choose individuals to state their case or make their argument before passing on to someone else.

activity
**GROUP WORK
(6.7)**

In groups of six, you are going to hold a meeting. You must elect a chairperson and a minutes secretary and prepare an agenda. You can choose the items on the agenda, but you could use this opportunity to evaluate some work you have done or discuss a proposed event or issue related to your course. Each member of the group should have input into the meeting. You should each contribute to the discussions that take place and each propose a motion on which you all vote.

Appropriate consultation of meeting delegates

Individuals that have been invited to attend a meeting are those that have a stake, or opinion, regarding particular issues. In any business there will be differing views and it is the purpose of a meeting to bring all those views together so that all of the participants are aware of the different ideas or viewpoints.

It is the chairperson's responsibility to give everyone an opportunity to say what he or she needs to say about an issue so that the rest of the group can hear their opinion. Only when everyone has had an opportunity to speak will the chairperson move on to encourage those attending the meeting to make a decision about what was being discussed.

Appropriate clarification of agreed conclusions

A 'motion' is a proposal at a meeting. In other words, it is an issue that needs to be discussed and then decided upon by those at the meeting. Motions that are voted upon are called 'resolutions'.

> *remember*
>
> Motions are proposals in a meeting and once the meeting has voted, the motion becomes a resolution.

Usually, motions will have to be written and signed by the proposer and supported by a seconder. If someone intends to support or propose a motion, they should ensure that they are well prepared for the meeting by ensuring that they:

- Have read all the minutes, reports, briefings and other documents relating to the issue.
- Know all the people at the meeting and are aware of any particular interest or objection to certain proposals or points of view. It may be necessary to gain the support of several people at the meeting in order for a motion to be carried forward.

Compilation, preparing and circulation of meeting minutes

During the meeting a series of notes have to be taken. These notes will later become the minutes of the meeting. These minutes are then distributed to all those who attended the meeting and a copy is filed. It is essential that an accurate written record of the meeting is provided for all those who attended and also for those who were unable to attend. At the next meeting, these minutes will be read under item two of the agenda and anything that needs reporting on as a result of the minutes will be dealt with under item three.

Minutes will be presented in the same order as the agenda and will include:

- A list of those present at the meeting.
- A list of those not present, but who sent their apologies.
- A statement that confirms that the minutes of the previous meeting have been read and signed as being a true record.

- An account of discussions that took place during the meeting.
- A note of tasks that were allocated to individuals.
- Reports that were received from individuals.
- Actions to be taken in the future as a result of the meeting.
- An account of any decisions that were made as a result of discussions.
- Details of individuals whom decisions taken my refer.

Minutes should be concise and precise, but they should not lose any accuracy in this process. Often a form of numbered listing is used against each minuted item, which helps to remind those present at the meeting about any decisions made or actions needed that they have to undertake before the next meeting. Figure 6.2 shows an example from a set of minutes.

The details of any motions voted upon or amendments made to these motions must be clearly detailed in the minutes.

Figure 6.2
An extract from a set of minutes

4. **Report from the Chief Safety Officer**
    Mr Mills reported that the recent government legislation concerning health and safety at work procedures would require careful consideration. The new procedures would be copied and distributed to all concerned. Mr Mills stated that he would like a sub-committee to be formed to study the legislation and report back at the next meeting.

    Mr Taylor, Mr Brenner and Ms Oliver volunteered to form the sub-committee and agreed to meet on Tuesday, 27 June 2-.

5. **Implications of possible new extension to the office block**
    Ms Oliver reported that she had seen the plans for the new office block and is concerned that not enough space had been allocated to each member of staff using that block. After some discussion it was decided that Mr Mills would speak to the architects and report his findings to the next meeting.

activity

INDIVIDUAL WORK (6.8)

Prepare your own set of minutes of the meeting you held recently. Make sure that your minutes follow the same order as the items on the agenda. Did you arrange another meeting in the future? If so, put the date of the next meeting in the appropriate place. Use numbered listing against each agenda item in the minutes if this is appropriate.

Was your note-taking efficient enough for the preparation of the minutes to be quite straightforward?

Compare the content of your set of minutes with those of members of your group in attendance at the meeting.

External meeting support

Some meetings may involve colleagues or managers having to travel to another part of the country. Check the diaries of those involved and make sure that the day and date of the meeting is convenient.

Travel information to the meeting location could include some of the following:

- A road map showing the location of the venue
- A street map with more detail
- Directions showing how to get to the venue using public transport
- Details of the meeting point and to whom they should report on arrival.

Accommodation may be necessary for those who are travelling some distance. Short meetings may have only the most basic of refreshments, but longer meetings may well have to have breaks.

activity
INDIVIDUAL WORK (6.9)

Using the Internet, find the website of a local hotel. Print out a map of the hotel's location. If it does not have a map on its website, visit www.multimap.com and type in the hotel's postcode. This will give you a basic map of the area. How useful is the map to someone that has not visited the area before?

Multimap.com
www.multimap.com

remember
Some large organisations employ other businesses to make their travel arrangements for them.

Before any travel arrangements can be made you need to find out whether the person travelling has any particular requirements.

When considering possible routes to a particular destination there are a number of alternatives. The further afield the destination is, probably the quickest and most direct route is by air. Isolated destinations are often difficult to get to and the traveller may have to make detours, stopovers or change aircraft to reach them.

activity
INDIVIDUAL WORK (6.10)

If it is 10.00 in London, what time is it in the following cities? You must use the 24-hour clock:

a) Harare.
b) Tokyo.
c) San Francisco.
d) Melbourne.
e) Cape Town.
f) Tunis.
g) Tel Aviv.
h) Quebec.
i) Buenos Aires.
j) St Petersburg.

Travellers may not necessarily want to go directly from the point of departure to the destination. They may wish to stop over and include an extra visit on the way. Certainly in the UK and for closer destinations in Europe, a car probably offers the most flexible and personalised opportunity for travel.

If the traveller is going to a destination abroad then there may be some other considerations to take into account. These include:

- Health – vaccinations and inoculations are required to protect the traveller against certain diseases in some countries.
- Insurance – it is advisable to take out travel insurance to cover medical fees, accidents and loss of personal belongings.
- Passports – a traveller must check that their passport is still valid. Some countries will not allow entry if the passport has nearly expired.
- Currency and travellers' cheques – obviously if the travellers' destination is an international one, it is advisable to take some foreign currency. Most of the countries within the EU use euros. Many of the banks also accept credit and debit cards, and local currency can be withdrawn from cash machines.
- Visas – if the traveller plans to travel outside the UK or the EU, they may need a visa to enter the country. The Foreign and Commonwealth Office Travel Service can provide information about visas.

Business travel is an extremely important part of normal business operations. A business traveller may need to take a number of documents and items with them, including:

- Briefing documents about the destination they are travelling to and the businesses that they will be visiting.
- Sales literature, including brochures and catalogues.
- Samples of products or descriptions of services.
- Display equipment, such as CDs, DVDs, posters and other marketing material.
- Business cards to be distributed to customers and suppliers as necessary.
- Addresses, contact names and telephone numbers of all customers, suppliers and other businesses or individuals the traveller may be visiting.

activity

INDIVIDUAL WORK (6.11)

Two people wish to leave Ipswich and travel to Prague for the following day. They need to be in Prague by 14.00.

a) Using the Internet, and assuming that they can get to any east or south-east airport in the UK, find them a suitable return flight (they expect to stay in Prague for three days).

b) Find them a hotel near the centre of Prague.

c) Book them a car for the duration of their stay in Prague. (You should end the procedure at the point where you are asked for your method of payment.)

Producing an itinerary confirming contact arrangements

An itinerary is a summary of the details and plans for a visit, including all times, accommodation and methods of travel. If a visit is a particularly long and complicated one, the itinerary will be very detailed and might consist of many pages.

The essential list for any itinerary needs to be drawn up after the following information has been gathered:

- The dates for the travel and the accommodation needed.
- Preferences about travel method and types of accommodation.
- The times and dates of meetings and appointments.
- Whether any seats need to be reserved or car hire included.
- Whether the travellers have passports or need visas, insurance or any other documents.

An itinerary should include:

- The dates of the travel and a breakdown of where the travellers need to be at any particular time during the visit.
- Departure and arrival times including addresses and telephone numbers as required.
- Details of each booked arrangement including table bookings at restaurants and entertainment.
- Every aspect of the travellers' journey including the return trip.

In order to support the itinerary the person organising it will have to ensure that:

- Any relevant tickets have been booked and are given to the traveller.
- Car hire details have been passed on.
- Insurance documents are ready.
- Any certificates relating to vaccinations or inoculations are carried.
- Passports and visas have been checked.
- An information pack about the area has been prepared.
- Taxis or hire cars for transfer to and from the airport or hotel have been arranged.
- Appropriate money is available, either in travellers' cheques, foreign currency or the business's debit or credit cards.

The itinerary should be as complete as possible and a copy should be given to each traveller. An ideal itinerary would take the following points into consideration:

- Schedules should not be too tight and the travellers should be allowed some time to themselves.
- It should take into account that time differences will affect the traveller if it is a long-distance or international destination.

remember

An ideal itinerary should take into account possible delays.

Figure 6.3

An example of an itinerary

ITINERARY		
For Susan Grafton		
25 January 2---		
Monday 25 January 2---		
Depart:	Norwich	09.30
Arrive:	London Liverpool Street	11.05
Hotel:	Regent Palace	
	Piccadilly Circus	
	London	
	Tel: 020 7273 6290	
Seminar: At the hotel		
	Registration	12.30
	Lunch	13.00
	Interpersonal skills	14.00
	Afternoon tea	15.30
	Plenary session	15.45
	Close	16.30
Theatre: The Adelphi Theatre		20.15
Tuesday 26 January 2---		
Seminar: At the hotel		
	Dealing with customers	10.00
	Coffee	11.00
	Role-play exercises	11.30
	Lunch	13.00
	Aggressive callers	14.15
	Afternoon tea	15.30
	Plenary session	15.45
	Close	16.30
Depart:	London Liverpool Street	18.00
Arrive:	Norwich	20.00

remember

Strangers to an area or country will need additional information and support in an itinerary.

- Allow time for delays in transport, particularly during holiday times and poor weather conditions.
- National, religious or local holidays and festivals should be taken into account as they may affect travel arrangements.
- It should always use the 24-hour clock and state that it is local time.
- Time should be allowed for waiting for connections at airports and ports.
- It should include flight numbers as well as check-in, departure and arrival times.
- If flying, the correct terminal should be stated.
- If travelling by rail, the correct platform number should be stated (if known).
- The name, address, fax and telephone numbers of each of the hotels booked should be included.
- Suggest times when it would be appropriate, given the time differences, for calls to be made to the traveller.
- A copy should be kept by the person organising the travel so that they know where the traveller will be and when to contact them if necessary.

case study

6.1

Business itinery

Rachel has a busy week in front of her. Over the next five days she must visit five European cities to meet with business partners. She needs to be in Cologne at 11.00 on Monday. She has to be back in London on Monday evening for a meeting with her business's director. She has to be in Paris for a meeting at 14.00 on Tuesday. On Wednesday she heads for Madrid where she has a meeting at 10.30. She then travels to Lisbon on Thursday where she must attend a meeting at 12.30. On Friday she needs to be in Athens for a meeting at 13.00. She hopes to be home by no later than 20.00. Luckily Rachel only lives 20 minutes away from Gatwick Airport and since all of the meetings are in the centre of the cities she is visiting she does not need a hire car.

activity

INDIVIDUAL WORK

Is Rachel going to be able to do this? Have a look on easyJet's website and find out whether her proposed itinerary is possible or not. If it is not possible, what changes would you suggest that she makes to her itinerary so that she can visit all five cities?

easyJet
www.easyjet.com

Processing, Retrieving and Archiving Information

The majority of organisations will have a centralised administration service or department. The main function of this department is to ensure that it supports all the other departments within the organisation and generally controls the storage, flow and dissemination of information throughout the organisation.

Figure 6.4

Processing, retrieving and archiving information

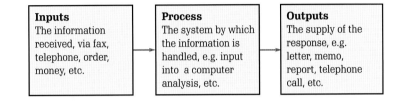

Inputs	Process	Outputs
The information received, via fax, telephone, order, money, etc.	The system by which the information is handled, e.g. input into a computer analysis, etc.	The supply of the response, e.g. letter, memo, report, telephone call, etc.

Process

The 'process' part of the Figure 6.4 can be split into two parts:

■ The storage of information (either manually or on computer)

■ The analysis of information.

The running of an organisation requires an organised approach if it is to be efficient and effective. Administrative jobs will be carried out at all levels of the organisation, but they all have similar tasks:

■ To provide support systems for all resources used by the organisation

■ To keep records relating to the activities of the organisation

■ To monitor the performance of the business's activities.

An administrative system would need to be in place to track the following types of business activities and to process the information related to them:

■ Purchases made

■ Sales made

■ Organisations and individuals with whom transactions have occurred

■ Dates of transactions

■ Payments received and those awaited

■ Records relating to personnel

■ Stock levels

■ Details of staff training and development

■ Accurate minutes of meetings.

The gathering of information, the storing of it and the coordination of the information requires certain skills. Breaking down information and then distributing it requires the individual involved to have a good knowledge of the business's structure and the job roles of those receiving the information. Security or restriction of information is also a key consideration.

Storage, retrieval and archiving
Storage and retrieval

The safe and secure storage of information and the easy access to or retrieval of that information is imperative if an organisation is to function successfully and efficiently.

The term 'storage and retrieval' can often be confusing when you have not worked in an office. In fact, it means 'filing'. Nowadays, storage and retrieval also includes the computerised systems of storing and retrieving information.

Another word for filing is 'indexing'. Obviously filing involves a logical and effective way of recording documents and storing them in an efficient system which will allow the easy retrieval of that information when required.

Filing is the basis of record-keeping and entails the processing, arranging and storing of the documents so that they can be found when they are required. The documents are placed in consecutive order and preserved in that system until they are required for reference. This can be carried out in any number of locations – a telephone directory is an index of alphabetical names and addresses. Your own address book is also a method of indexing in alphabetical order.

Paper-based filing systems

So what are the basic techniques required to ensure that the storage and retrieval of information and documents is efficient? Let us look at this in some detail by considering the following points that help you adopt good filing practice:

- Ensure that the papers which have been passed for filing have been marked in some way to indicate that they are ready for storing.

- Sort the papers into order so that they are grouped in the required way.

- Remove any paperclips and staple documents together.

- Each individual file should be in date order, with the most recent documents at the top or front.

- Be careful with the documents – curled edges can easily become torn.

- File daily if possible – this makes it less of a chore and also ensures that the files are up to date.

- Follow organisational procedure regarding 'out' or 'absent' cards. These are cards that are inserted into a file if the paperwork contained in the file has been removed by a member of staff.

- Follow up all overdue files regularly when they have been borrowed by another member of staff or department and not returned on time.

- Use a cross-reference system whenever a file is known by more than one name.

- Thin out the files when necessary.

- Be aware of health and safety regarding filing cabinets. For example, always close drawers after you have used them, and lock drawers and cabinets before leaving the office at night.

- Always ask for help if you are unsure where something should be filed.

The alphabetical method is the filing of documents according to the first letter of the surname. It is the most common method of classification used in businesses. This is normally the first letter of the surname of the correspondent. Some rules for alphabetical filing include:

- Consider the first letter of the surname and then each letter after that, for example:
  - Black, Brian
  - Blake, John
  - Blakemore, Margaret.

- If the surname is the same, place the first name or initial in alphabetical order, for example:
  - Smith, David; Smith, John; Smith, William.

If the surname and the first name are the same, file by second name or initial, for example:

  - Jones, Brian A; Jones, Brian D; Jones, Brian P.

- Treat surname prefixes as part of the name and all names beginning with M', Mc or Mac as if they were spelt with Mac, for example:
  - McBride, Angus; McGregor, William; MacMasters, Peter.

- File all 'saint' surnames beginning with St as if they were spelt 'Saint', for example:
  - St John, Ian
  - St Luke's Church
  - St Mary's Hospital.

- Ignore titles, for example: Brown, Sir Andrew
  - Grey, Lady Jane
  - Simpson, Major David.

- Ignore words like 'The' and 'A' in the name of an organisation, for example:
  - Card Shop, The
  - Office Equipment Centre, The
  - Tea Shoppe, The.

- Numbers should be filed as if spelt in full, for example:
  - 55 Club, The (would be filed under 'f' for 'fifty')
  - 99 Boutique, The (would be filed under 'n' for 'ninety')
  - 111 Association, The (would be filed under 'o' for 'one').

A quick way of putting a list into alphabetical order is to put them into numerical order first, by writing the number of the position the entry will be in an alphabetical list next to the relevant entry and then writing the list out again in numerical order.

The numeric classification method of filing is linked by means of index cards to the alphabetic method we have just looked at. Each document or folder is given a number and is filed in number order. The information contained within the files is sorted into alphabetical order. The index cards contain the number of each document or folder and a summary of what is contained in that document or folder. They are also filed numerically.

Chronological filing means that documents are stored according to the date, with the most recent date being at the front or top of the file. A sales representative might use the chronological system of filing paperwork according to the dates they have arranged meetings with customers.

---

activity
**INDIVIDUAL WORK
(6.12)**

Place the following list of names in alphabetical order:

Hutchinson, David	Hurle, Peter
Conway, Malcolm	Aliffe, Burt
Hunt, Peter	Smith, Marie
Woodhouse, John	Smith, Delphine
Jackson, Nick	Wright, Susan
Sutherland, Joshua	Canwell, Rosie
Hewitt, Ernest William	Greene, Susan
Hewitt, Diane Elizabeth	Green, Samantha
Canwell, Stuart	Leggett, Michael
Canwell, Alun	

---

activity
**INDIVIDUAL WORK
(6.13)**

Place the following list of numbers in numerical order:

134	88	95	109	245	180	21
176	333	378	310	213	76	209

Place the following list of dates in chronological order, putting the most recent first:

25 January 1999	20 July 2002
17 September 2001	15 November 2002
1 August 2003	18 November 2003
15 June 2000	21 September 2001
27 June 2000	18 June 2000
11 November 2001	24 August 2003
6 May 1999	21 December 2003

The term 'archiving' means storing away old files in another location, for example another room, cupboard, storage area or another building belonging to the business. Archiving does not mean throwing away. Old files may be needed again in the future and only need to be archived until they become current again.

There will be procedures in place that have to be followed, mainly because someone with authority will have to decide when a file becomes an old file. A file could be an old file if, for example, the information in it:

■ Relates to a previous customer or business the organisation used to deal with.

■ Relates to an employee who has now left the business.

■ Is now out of date.

Obviously, after filing paperwork away, either you or someone else must be able to find it again when it is needed. Being able to find the right information in a filing system is known as retrieving information and this would be done to:

■ Add more information to the contents of the file

■ Obtain some information from the contents of the file.

If someone takes individual documents from a file the papers may go missing forever. You should never allow just one or two pages to be taken from a file unless:

■ Most of the information contained in the file is confidential and the person needing the one or two documents cannot see the rest of the confidential information.

■ The information contained in the file is too large to take away.

There are some golden rules for making sure that information from a file does not get lost or refiled in the wrong place:

- Record the fact that information has been taken from the filing cabinet by inserting an 'out' or 'absent' card in its place.

- Use a log sheet to record the fact that the file has been borrowed, who took it and when they took it, where they have taken it and when they have agreed to return it.

- Keep information on the log sheet up to date and chase up any files that are not returned on the agreed date.

All information stored on computer must also be protected. Organisations are more likely nowadays to use this method of filing their records because it is easier to store and retrieve documents. They must ensure that:

- Back-up copies of documents are made and stored safely.

- Passwords are used by the staff using the computer, and these should be changed regularly.

- User codes are used if necessary. Only those who are authorised to access the information know these codes, which often only relate to specific files or documents stored.

> **remember**
>
> Many organisations routinely back up all of their computer network at the end of each day.

The business will have chosen its system for the preparation, storage and retrieval of data for a number of different reasons. It will then train the employees who will be using this equipment and software so that they are aware of the importance of:

- Accuracy and checking – given the fact that any computerised system is only as accurate as the data it receives, there is always the possibility that the information is inaccurate as a result of human error.

- Cost – most organisations will use data-handling systems in order to cut costs. The more time that can be saved by not having to repeat tasks or sort out problems, the more money that will be saved.

- Speed and accessibility – in most cases, the use of data-handling systems means that information can be processed much faster than it could using a manual system.

> **activity**
> **INDIVIDUAL WORK**
> **(6.15)**
>
> We have now looked in some detail at the ways in which businesses can store their information paper-based and electronic and the right people can retrieve it at the right time.
>
> Compile two tables, one for paper-based storage and retrieval and the other for computer-based storage and retrieval. Each table should have two columns headed 'Advantages' and 'Disadvantages'. Complete the table with your thoughts about the two methods. Which method has the most advantages?

progress check

1. Why might administrative support be of value to managers?

2. What kind of administrative support would be needed for arranging an event?

3. Name one additional feature of a good diary.

4. What is a callback facility?

5. What documents would need to be prepared for a meeting?

6. What kind of travel information would a person need if they were visiting a location for the first time?

7. What is an itinerary?

8. State three different sorts of information that comes into a business.

9. State three different sorts of information that goes out of a business.

10. Give five features of good filing practice.

Personal Selling

This unit covers:

- the purpose of sales personnel
- how to prepare for personal selling
- demonstrating the personal selling skills and processes
- closing sales techniques and how to identify customers' objections

This unit aims to assist you in understanding the role and importance of personal selling. You will learn how sales teams work and the nature of personal selling. You will learn how to prepare for selling and how to develop your personal selling skills. Importantly, you will also appreciate the importance of legislation that impacts on selling.

The final part of the unit looks at closing a sale, or effectively persuading the customer to purchase the product or service. You will look at the techniques and processes used and how to deal with customers who are still unsure about making a decision. You will also understand how important it is to follow up sales and to record useful customer information which can be used in the future by the business.

grading criteria

To achieve a **Pass** grade the evidence must show that the learner is able to:	To achieve a **Merit** grade the evidence must show that the learner is able to:	To achieve a **Distinction** grade the evidence must show that the learner is able to:
P1 describe the purpose of sales personnel and the knowledge and skills required for personal selling	**M1** demonstrate an independent approach to a major part of their work, showing confident and effective personal selling skills	**D1** demonstrate excellent and confident personal selling in at least three different situations
P2 describe the legislation which affects personal selling	**M2** explain how legislation might affect personal selling in two different situations	**D2** evaluate the preparation to support personal selling and the personal selling skills and processes carried out in two different situations
P3 describe the preparation needed to support personal selling in two different situations	**M3** compare and contrast personal selling skills and processes used in two different situations	

grading criteria

To achieve a **Pass** grade the evidence must show that the learner is able to:	To achieve a **Merit** grade the evidence must show that the learner is able to:	To achieve a **Distinction** grade the evidence must show that the learner is able to:
P4 demonstrate personal selling skills and processes in two different situations		
P5 demonstrate the process of closing sales in two different situations		
P6 demonstrate how to respond to customers' objections in two different situations		
P7 describe the reasons for following up sales and recording customer information		

The Purpose of Sales Personnel

For many organisations sales teams are key groups of people that can affect the success or failure of the organisation. It is these individuals that are responsible for the business's point of contact with their customers.

remember

Sales teams are often the point of contact between the business and its customers.

Some organisations rely on their sales teams to go out and find customers, whilst others use marketing and advertising to attract customers to their premises and then rely on sales teams to close a sale with these visitors.

Sales teams have many different purposes. Broadly these can be broken down into the following categories:

■ Increasing business sales – this could involve actively looking for customers and visiting them, or dealing with customers that visit the business and trying to convince them to purchase products and services. Sales teams will be given targets to increase sales revenue.

■ Helping the business to remain competitive – this means feeding back information that they may receive from customers or other sources with regard to the pricing and customer service offered by competitors. Businesses will try to match competitors' prices.

- Providing information and services to customers – whether the sales person is visiting the customer or the customer has come to the business, they may well need assistance before they can make a decision about a purchase.

- Developing customer care – this is an increasingly important function of a sales team. By using a good standard of customer care the business can continue to serve that customer.

- Gathering feedback – customers will routinely offer their opinions on the quality of the business's products and services. They will compare these with those of competitors.

Although the primary benefits of a good relationship with customers are to the business in terms of sales and profit, it is not just the business that will benefit. Employees benefit if the business has a good relationship and is making sales as their jobs will be secure and they will have the opportunity to increase their income. Many sales teams are paid on the basis of a set, low wage, which is topped up by bonuses based on the amount of products and services they have sold. If the business gets the sales process right and supports it with high-quality customer care then there are key advantages to customers.

---

activity
GROUP WORK
(7.1)

Choose a business, such as an electrical shop or a record store. How might the sales teams in these types of business keep up to date with new products? These types of sales teams need to be constantly aware of new technology and releases. Do you think they do this themselves or are they given training and support by the business?

Knowledge and skills required

Training is essential in order to create and maintain an effective sales team. A sales team may have several different types of training, including:

- Product knowledge – this is essential as the sales person will have to know about the organisation's products, their benefits, how they work, how they compare with competitor's products and their relative strengths and weaknesses.

- Motivation – this is a very broad type of training but it essentially means giving the sales person a reason to be positive about their job. This may include setting realistic sales targets for them so that they can earn extra income from bonuses.

- Closing a sale – as we will see later in this unit, closing a sale is one of the trickiest skills required. A sales person will have to overcome any objections or delaying tactics used by a customer and ensure that the sale is made.

■ Keeping up to date – in addition to having knowledge of the products and services offered by the business, a sales person also needs to be aware of current and future developments in products and services and their implications to those currently on sale.

■ Good sales habits – many businesses will have set procedures and will attempt to ensure that the sales person is truthful and honest during the sales process.

Like any job, being a member of a sales team can be frustrating and sometimes difficult. Businesses know that these individuals are at the front end of their efforts to sell products and services. They therefore need to be motivated individuals who are not only good at their job but also have a passion to sell products and services.

Sales teams are often offered sales incentives, particularly if they sell specific products and services with a higher profit margin for the business. One of the ultimate motivating techniques is to offer sales teams career development so that they can become sales managers or departmental or shop managers.

activity

GROUP WORK (7.2)

As we have seen, product knowledge is important. Try this out for yourselves:

Come up with five key features of the following:

a) Toothpaste.

b) Satellite navigation system.

c) A new fragrance for men.

remember

Consumer law aims to regulate the relationship between sellers and buyers.

Legislation affecting personal selling

Sale of Goods Act 1979/1995

Traders must sell goods that are as described and of satisfactory quality. If consumers discover that products do not meet these requirements they can reject them and ask for their money back. They can also ask for a repair or replacement or claim compensation.

The Sale of Goods Act has been replaced by the Sale and Supply of Goods to Consumers Regulations (2002). Under the new regulations, consumers can now demand repair, replacement, partial or full refund on any goods that were faulty or defective at the time of purchase.

Supply of Goods and Services Act 1982

This law states that certain terms are implied in every transaction for the transfer of goods and that the goods must:

- Correspond with the description given
- Be of satisfactory quality
- Be fit for the purpose for which it was sold.

Consumer Protection Act 1987

This safeguards consumers from products that do not reach a reasonable level of safety. The main areas dealt with are:

- Product liability – allows injured persons to sue producers, importers and own-branders for death, personal injury or losses. Defective products are defined as being those where the safety of the product is not such as persons generally are entitled to expect.

- Consumer safety – requires producers and distributors to take steps to ensure that the products they supply are safe, that they provide consumers with relevant information and warnings, and that they keep themselves informed about risks.

---

activity

INDIVIDUAL WORK (7.3)

Read the information regarding consumer protection laws and then answer the following questions:

1. You purchase a CD player from a local shop using your credit card. Four weeks later it stops working. What can you do?

   a) Nothing – it is just bad luck.

   b) Go back to the store and reject the item.

   c) Try to fix it yourself.

2. A relative has bought you a games console for your birthday. You open it straightaway and it appears to be faulty. What are you entitled to?

   a) Nothing, it should have been checked at the shop.

   b) A full refund, but only the relative can take it back.

   c) The shop has to offer you a replacement.

Consumer Credit Act 1974

The Consumer Credit Act 1974 regulates consumer credit and consumer hire agreements for amounts up to £25 000. Its protections apply to agreements between traders and individuals, sole traders, partnerships and unincorporated associations, but not agreements made between traders and corporate bodies such as limited companies.

A new Consumer Credit Bill was announced in November 2004. The key benefits of the new law will be that it:

- Protects consumers and will create fairer and more competitive credit
- Improves consumer rights and redress
- Improves the regulation of consumer credit
- Extends protection to all consumer credit.

Trade Descriptions Act 1968

The Trade Descriptions Act 1968 aims to prevent misleading descriptions of all goods and services. The Act protects consumers from misleading or false descriptions of goods.

The law applies to suppliers, manufacturers and retailers of goods, as well as services, facilities and accommodation. The law states that it is the business's responsibility to ensure that the goods, services, facilities and accommodation sold or provided are not falsely described. Legislation on misleading prices was made under the Consumer Protection Act 1987.

Preparing for Personal Selling

Even if you were attempting to sell products on a market stall, you would need to know something about your potential customers and their expectations. You would also need to know about the laws and regulations that have an impact on personal selling.

Identifying and finding potential customers

Different businesses use different methods with which to find potential customers. All these methods focus on identifying who the customers are and then convincing them to invest their time and attention whilst the sales person tries to convince them that they need the product or service. Some are more or less effective, depending on what is being sold, and many businesses will use a combination of techniques. Typical techniques include the following:

> *keyword*
>
> **Call centre**
> – An office environment in which staff have access to telephones and computers and use computer software to make calls to potential customers.

- Cold calling – this involves telephoning or visiting a potential customer without having warned them that you will contact them. These are notoriously difficult situations as the person you may need to speak to may not be there.
- Face to face – these types of sales usually take place in a retail environment. A customer may come in with the desire to purchase a product or service and, perhaps, needs very little encouragement or assistance in making the final decision to buy.
- Telemarketing – this involves actively trying to sell products and services via the telephone, usually using **call centres** with dedicated sales staff. The call centres will use a database of customer names and numbers and systematically ring every single person on the database.

activity
GROUP WORK
(7.4)

Have you ever received a telephone call from a call centre? You may have answered the call, or perhaps one of your family did? If you remember the last one, how appropriate was the product or service being offered? How would a business such as this identify the correct customer for particular products and services?

Preparation

In order to succeed, businesses must be alert and responsive to the needs and preferences of today's consumers who are more demanding and discerning than ever.

This also means that the business needs to be creative, delivering quality and value for money. Consumers now expect the highest possible standards of customer care. This means proper policies and procedures for dealing with enquiries and complaints should things go wrong. It requires staff who are properly trained and equipped for dealing with customers with special needs and those from minority and ethnic backgrounds.

Understanding consumer protection legislation

Many businesses do not provide any customer information about their policies for refunds, complaints and customer care. In many cases where information is provided, the nature of it and how it is provided is very much dependent on the size of the business.

Information about the business and its customer care policies should be readily available and easily accessible.

Generally, business awareness of consumer protection legislation is poor. Many businesses are unsure if there is a specific body dealing with complaints for their business or industry.

It is important that businesses are familiar with consumer protection arrangements generally and not just the bodies relevant to their business. It also means that employees need to be aware and it is the responsibility of the business to inform them and keep them up to date with the legislation.

activity

INDIVIDUAL WORK (7.5)

How might a retail store or chain ensure that its sales staff is kept up to date with consumer protection legislation?

Business and retail customers and professionally trained buyers

Depending on the size of the business, some of the sales staff may only deal with retail customers whilst others will deal with the local businesses.

Businesses tend to buy in greater quantities than retail customers and they may also have accounts with the business and be given credit terms. Therefore, an organisation that supplies other businesses with products and services will encounter professional business buyers who will often wish to negotiate prices, delivery, credit terms and discounts.

Supply constraints

It is not always possible for a business to have adequate stocks of products to meet the demands of its customers. Retail stores, in particular, are reliant upon their suppliers to be able to deliver products as and when they are ordered.

Some customers will want to purchase and take products away immediately, and it is the role of the sales staff to try to make the sale, even if the products are not in stock, rather than risk the customer purchasing the product elsewhere. They will expect to be given a firm date as to when the product will be available and also wish to be advised if that date changes.

Product knowledge

Just as sales staff need to be aware of the business's policies on dealing with customers and have knowledge of consumer protection legislation, they also need to be seen as an expert, or at least knowledgeable, about the products that they are selling. Customers will often ask sales staff for their opinion of various competing products.

Many businesses have a policy towards this service to customers and will often steer the customers to products that provide the business with a greater profit margin.

Business customer sales histories

If a business deals with other businesses, then they will have fuller and more accurate records of the previous purchases made by those customers. These customer records will contain the following information:

- How often they make purchases
- How much they are likely to spend in a single order
- What kind of products or services they buy
- The names of the buyers
- The address and contact details
- The method of payment
- Any delivery requirements
- The discounts offered.

activity
INDIVIDUAL WORK (7.6)

Using Microsoft Word, design a simple customer record card for business customers. It should contain spaces to include all the information listed here.

remember

Many high-street stores and supermarkets routinely monitor their competitors' prices.

Pricing policies

Normally, retail customers only receive discount from shops if the products have already been discounted by the store and are available at that price to anyone. When a store deals with business customers, however, they will have a range of discounts, usually dependent upon how important the customer is to the business.

A business does need to ensure that each product's price covers all of the costs incurred by the business in buying it from a supplier and selling it. The business's customer records will detail the amount of discount normally given to that business. A business may actually ask for a larger discount than usual, and in such cases it would be the responsibility of the manager to decide whether or not this additional discount can be given.

activity
INDIVIDUAL WORK (7.7)

A stationery supplier buys in boxes of five reams of photocopy paper for £6 a box. The normal retail price is £12 a box. The minimum profit margin the business expects is £3 on each box. A major customer wants to buy 100 boxes, but is demanding a 60 per cent discount off the retail price. Would the store be able to offer this discount and maintain its profit margin?

Customer service training

Where training is provided, this tends to be either general or in areas such as the business complaints-handling policies. Once again, the level of customer service training depends on the size of the business, and larger businesses are much more likely to provide staff training of this nature.

Businesses do realise that better staff training will eventually be reflected in increased consumer satisfaction. However, the vast majority of businesses do need to provide more staff training in dealing with customers with a disability or from ethnic and other minority backgrounds.

Different clients and range of customer requirements

Sales staff in a retail store will have to provide assistance to a wide variety of different customer types. Not all customers will be alone. Many will be part of a group comprising people of different ages. Younger people respond to a less formal approach and want more of a relaxed interaction with the sales staff. Older customers may want a more respectful and professional approach.

Sales staff also need to be aware of the fact that they could easily offend customers from different cultural backgrounds. All customers need to be treated with respect. Some have different dress codes and preferences. Non-English-speaking customers can present a challenge to sales staff, although increasingly in many stores important information, particularly regarding customer service, has been translated into different languages.

Essentially, a business may have to deal with the following types of customers and situations:

- Single individuals who may well be better off than married couples or those with children.
- It is common for families or groups of adults, or even groups of children, to become regular customers. The store needs to be family friendly.

- Customers will be of different ages and the store will have to cope with their different demands.
- People from different cultural backgrounds who can be either UK citizens or visitors from overseas.
- People with disabilities who will need to be able to enter and move around the store easily. People with visual impairment may need assistance. Those with literacy or numeracy difficulties may require help reading signs or information on products.

Negotiation skills, courtesy and efficiency

In addition to customers needing advice about different products, a sales assistant's role is ultimately to persuade the customer to part with money in exchange for the products. Sales assistants consider it a failure, having had a conversation with a customer about a range of products, for that customer then to leave the store without making a purchase and potentially buying the products elsewhere. While sales staff need to be aware of how they provide customer service, their primary goal is to sell products.

Some customers may need encouragement and persuasion before they decide whether to purchase a product or not. To successfully make a sale, a sales person needs to:

- Establish a rapport with the customer
- Find out what the customer is interested in
- Describe the major benefits of the product
- Overcome any objections to purchasing the product
- Answer any questions
- Close the sale.

Most customers will need help and assistance. Sometimes the help may be of a practical nature, such as demonstrating how a product works. However small the request for assistance might be, customers must feel that they are valued and that the staff actually care about them.

---

activity
GROUP WORK
(7.8)

a) Why might it be important to a retail business that their customers feel valued and that the staff care?

b) What are the implications to the business if the customers do not feel valued and the staff give the impression that they could not care less about them?

Referral procedures

In some cases, a situation may arise with a customer that cannot be resolved and the situation will have to be passed on to a more experienced or senior member of staff. Referral procedures differ from store to store, but usually there is a senior or experienced sales person available to ask for advice or to take over the situation.

Typical referral situations include:

- A customer with a complaint that cannot be dealt with using the normal complaints procedure.
- A customer who is abusive or rude.

- A customer asking questions about aspects of the product that the sales staff are unable to answer.
- A customer making requests that are outside the authority of the sales staff.

Return and exchange policies

Normally a business will have a policy which allows a customer to return the item for an exchange or refund if they are not completely satisfied with their purchase. Usually, all articles in saleable condition are accepted for credit or exchange within 30 days of purchase. Cash refunds will be made only to the purchaser.

Some businesses will adopt a more complicated policy. If the goods are damaged or faulty, customers will need to contact customer services as soon as possible. Customer services will then arrange a replacement or a refund. Usually, customers will need to contact customer services and arrange for the goods to be returned within seven days for a refund.

activity
INDIVIDUAL WORK (7.9)

Find out about the returns policy in one of your local stores.

Preparation of the physical sales environment

As we will see, the layout of stores can either determine how comfortable staff and customers are, or it can be designed to ease the flow, aid security measures or simply make the premises more accessible.

Accessibility, furnishings and décor

By law, all stores that are open to the public have to have disabled access. This means that ramps and lifts have been constructed to comply with these laws. Ramps and lifts are, of course, of great value to people with small children and to older people.

Access is important. It should be easy for the customer to enter the shop and not have to hunt around for the entrance. Often the doors to shops are kept open or work electronically with sensors to detect movement outside.

Once inside the store, the customer needs to have enough space to move around. There must be sufficient room between the aisles or products, and everything needs to be clearly marked. Many larger stores have floor plans and notices telling the customers where certain items are located. Supermarkets have signs above the aisles to show the customers where to find regularly purchased items.

The store should be at the right temperature, it should have sufficient lighting, and customer service points and cashier tills need to be marked. In addition, the store needs to mark the emergency exits and, if there are any, the customer toilets.

remember
Comfortable, spacious and relaxed sales environments encourage customers to shop and buy more.

The layout of the store is usually designed to encourage the flow of customers. Stores will avoid locating several regular-purchase products in the same place to prevent bottlenecks. They will locate these products around the store, also in the hope that as customers pass other products they will buy them as well.

The look of the store is also important. Many chains have a common look to all of their stores and indeed the layouts are very similar. Colour, use of lights, carpets, rest areas and other features are all designed to help the customer feel comfortable.

activity
**INDIVIDUAL WORK
(7.10)**

Think about one of the stores you visit on a regular basis. How is it laid out? Are things easy to find? Do the furnishings and décor make you feel comfortable?

Use of music

Many retailers use music to help customers feel relaxed and believe that they are in familiar surroundings. Research on music and consumer behaviour has, however, almost completely ignored the potential effect of in-store music on purchasing and particularly on product choice.

activity
**INDIVIDUAL WORK
(7.11)**

What kind of music, if any, is played in your favourite store? What effect does it have on you?

Health and safety hazards

All employees need to be clear about the responsibilities they have to make sure that the store operates in a safe and careful manner. Just as it is easy for members of staff to injure themselves at work, it is also possible for customers to have accidents in the store.

Routes around the store need to be kept clear. Cables, products that have not been put on shelves, or displays and any other obstacles need to be cleared from areas through which the customers pass. In many stores selling electrical goods, there is an additional hazard from trailing wires, the electricity supply itself and children with drinks close by.

There can be a huge number of potential hazards to customers in any retail store. A business will need to have insurance in order to cover it for claims by customers should they injure themselves or damage their property while on the premises.

Security personnel

Many stores prefer store detectives to uniformed guards so that thieves do not know that they are being watched. Store detectives are highly skilled at blending into the background inside stores. Their role is to observe customers' behaviour by acting like normal shoppers, aiming not to arouse suspicion. If they see a

customer stealing from the store, then they will follow the customer until they have shown they have no intention of paying for the goods, and then arrest them for theft.

Policies within stores differ, but the detective may detain the offender until the police arrive, or may issue a formal warning and banning order and then escort the offender from the premises.

Store detectives are ideal for larger stores with poor CCTV coverage. When a store is too big for a uniformed officer to observe all areas, a store detective will generally be more effective.

Uniformed security officers act as a deterrent to criminal activity, and provide a useful link between a business and its customers. Often the first person a customer will see when they enter a shop is the security guard; therefore first impressions are absolutely vital.

activity
INDIVIDUAL WORK
(7.12)

Visit the IPSA website and answer the following questions.

a) When was IPSA formed?

b) What are its purposes?

c) What kind of members (individuals and organisations) does it have?

Market competition and buyer behaviour

All businesses face competition from a large number of other businesses. In a retail environment, this may mean a competitor having a wider range of products, selling products at a lower price, being more accessible to customers or simply having a better reputation.

If the business fails to react to actions taken by its competitors, it runs the risk of not attracting as many customers. If the customers are not entering the store, then the sales staff cannot sell products to them.

The competition could be offering their customers any of the following, which will affect the way customers view the business and have an influence on where they choose to shop:

■ More convenient parking, close to the store, with disabled and parent/toddler parking spaces.

■ More advertising in the media to attract customers to the store.

■ A sale or discounted prices on various products.

■ A wider range of products.

- Packing, car loading and delivery services.
- A wider range of services to customers, including refreshment area, children's play area, more tills, a good supply of trolleys, wider aisles, clear signposting.
- More and better-trained staff.

Demonstrating the Personal Selling Processes

Once the sales person has contact with a potential customer, all of the efforts of the business have succeeded. It is now the role of the sales person to convert contact with the customer into a positive sale. This means that responsibility for closing the sale rests with a single person and their own skills and ability to follow an effective selling process is of vital importance.

Businesses may have set procedures as to how the interaction between the sales person and the customer develops. The end result involves closing the sale, responding to objections and carrying out any follow-up work.

Personal selling skills and the selling process
Effective sales presentations

Sales staff play a crucial role in convincing customers to part with money for products and services. They do this by having sales conversations with the customers. These can take place either face to face or via the telephone. There are a number of different types of presentation, including:

- Sales promotions, which encourage customers to make repeat purchases, build up long-term customer loyalty and encourage new customers to visit the store. They include price reductions, vouchers, coupons, gifts, competitions, lotteries and cash bonuses.

> **remember**
>
> Without a trained and well-motivated sales force, a business cannot expect customers to purchase their products or services.

- Sales seminars, which are usually aimed at the sales representatives themselves or business buyers. They provide information about the products and services, along with a demonstration.

- Product launches, which are also aimed at broadening the appeal of particular products or services and, in some cases, the opening of a new store. These are aimed at attracting customers to the store or encouraging them to try new products and services.

Sales presentations are supported by a number of different forms of display which are designed to make the product more attractive and the store more interesting. Examples of displays that support sales presentations are:

- Window areas – These can include posters stuck to the glass or boards in the window area, a pelmet with the product's name pasted along the edges of the window, empty product packs attractively stacked, life-size cut-outs of product characters or personalities and illuminated displays with flashing lights.

- Point-of-sale – this is the area near the cash tills. Examples include cut-out displays, posters announcing special offers, a pelmet along a shelf, empty packs, dump bins placed near the tills with a selection of products, wire stands for smaller products, portable displays and dispenser boxes for leaflets and brochures.

- Public places – these could include illuminated displays, display stands, leaflet dispensers, video screens and TVs.

- Advertising sites – these would be placed near areas where potential customers visit or pass, including bus and railway stations, airports, on buses and trains or outside buildings.

activity
INDIVIDUAL WORK
(7.13)

Note down how many different advertising messages you see on your way home from school or college. Where are they directing you to go to purchase products and services? What made you notice them?

It is the personal selling skills of an individual sales person that may make the difference between success or failure. There are several key aspects to personal selling skills, including:

- Making a good impression – this is important from the outset, that the customer feels at ease and is comfortable with the approach being made by the sales person.

- Appropriate dress – although some businesses may have uniforms, others will have dress codes. Clothing should be clean, neat and follow the set dress codes of the business.

- Positive attitude – an enthusiastic approach to every customer. Whether it is nine in the morning or nine at night, the sales person should make the customer feel valued and important.

- Good manners – the customer will not expect the sales person to use bad language, jargon or be too familiar with them.

- Professionalism – customers will expect a knowledgeable, polite and helpful individual who can help them make a purchasing decision.

- Courtesy and consideration – a sales person needs to listen to a customer and not to bully them into making a purchase. A polite, paced and considered approach is far more effective than giving the impression that there is little time for the customer.

- Personal space – many people do not like to be crowded and prefer to have a conversation across a counter or a desk.

- Eye contact – the sales person needs at least to give the impression that they are paying attention to the customer.

activity

GROUP WORK (7.14)

Can you think of a situation where you have encountered a rude sales person? Did it put you off buying products or services? Have you encountered a sales person with a good range of personal selling skills? How did you react to them?

keyword

Point-of-sale (POS)
– The physical location in a store where the customer purchases products and services, such as a cash register or payment point.

Setting up a sales promotion

Sales promotion is an example of a 'below-the-line' marketing activity, i.e. it is a discreet (not so obvious) marketing method, like public relations. Compare this with advertising which is considered to be 'above-the-line', i.e. it is an overt (open or obvious) marketing method. Usually, the sales promotion effort is concentrated either on pack (on or within the packaging) or at the **point-of-sale**.

Before we consider some sales promotion techniques, we should fully consider the functions of sales promotion campaigns, which include:

- To encourage stockists to order the product or existing stockists to increase their orders.

- To encourage the customer to try the product or increase their level of purchasing.

- To counteract the effects of the competition. When a competitor either launches a new product or is running a sales promotion for an existing one, there is the danger that some of the market share could be lost.

■ To improve the distribution network and enhance the sales representative's journey cycle. If the campaign works, the supplier will be able to acquire more customers in a given area and vastly improve the efficiency of the sales representative's journey cycle by having an increased number of customers in the territory.

■ To revitalise or relaunch a product that has become rather stale in the eyes of the customers.

> **activity**
> **INDIVIDUAL WORK**
> **(7.15)**
>
> A business has not run a sales promotion for its major product for some months. It discovers in the trade press that a competitor is about to launch a new sales promotion in six months' time. Which of the reasons given above might prompt the business to launch their own sales promotion?

Some of the more common forms of sales promotion include:

■ Free samples – either given out in a retail outlet, attached to another product, on the front of a magazine or posted through customers' letter boxes.

■ Cut-price special offers – products would be despatched with preprinted price reduction flashes on the packaging.

■ Two for the price of one – either two products attached to one another, or the price of one of the items is deducted at the point-of-sale (checkout).

■ Free gift on pack – a version of a 'premium offer', either on or in the pack itself or given out at the cash desk.

■ Free gifts on proof of purchase – requiring the customer to collect a number of tokens or wrappers.

■ Self-liquidating premiums – the customer receives a coupon on the pack offering a reduction in price for the next purchase of the same product.

■ Competitions – a variety of different 'games' of skill and judgement.

■ Personality-based promotions – linking the product with a well-known personality.

> **activity**
> **INDIVIDUAL WORK**
> **(7.16)**
>
> Think of a sales promotion that you might have been tempted to try. What type of sales promotion was it?

> **remember**
>
> Sales promotions aim to tempt customers to purchase the product or service and, having done so, continue to buy it after the promotion is over.

Any sales promotion campaign needs to be supported by a concerted effort on all fronts. In other words, the organisation needs to have the following in place before the launch of the campaign:

■ The customer response structures need to be in place.

■ Sufficient stocks need to be available in the outlets and in reserve to cater for demand.

- The sales representatives should be well briefed so that they can brief the retailer.

- Any response mechanism should be clear and easy to use by the customer.

- Special point-of-sale materials should have been created and distributed to retailers.

- The on-pack messages need to be clear and stand out well.

- The distributors and retailers should be given incentives to be part of the promotion.

Sales promotions are often referred to as 'push and pull' strategies (see Figure 7.1). The rise in sales prior to the sales promotion is caused by the business selling extra products as the retailers anticipate higher sales as a result of the promotion. After the sales promotion there is a further increase in sales as customers who have tried the product during the promotion continue to buy it and recommend it to others.

Figure 7.1

Push and pull strategies

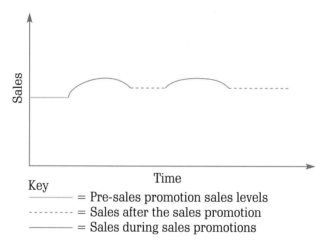

Key
- - - - - - - = Pre-sales promotion sales levels
- - - - - - = Sales after the sales promotion
———— = Sales during sales promotions

Obviously, either during or directly after the sales promotion campaign, the organisation will need to assess its effectiveness and impact on the sales of the product. Typically, the following data would be used to assess this:

- The increase in sales volume of the product.

- The number of new customers created.

- The repeat purchase rate of customers.

- The profit per unit during and after the promotion.

- The performance of the promoted product against a similar product that did not have a promotion.

- The attitude, or change in attitude, towards the product (both the customer and the retailer).

- The additional profit gained from the new purchasers of the product.

- The sales revenue, profit and volume of sales against the promotional costs.

- The increase in the number of retailers stocking the product.
- The improvements in the distribution system and the sales representative's journey cycle as a result of the promotion.
- The effect on goodwill (both customers and retailers).
- The increase in the amount of point-of-sale materials/displays used by the retailers.

activity
INDIVIDUAL WORK (7.17)

A business wants to launch a sales promotion campaign. It wants its existing customers to buy more, attract more customers and encourage more retailers to sell the products. Which items in the above list does this sales promotion hope to address?

We will now look at the incentives that can be used to encourage both retailers and sales representatives involvement. We begin by looking at the retailer, who would be offered:

- Extended credit terms
- Retailers' associated competitions/promotions
- Cash discounts
- Case bonuses (such as one extra box for every 12 ordered).

Sales representatives would normally be offered:

- Cash payments for achieving sales targets attached to the promotion
- Prizes (such as holidays, etc.) for particular target achievements
- 'Best salesperson of the month' prizes
- Team prizes for the best-performing region.

Finally, an integral part of the sales promotion and, for that matter, a vital role of the sales representative's regular visits to a stockist is to provide (and encourage the use of) a variety of different window displays, point-of-sale materials and other merchandising tools. These promotional tools would include:

- Point-of-sale materials, including posters, leaflets and aisle banners.
- Shelf-strips, which can be attached along the shelf or used to attract attention.
- Posters designed for windows and doors.
- Freestanding or wall-mounted displays.
- Dump bins (floor or shelf-mounted containers).

activity
INDIVIDUAL WORK
(7.18)

During your next visit to a supermarket or large store, look out for point-of-sale material. What kind is being used? Is it well placed and does it attract your attention?

Organising a sales promotion

As we have seen, a business may have several reasons for launching a sales promotion. In this section we will look at the various choices and the preparation that needs to take place before launching, or even designing, the promotional campaign.

Above-the-line and below-the-line methods

Traditional advertising media such as press, radio and TV are known as above-the-line. Non-traditional media such as sales promotions are known as below-the-line. Below-the-line elements of marketing include:

remember

These methods represent all of the ways in which a business tries to convince customers to purchase their products and services.

■ In-store vouchers and special offers.

■ Loyalty card offers that encourage repeat purchases or encourage someone to purchase a product that they would not normally buy.

■ Competitions, both in-store and on the back of packaging.

■ Packaging which is used to attract the buyer's attention.

Above-the-line marketing includes:

■ The press, including newspapers and magazines – the advertisements can be very detailed.

■ Television advertising that reaches large audiences.

■ Radio advertising, there are many new national, regional and local independent radio stations to reach particular audiences.

■ Cinema advertising – effective, with good sound and colour, often used to test advertisements that will later be screened on television.

■ Posters and billboards which can be sited near road junctions, shops, travel centres and other locations where there is a large amount of passing 'traffic'.

■ The Internet – the newest form of advertising and quite effective if it reaches the right audience.

■ Mobile advertising, which includes trucks and lorries bearing the names and messages of shops and businesses. This also includes the increasing trend to send text messages to mobile-phone users.

Closing Sales Techniques and Identifying Customers' Objections

All the efforts of the business and the sales team have led up to this point. In this last section of the unit we look at overcoming the final objections the customer may have when deciding whether to purchase a product or service. Once whether these final objections have been overcome then the sales person can concentrate on closing the sale.

Closing sales

Closing a sale is the ultimate goal of a sales rep. A sale is closed when the product has been exchanged for payment. To reach this stage, the sales rep will have dealt with any objections, queries or questions the customer has posed, and convinced them to make the purchase.

Once the sale is closed, the sales rep will always ask whether there is anything else that they can help the customer with. They will thank the customer and the interaction with the customer at this stage will be over.

The sales person needs to recognise when to close the sale. They can notice that a customer is ready to do this when they do one of the following:

- Lean forward and listen intently
- Agree with everything the sales person has said
- Call another person over for final confirmation.

There are several different closing techniques, which include the following:

- The direct close is extremely blunt and is, in effect, 'Do you want to buy this product?'
- A summary close begins with the sales person summarising all the benefits and matching the needs and desires of the customer.
- The indirect close is rather more laid back, and after the product or service has been described the sales person asks what the customer thinks about it.
- The silent close is when the sales person says something puts a question to the customer and then waits for the response.
- The alternative close offers the customer different options, such as another colour, size or shape of product.
- The presumptive close is when the sales person tells the customer how much they will enjoy or benefit from the product or service.

> **remember**
> The ultimate goal of the sales person is to close the sale; at that point, the product or service is exchanged for payment.

Responding to objections

Studies indicate that a customer will say no on average five times before they actually decide to buy. As a general rule, customers are hesitant to commit to purchasing a product or service until they have convinced themselves they need it and that they are getting it at a fair price.

When the customer voices an objection the salesperson should treat it with respect and hear them out. Interrupting when they should be listening is a significant factor in the loss of trust and rapport.

It is vital for the salesperson to understand the customer's specific concerns:

■ Hearing out the customer – pay full attention and avoid the temptation to think about your response while they are speaking. Learn to be an active listener.

■ Feed back to the customer – by repeating the customer's position, the customer will often answer their own objection.

■ Answer the objection – the sales person should be prepared to provide additional information.

■ Ask for the customer to confirm the sale – the salesperson may have to ask several times, so they should vary the closing questions.

Following up sales and recording customer information

Many businesses carry out transactions with their customers and the only information they retain is a cheque or credit card receipt. This means that they have not captured any information about the customer that could be of value to them in the future.

In retailing, a large number of individual stores and chains have customer loyalty cards. Each time the customer uses their card, the business puts the details of their transaction with the business onto the customer record database.

When dealing with business customers, particularly those that have credit terms, a business will have to retain contact details. Invoices, statements of account and reminders need to be sent out from time to time. In addition to this the business will use their customer contact database to generate letters to all of their customers, telling them about new products and services or special offers.

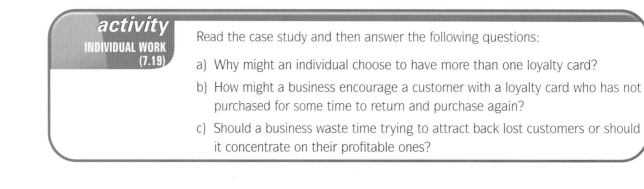

activity
INDIVIDUAL WORK
(7.19)

Read the case study and then answer the following questions:

a) Why might an individual choose to have more than one loyalty card?

b) How might a business encourage a customer with a loyalty card who has not purchased for some time to return and purchase again?

c) Should a business waste time trying to attract back lost customers or should it concentrate on their profitable ones?

After-sales service recognises the fact that the organisation's relationship with the customer does not end with placing the product in a carrier bag and taking their money. The organisation will be keen to provide:

- Friendly and supportive advice, either in-store or via a helpline
- Stocks of spare parts
- An efficient maintenance service.

These features are designed to encourage the customer to make repeat purchases with the business. In addition to the provision of repairs, maintenance and advice, after-sales service has become an integral part of a business's marketing and customer service provision.

Nationwide or international dealer network information

Many retailers are part of a chain, which means that after-sales service can be delivered at any location where the chain has an outlet, regardless of where the product was purchased. This form of nationwide network provides a far more convenient way for customers to receive after-sales service. Manufacturers also have similar arrangements. Other businesses use the services of independent dealers to carry out their repairs and after-sales service, particularly if they do not have outlets of their own in a particular area.

Preparation for returns

remember

Businesses, such as Marks & Spencer, have a very open returns policy and immediately give a refund or exchange the goods.

Any outlet in a chain, or indeed part of a dealer network, needs to be prepared to provide after-sales service to customers. This service must include the ability to repair, replace or even give a refund, depending on the circumstances. The returned item will eventually find its way back to its original manufacturer, but at the point of contact with the customer it is the member of the retail chain or the dealer that will have to carry out the necessary interaction, customer service and after-sales service with the purchaser.

Dealing with complaints

Customer dissatisfaction may lead to complaints and requests for assistance. Reasons for dissatisfaction can include:

- A product or service that is either faulty or not suitable
- A product that the business does not stock or which is out of stock
- Poor service
- A problem that no one seems able to assist the customer with.

It is usual practice for complaints to be referred to a manager who has the power to act on them and make an on-the-spot decision to deal with the situation. There are some key points to remember in the event of a complaint:

- Do not interrupt. Give the customer the opportunity to explain the situation.
- Always appear to be sympathetic to the customer.
- In particularly complicated cases, make sure that all details are written down.
- Check with the customer the main points of their complaint.
- Even when the customer is rude or abusive, stay calm and polite.
- Refer the matter to a senior member of staff if necessary.
- Never give the customer a vague answer or an unbelievable excuse.
- Do not directly blame another member of staff.
- Do not lose your temper.
- Remember, it is a problem as far as the customer is concerned and it should be taken seriously.
- Always tell the customer exactly what is happening, particularly if this involves having to refer it to another member of staff.
- Never make promises that cannot be kept by the business.

activity
GROUP WORK (7.19)

With a partner, try the following exercise. One of you will be an employee at a business and the other will be a customer who has a complaint. The idea of the exercise is for the employee to calm the customer and the customer must try to make the employee lose their temper! The complaint is that the kettle purchased yesterday is faulty and caused a minor fire in the customer's kitchen.

An organisation that is concerned with improving its customer service will carefully check all the complaints they receive. It will want to know how often different customers complain about the same thing. If it finds that complaints about the same subject occur regularly, then it will attempt to improve the situation.

Depending on the type of complaint, this could be a simple letter of apology or it could involve:

- The letter plus an offer of a refund.
- The letter plus an offer to replace faulty products or services.
- The letter plus an offer of a cash payment to reimburse the customer for any problems or inconvenience.

Obviously the organisation will have to investigate the complaint. It will be interested to find out whether the complaint was a result of some action by an employee or group of employees. If this is the case, then it will want to reassure the customer that the individual will be suitably disciplined.

Even if, after its investigations, the organisation discovers that the customer has no real cause for complaint, it will still want to respond to the customer. Often it will:

- Apologise to the customer for the fact that they have found cause to complain.
- Make a 'token' offer to the customer. This could be a voucher to be spent at the organisation in the future.

All letters of complaint should be handled as quickly as possible. Even when an enquiry or investigation has to be undertaken before a solution is found, the customer should be kept informed as to what the organisation intends to do and when it intends to do it.

Repairs and replacement parts

> **remember**
> It is often difficult for businesses to offer a replacement if the product is no longer sold.

A customer complaint might occur some weeks or months after the original purchase. Usually, in the early stages after a purchase, a customer will demand and the business will provide a replacement or a refund. After a certain point, however, it is more likely that the product may need repair. Depending upon how long ago the purchase was made and whether it is covered by a guarantee or warranty, the retail outlet will take responsibility for sending the faulty product back to the manufacturer, who will carry out the repair and then send it back to the retailer, who in turn will inform the customer that the repair has been carried out.

Other businesses run repair services that require a specialist to visit the customer and carry out the repair on site. The cost of the repairs would be covered under the guarantee or warranty of the product, if this has not expired. The problem arises when the product is no longer being made and replacement parts become difficult to obtain.

Recommendations, publicity and customer dissatisfaction

As we have seen, a positive experience by a customer can lead to them recommending the business to others. A negative experience with a business can result in customers warning other people not to use that business.

The main reasons behind customer dissatisfaction are:

- Uncaring, negative attitude of employees and management
- Dissatisfaction with the treatment received
- Failure to return customer calls
- Employees not given the power to make decisions
- Poor handling and resolution of complaints.

These can be summarised under the following headings:

- Performance of the staff, business or product
- Unrealistic expectations of the staff, business or product
- Misunderstandings.

Personal Selling

In order to deal with these issues, a business needs to realise that:

- The customer is the most important person in the business.

- The customer is not dependent on the business; the business is dependent on the customer. The business therefore works for the customer.

- The customer is not an interruption of work. The customer is the purpose of the work.

- It is the employees' job to satisfy the needs, wants and expectations of the customers and, whenever possible, resolve their fears and complaints.

- The customer is the lifeblood of the business and deserves the most attentive, courteous and professional treatment the business can provide.

All of these issues can be addressed by making sure that customer service is delivered to the highest possible standard, that products and the level of service are described accurately, and that any information given to the customer is correct. In other words, better and clearer interaction with customers can address the majority of reasons why a customer can become dissatisfied.

activity
**GROUP WORK
(7.20)**

As a group, explain any after-sales service you may have had to ask for from a business.

What was your experience of that after-sales service? Did it leave you with a positive or negative image of the business?

Individually, try to find a customer care and after-sales service leaflet or brochure from a business local to you. Many supermarkets and retail chains have customer service information available. Argos is a good example as it gives its customers details about the refund and exchange policy.

*progress
check*

1. Name three purposes of a sales team.
2. Give an example of good sales habits.
3. What is a cold call?
4. Name three Acts related to personal selling.
5. Why is it important for a sales person to maintain a positive attitude?
6. Why should a sales person ensure eye contact with their customers?
7. What is a point of sale?
8. What is meant by the term 'closing a sale'?
9. What is a presumptive close?
10. How might a sales person overcome customer objections?

Doing Business Online

This units covers:

- different online business activities
- the business feasibility of going online
- the operations of an online business
- the benefits of an online business presence

Websites can reach a global market and to a large extent they wipe out the advantage that larger businesses have over small businesses. Customers can be attracted to websites around the clock, and in many cases, for small and specialist businesses, an online presence is ideal to reach a small and scattered group of customers.

This unit looks at the various types of online business activity, the benefits of an online presence and how it can help a business to achieve its aims and objectives. It also looks at how feasible it is for an average business to develop an online presence.

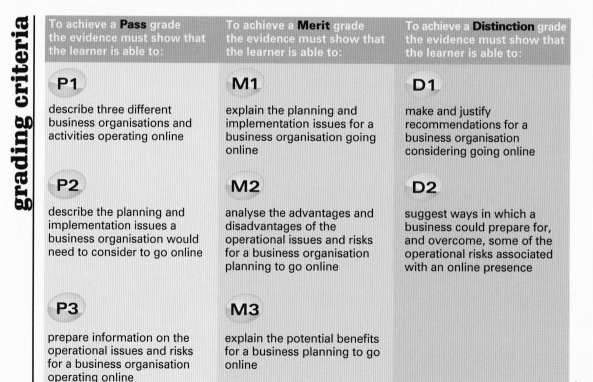

grading criteria

To achieve a **Pass** grade the evidence must show that the learner is able to:	To achieve a **Merit** grade the evidence must show that the learner is able to:	To achieve a **Distinction** grade the evidence must show that the learner is able to:
P1 describe three different business organisations and activities operating online	**M1** explain the planning and implementation issues for a business organisation going online	**D1** make and justify recommendations for a business organisation considering going online
P2 describe the planning and implementation issues a business organisation would need to consider to go online	**M2** analyse the advantages and disadvantages of the operational issues and risks for a business organisation planning to go online	**D2** suggest ways in which a business could prepare for, and overcome, some of the operational risks associated with an online presence
P3 prepare information on the operational issues and risks for a business organisation operating online	**M3** explain the potential benefits for a business planning to go online	

grading criteria

Different Online Business Activities

It is difficult to assess the value of Internet-based business throughout the world. Some estimates suggest that the total value of electronic commerce worldwide has already exceeded $208 billion. Of this, around 88 per cent is commerce between businesses. Growth areas include wholesale and retail, estimated at around $89 billion per year.

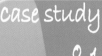

case study 8.1

Get into the net

Some 20 million Britons were predicted to do their shopping on the Internet during 2004.

UK shoppers spent around £17 billion online in 2004, rising to £80 billion by 2009. The Chief Executive at Tesco said: 'You only have to look at the business we did last December to see how fast the online operation is growing. We did as many sales in December as we did in the whole of 1998.'

According to Sainsbury's Bank, which saw a 600 per cent increase in Internet banking customers over the years 2000–03, banking services are expected to see the next big increase in revenues. The bank predicts a big increase in the number of financial products purchased online.

Sainsbury's estimated that there was a 31 per cent increase in online purchasing of financial products in 2003 and that this was set to continue. Some 3 million UK adults now buy their financial services online.

a) If the approximate population of the UK is 60 million, what was the average spending per person in 2004 and the prediction for 2009, based on the figures given in the case study?

b) If 3 million adults bought their financial products online in 2003, what will be the figure in 2004, assuming that the increase was the same as in the previous year?

Auctions

Auctioning items is no new thing, but it has become an extremely popular activity online. In auctions, the seller sets a low starting price and a group of buyers bid gradually higher prices until a winner is announced.

Today a large part of e-commerce is comprised of online auctions, selling practically anything to worldwide buyers every day of the week. There is an increasing number of auction sites, but the largest is eBay.

Banking

The number of online banking customers seems to be growing at a rate of around one million a year, with the online banks concentrating on new services and products to offer customers. Banks are keen, for cost reasons, to move as many of their customers as possible away from the expensive high-street branches, and instead make them online customers.

Chat rooms

Chat line users are amongst the heaviest users of the Internet. A chat room is a place on the Internet where people with similar interests can meet and communicate by typing messages to one another on their computers.

case study 8.2 — Internet chatters

A recent survey found chatters to be online more than 17 days a month, and also discovered chatters to be heavy users of other Internet protocols, particularly audio-video streaming (used by 54 per cent of chatters), secured connections (92 per cent) and instant messaging (59 per cent). Not surprisingly, chatters send and receive more than twice as many emails as the general Internet population.

Chatters clicked on an average of 4.8 banners in one month, which is almost double that of the general Internet population, and their unique page views are also more than double the overall Internet population.

The Internet sectors with the highest concentration of chat users are the personals, with more than 16 per cent, and the movie sector (15 per cent). Science and technology (14 per cent), the family sector (13 per cent), and the adult sector (12 per cent) are also popular with chatters.

activity
INDIVIDUAL WORK

What do you understand by the following terms used in the case study?

a) Internet protocols.

b) Audio-video streaming.

c) Secured connections.

d) Instant messaging.

Gambling

remember

Gambling is one of the fastest-growing Internet activities.

The major UK bookmakers all now have substantial online operations. Ladbrokes, William Hill and Coral have all gone heavily into the sports betting market, which only requires a betting licence. Most sites also offer casino games, although these casino games sites cannot currently be hosted in the UK and so are hosted offshore.

case study 8.3 — Online betting

Sportingbet is a pure online operator and has grown rapidly to be one of the largest operators in the world, with 608 000 customers in 150 countries. Its turnover to year-end March 2002 was £991.5 million, up from £324.7 million in 2001 with a profit before tax of £5 million compared with a loss of £4.2 million in 2001. Betfair, which matches bets between private individuals, has also experienced substantial growth since its launch.

activity
INDIVIDUAL WORK

Read the case study and answer the following questions:

a) If Sportingbet has 608 000 customers in 150 countries, what is the average number of customers per country?

b) What is meant by 'turnover'?

Job searches

Online job searching has become one of the ways of finding a career. Internet technology allows searches for job openings as they occur. Many organisations now invite online applicants, which allows them a much wider geographical range of potential applicants.

Many career-hunting sites allow applicants to submit their CVs directly to the companies, making the application process much easier. Most search pages can even provide helpful information on relocating after being accepted for the job. There are many ways to find a career, a job and a future just by looking online, but only around 4 per cent of Internet users actually find their jobs online.

activity
INDIVIDUAL WORK (8.1)

Visit the website of Total Jobs – just one of the many online job search services – at www.totaljobs.com. How would you use this service to find a job as a trainee manager in retailing in your region of the country?

Total Jobs
www.totaljobs.com

Last-minutes services

In a world where many people have busy work and home lives, last-minute services provide the answer to their lack of time to spend looking for gifts and holidays. On these sites, a bewildering range of products and services are displayed and the user only has to specify the type of product or service they are looking for within the criteria offered on the website. Criteria such as price, time

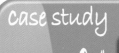

Lastminute.com

Lastminute.com was founded by Brent Hoberman and Martha Lane Fox in 1998. The website (www.lastminute.com) was launched in the UK in October 1998. An Australian version of the website was launched in August 2000 in conjunction with travel.com.au, the joint-venture partner for Australia and New Zealand. A further joint-venture agreement was signed for an operation in South Africa in May 2000.

Lastminute.com aims to be the global marketplace for all last-minute services and transactions. Using the Internet to match suppliers and consumers at short notice, lastminute.com works with a range of suppliers in the travel, entertainment and gift industries, and is dedicated to bringing its customers attractive products and services. Lastminute.com carries almost no inventory risk, selling perishable inventory for its suppliers and, where appropriate, it protects suppliers' brand names until after purchase.

It also aims to inspire its customers to try something different. Since 1998, the company believes that it has developed a distinctive brand, which communicates spontaneity and a sense of adventure, attracting a loyal community of registered subscribers.

activity
INDIVIDUAL WORK

Read the case study and answer the following questions.

a) What do you understand by the term 'joint venture'?

b) What do you understand by the term 'distinctive brand'?

c) What is a registered user?

(of a holiday or required delivery for example), colour, brand name and a host of other choices narrow the search parameter. The user choose and pay online.

Lastminute.com
www.lastminute.com

Procurement and sourcing

E-sourcing involves using the Internet to locate and slect suppliers or providers of products or services.

E-procurement is the purchasing of goods and services using the Internet. E-procurement systems are designed to simplify the procurement process by reducing unnecessary administrative tasks and paperwork. In theory, this should improve the purchasing cycle.

Electronic supplier catalogues provide customers with a single searchable source of products and services. Orders created by users are sent electronically to the respective suppliers for action and delivery.

The major advantages of e-procurement and e-sourcing are that:

- On average a business can negotiate a 14.3 per cent reduction.
- It takes half the time to find the right products or services.
- It takes fewer people less time to find the right products and services.
- A business buying products and services can then sell the products and services to their own customers much quicker.
- It is no longer the case that a business has to buy from a local or even national supplier, it can 'shop' for products and services around the world.
- A business can always buy the best it can afford, not just what is available.
- By dealing with more suppliers the business can forge a close relationship with those that provide the best products or services.
- A business can learn from the experiences of other businesses in carrying out e-procurement and e-sourcing the right way.
- Those involved in the sourcing will quickly learn the problems involved.
- The business will be able to access more information about its competitors and the markets they serve.

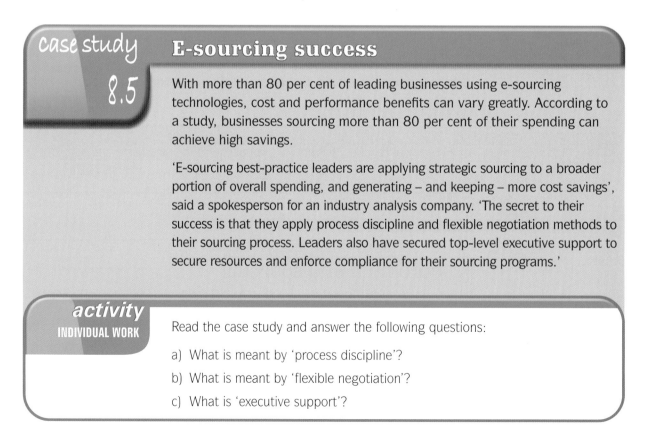

case study
8.5
E-sourcing success

With more than 80 per cent of leading businesses using e-sourcing technologies, cost and performance benefits can vary greatly. According to a study, businesses sourcing more than 80 per cent of their spending can achieve high savings.

'E-sourcing best-practice leaders are applying strategic sourcing to a broader portion of overall spending, and generating – and keeping – more cost savings', said a spokesperson for an industry analysis company. 'The secret to their success is that they apply process discipline and flexible negotiation methods to their sourcing process. Leaders also have secured top-level executive support to secure resources and enforce compliance for their sourcing programs.'

activity
INDIVIDUAL WORK

Read the case study and answer the following questions:

a) What is meant by 'process discipline'?

b) What is meant by 'flexible negotiation'?

c) What is 'executive support'?

Product supply

The supplying of products is an enormous business on the Internet. Not only do consumers purchase a wide range of products from a variety of different online companies, but other businesses purchase their own consumables and other products essential for their work.

In 2005, UK consumers spent £19.2 billion, up 32 per cent on 2004. A total of 24 million UK consumers shopped online. Just in the 10 weeks leading up to Christmas 2005, shoppers spent £5 billion online. This was a rise of 50 per cent on the previous year.

Spending online is likely to grow by 36 per cent in 2006, with total sales figures of £26 billion.

Consumers are not only embracing online shopping, they are also increasingly keen to conduct all types of transaction via credit card rather than cash. This degree of progress has pushed the UK to the forefront of credit card security technology.

case study 8.6 — Boom in online shopping

Internet shoppers spent an average £770 each in 2004 on goods and services, according to a survey by YouGov, commissioned by the Alliance & Leicester bank.

The survey found that almost 50 per cent of shoppers bought a holiday, flight or hotel stay over the Internet, while 45 per cent purchased CDs and other forms of music online. Thirty-nine per cent of those polled by YouGov said they had bought shoes or clothes over the Internet and 34 per cent had purchased electrical items. Eighty-seven per cent of shoppers said they had bought much more on the Internet in the last year than they did five years ago, the survey found. Over a third of those polled said they buy goods and services online every couple of weeks.

activity
INDIVIDUAL WORK

Read the case study and answer the following questions:

a) What was the average spending per month on online shopping?

b) What was the most popular purchase online?

c) Why might there have been such a large increase in the number of people buying online compared to five years ago?

Research

While the majority of consumers research products online, they make their purchases in actual high-street stores. Around 65 per cent of Internet users regularly practise this 'cross-channel shopping', and 51 per cent purchase something this way every three months. Cross-channel shoppers are younger, wealthier and more experienced online. They purchase a wide variety of products, with the category of books/music/DVD/video games being the most popular (64 million cross-channel transactions in 2005).

Around half of all cross-channel shoppers switch brands before they purchase offline, and they spend an average of £80 on additional products once they are in the store. Ultimately, the average cross-channel shopper spends £238 on products they research online and buy offline, which adds up to £5.6 billion per year.

It is not only customers who carry out online research: it is a growing area of marketing and market research. Internet research is a global phenomenon with estimated spending of £416.5 million. Experts suggest an annual growth rate of more than 250 per cent.

Around 75 per cent of Internet research spending is devoted to better understanding of attitudes and activities of consumers, while 25 per cent is spent on business-to-business efforts.

Most online research is generally carried out via web pages and emails. Web surveys can incorporate radio buttons, data entry fields and check boxes, which help researchers to take responses from respondents easily and according to requirement.

remember

Spending time comparing prices on the Internet will often lead to substantial savings.

case study 8.7 — Buying online research

Only a few years ago, buying market research reports involved the purchase of a complete hard-copy report. Today, publishers are offering web access, through their branded sites, to reports and databases and immediate downloading of reports or extracts. Many businesses are now offering extracts – the so-called 'slice and price' option – to broaden the customer base to those who are willing to pay £20 or more for a specific piece of information, such as market size or competitor details, but are unwilling to pay for the complete report. These 'slice and price' options usually comprise chapters or sections of reports. Credit card payment makes the transaction simpler.

Datamonitor, for example, has packages for markets such as healthcare and IT. Datamonitor's core product is no longer its off-the-shelf reports but its Strategic Planning Programme that costs £20 000 a year for a single-user licence. This gives access to reports, weekly briefings, analysis and interactive forecasting models.

Read the case study and then visit the following websites:
www.marketresearch.com; www.mindbranch.com; www.ecnext.com.

What kind of products and services do they offer?

MarketResearch.com
www.marketresearch.com
MindBranch
www.mindbranch.com
ECNext
www.ecnext.com

Games and music

Recent figures show that gaming is becoming more and more popular in the UK. In 2002, the UK spent over £1 billion on their passion for games. Things have come a long way from the first game, 'Space War' (1961), and now over a thousand new games come into the shops every year.

A few years ago, a software program called Napster was created and then closed down for allowing the illegal sharing of copyrighted material, mostly music files. Conservative estimates put the number of Napster users at 40 million just 18 months after it was created, a figure which was achieved despite a lack of any real advertising.

By 2003, there were signs that the music industry was beginning to catch up. In April 2003, EMI was the first of the big five record companies to make the majority of its music available online (90 per cent or around 140 000 tracks).

There are two ways of buying and downloading music from the Internet – by subscription or pay-as-you-go.

case study
8.8

Subscription vs pay-as-you-go

Subscription-based services are now available that offer many of the features of Napster-type programmes with the difference that they are completely legal, if not free. Internet music subscription services are widely available from MSN, Freeserve, HMV, BT and many others. The most common pricing structure is 500 credits for a £4.99 monthly fee. With these credits, users have a choice: stream tracks at a cost of 1 credit each, download tracks for 10 credits each or burn to CD for 100 credits. The pricing encourages users not to create physical copies of the music, but instead, access them on demand. The tracks downloaded using subscription services are encrypted so they cannot be played by others or by non-subscribers.

activity

INDIVIDUAL WORK

Read the case study and then, using a search engine, find out the names and web addresses of five major providers of downloadable music. What are the payment options for users? Which offer the most value for money and flexibility for users?

Virtual property tours

A simple search engine query reveals over 600 sites offering virtual property tours. Largely, the online tours are provided by a wide variety of different estate agents as a back-up to the more conventional visit to a property. Virtual tours allow anyone with Internet access to view what they would see if they were actually visiting a property.

Sector

Obviously, there are many thousands of organisations and businesses that operate either solely on the Internet or have websites to support their other activities. In this section we will look at three examples of different types of organisation and how they fit into each of the three major sectors.

Public sector

NHS Direct Online is a website providing high-quality health information and advice for the people of England. It is unique in being supported by a 24-hour nurse advice and information helpline.

activity

INDIVIDUAL WORK
(8.2)

Using the website www.nhsdirect.com find out the answers to the following questions:

a) What does it recommend when a baby has a rash?

b) What is the nearest pharmacist to your home?

c) Using the Best Treatments options, what is recommended for back pain?

d) What is HealthSpace?

NHS Direct Online
www.nhsdirect.com

Private sector

Amazon was one of the pioneers of online sales. Amazon.co.uk is the trading name for Amazon.com International Sales, Inc. and Amazon Services Europe SARL. Both companies are subsidiaries of Amazon.com, one of the leading online retailers of products. The Amazon group also has online stores in the USA, Germany, France, Japan and Canada.

Amazon
www.amazon.co.uk

Voluntary and non-for-profit sector

Charity Choice is an encyclopaedia of charities on the Internet, listing over 9000 organisations in the UK. The Charity Commission's website has a list of registered UK charities, including links to the web addresses where available. The National Council for Voluntary Organisations (NCVO) is the umbrella body for English voluntary organisations. Its website has over 2000 members listed in its links to the voluntary sector online.

Charity Choice
www.charitychoice.co.uk
Charity Commission
www.charity-commission.gov.uk
NVCO
www.ncvo-vol.org.uk

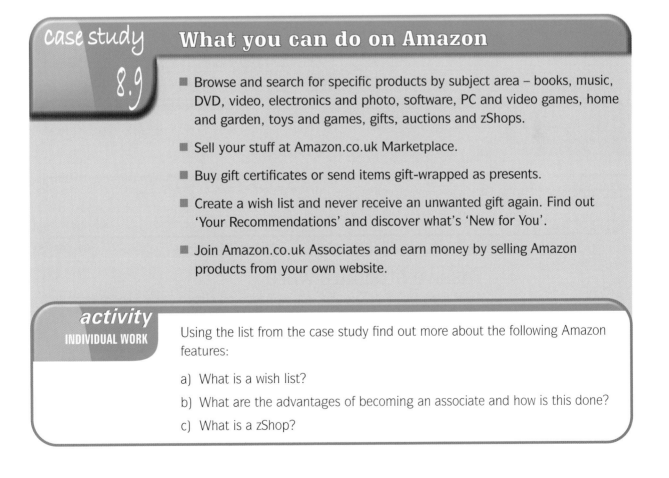

case study 8.9 — What you can do on Amazon

- Browse and search for specific products by subject area – books, music, DVD, video, electronics and photo, software, PC and video games, home and garden, toys and games, gifts, auctions and zShops.

- Sell your stuff at Amazon.co.uk Marketplace.

- Buy gift certificates or send items gift-wrapped as presents.

- Create a wish list and never receive an unwanted gift again. Find out 'Your Recommendations' and discover what's 'New for You'.

- Join Amazon.co.uk Associates and earn money by selling Amazon products from your own website.

activity
INDIVIDUAL WORK

Using the list from the case study find out more about the following Amazon features:

a) What is a wish list?

b) What are the advantages of becoming an associate and how is this done?

c) What is a zShop?

Levels/types of online presence

First and foremost, a business needs to define the specifications for its website content. There are two major kinds of content to be considered, static or dynamic content, summarised in Table 8.1.

Registered site viewers can generate a highly accurate and targeted source for online marketing activities.

Table 8.1 Static and dynamic website content

Static content	Dynamic content
Company identities, including logos, slogans, corporate messages, etc.	A database has to be set up. The data will include important information such as product categories, description, sizes, colours, codes, materials, prices, images, etc.
Company information, including history, organisation, company culture, personnel, contact information, etc.	Database design has to coincide with the display format and design of your online storefront.
Business information, including ordering procedures, shipping, credit terms, etc.	Consideration will also be given to incorporating ease of updating the data to minimise the cost of ongoing maintenance.
General product information, including quality, material, sizing guide, what is new, etc.	

activity

INDIVIDUAL WORK (8.3)

Using the Internet, visit www.charitychoice.co.uk.

a) What is the purpose of this website?

b) How many UK-based maritime charities are there and how many of them have their own website?

c) What is the Charity Choice Directory?

Passive brochure ware

A website can either be a dynamic tool focused on achieving a specific set of business objectives or it can be a passive electronic brochure.

Most shop websites today take the passive brochure ware approach. Although generally not very effective, this type of site can help keep the shop's image current and offer some convenience to existing customers.

A dynamic website features helpful, frequently updated content that keeps customers returning to the site. A dynamic website offers what is known as 'actionable' tools that allow the business to communicate with their customers.

remember

Downloadable and printable catalogues and price lists produced as Adobe pdf files can replace expensive colour printed catalogues.

Complementing offline services

If a business is successful online, then why might it be so important to have an offline, or conventional, presence? Customers seem to think that it is important, as recent research has uncovered.

A physical 'bricks and mortar' presence is still important to many consumers. Around 50 per cent of all customers rated having a physical offline presence as 'very or somewhat important', with only 15 per cent stating that it was not important at all.

Mail order

The simple fact that Internet-based businesses are not conventional stores means that they need to deliver the majority of their products and services by mail order. At the top of the list of complaints received by Trading Standards officers around the UK are the non-delivery of Internet goods and mail order problems.

Online transactions

Primarily, customers will use credit and debit cards as well as direct fund transfers. Many businesses use online transaction solutions including online credit card transactions and product cataloguing. These can be incorporated into the web design and development services to produce a fully functional e-commerce site, which is easy to use for both the customer and the supplier.

Interactive customisation

Increasingly online businesses focus on customer interaction, with an emphasis on organisation and ease of navigation, to make sure they have a pleasant experience with the website.

To complement this, businesses also concentrate on the customer's interface. These interfaces allow the customisation of websites to appeal to their customers' needs. **Cookies** offer an innovative means to collect data on the demographics and behaviour of web users. Site visit statistics can be estimated more accurately by using cookies; cookies also allow the customisation of websites without making the user reset preferences every time the site is revisited.

keyword

Cookie
– A small text file that is placed on the user's hard drive by a web server. It is a code that is uniquely the user's and can only be read by the server that sent it.

activity
INDIVIDUAL WORK (8.4)

Visit a website, such as www.amazon.co.uk, and register as a user. See what options there are to customise the page to suit your tastes and interests. Visit the same website on another occasion and see if it has 'remembered' your customisation.

The Business Feasibility of Going Online

Most small businesses can benefit from the range of technologies available online. A website can assist a business in a number of different ways:

- Improved productivity
- Easier communications
- Higher profile
- Ability to sell online.

Increasingly businesses are trying to incorporate their online activities with their existing administrative systems to increase their efficiency and improve their customer service.

Planning and implementation issues

The latest figures on the number of UK businesses either online or planning to go online indicates that the vast majority of businesses have some kind of Internet presence.

Table 8.2 Planned web access (% of businesses online/planning to go online in 2005)

No. of employees	All size bands	10–49	50–249	250–999	1000+
Online in 2004	89.6%	86%	97.6%	9.3%	99.08%
Planning to go online in 2004	10.4%	14%	2.4%	0.7%	0.2%

Source: ONS's 2004 e-commerce survey of business (published 22 Aug 2005)

Table 8.3 Business using broadband connection (% of businesses using broadband connections during 2005)

No. of employees	All size bands	10–49	50–249	250–999	1000+
Fixed broadband connection	75.1%	39.9%	81.7%	80.5%	95.3%

Source: ONS's 2005 e-commerce survey of business (published 22 Aug 2005)

Choosing a domain name

Buying a **domain name** has plenty of potential pitfalls; here are some of the major ones and points to remember:

- If you are buying a .co.uk domain name (e.g. newbusiness.co.uk), make sure you also buy the other main TLDs (Top Level Domains) for the same prefix, such as '.com', '.net', etc.

keyword

Domain name – A website's address on the Internet. It needs to be registered by a business, organisation or service, just like a business name. It allows potential customers to find the business's web address and website easily.

- If you do a domain name search and find that only the .co.uk is available for your chosen prefix (e.g. newbusiness), it may be worth your while choosing another domain name prefix.

- It is possible that your small business may grow into different areas of interest, so it may be an idea not to make your domain name too specific to one area of your expertise.

- Keep your domain name as short as possible and simple – it needs to be memorable and preferably not contain hyphens.

- A few web promotion businesses suggest inserting your major keywords into your domain name wherever possible to help with your search engine rankings.

- Allowed characters – domain names can only contain letters, numbers and dashes. Spaces and symbols are not allowed.

- Domain names are not case-sensitive.

- Choose a reputable domain name supplier.

- You should ensure that your domain name is not a commonly known brand name or trademark.

- Make sure you keep your contact information up to date. Although your domain name supplier is bound to contact you when a domain name comes up for renewal, it is your responsibility to make sure it is renewed.

Set-up issues

The cheapest way for a business to develop its own website is to build one itself. With web authoring tools, a business does not need to have a high level of expertise. A more professional approach should provide the following advantages:

- The design will fit in with the business image

- Information can be found easily by a visitor to the site

- The site can incorporate features such as searches and databases

- The website will be submitted to the search engines.

Budgets are important and even more difficult to control if you are using an outside specialist. Even if the business is using its own expertise, it is a good idea to identify exactly what is required from the websiste in a brief. This should include:

- The objectives of the website

- The target groups of customers

- The overall image of the business and the website required

- The use of current company designs, typefaces, logos and colours

- How you will monitor who is using your site

- The overall budget and the maintenance costs

- The timescale to launching the website.

Low-cost availability of web authoring tools

Competition has driven down the price of the tools needed to create websites. Table 8.4 shows a selection of some of the cheaper alternatives.

Table 8.4 Web authority systems

Web authority system/website	Features
Adobe GoLive CS www.adobe.com Click on 'Products' and 'Web publishing'.	Adobe GoLive CS (customer solution) software is designed to create professional websites, and it is easy to use with other Adobe software. Setting up new pages is simple using the WYSIWYG layout view and simply dragging a layout grid onto a new document and setting the required width. Text can be formatted using HTML tags or by using GoLive's dedicated CSS (cascading style sheet) Editor, which allows the user to create and edit their own styles with real-time visual feedback. GoLive's comprehensive sets of authoring features are ideal for those working in a print and graphics environment. The product's integration with Adobe's Creative Suite can provide a very powerful, all-in-one solution.
Dreamweaver www.macromedia.com Click on 'Dreamweaver' under 'Products'.	Macromedia Dreamweaver is a WYSIWYG system which allows users to see how the pages look before they are uploaded. It is also possible to work with HTML using a single click. The HTML is colour coded so users can track them in a split screen with the design. Dreamweaver has CSS support and a tool to help users build CSS documents that is easy to use and understand. Positioning styles are also available so that the site is XHTML compliant. Opening files such as CGI and Perl is much easier with Dreamweaver as there is a built-in colour coding for PHP, ASP.Net and XML. Dreamweaver offers all the power and control that a designer could want, combined with the speed and production tools useful for developers.
BBEdit www.web.barebones.com	BBEdit, provided by Bare Bones Software, Inc., is a text and HTML editor available for Macintosh only (non-WYSIWYG). This editor offers great functionality and control over HTML code. As a powerful text editor, it offers features such as multiple undo, multi-file find and replace, the capability to read all DOS/Unix/Mac files up to 2 GB in size, and more. At the same time, acting as an HTML editor, it offers HTML specific features such as floating tool palettes, syntax colouration, and HTML syntax checking. Using this editor with a browser is as simple as clicking a button, allowing one to view a web page as it is created.
Microsoft Front Page www.microsoft.com/ frontpage	Microsoft's FrontPage is a WYSIWYG system that allows users to create and build dynamic and sophisticated websites. The biggest advantage is that users will be familiar with Office tools. New layout and graphics tools make it easier to design exactly the site needed, and at the same time enhanced publishing features and options help users to get the web pages online quickly and simply. FrontPage also has wizards for interactive and dynamic features including live links to databases, discussion forums, search forms, hit counters and navigation bars. Using Microsoft Windows SharePoint Services and Windows Server 2003 connected to FrontPage, it is possible to modify and present live data from a range of sources, including XML, to build rich, interactive data-driven websites in a WYSIWYG editor.
Nvu www.nvu.com	Nvu is designed for Linux Desktop users as well as Microsoft Windows and Macintosh users. It uses WYSIWYG for editing of pages, making web creation straightforward. Nvu has integrated file management via FTP. Users simply log on to their website and navigate through the files, editing web pages on the fly, directly from the site. It has reliable HTML code creation that will work with all of today's most popular browsers. It is possible to jump between WYSIWYG Editing Mode and HTML using tabs. Tabbed editing is used to make working on multiple pages much more user friendly. It has powerful support for forms, tables and templates. It is claimed that Nvu is the easiest to use, most powerful Web Authoring System available for Desktop Linux, Microsoft Windows and Apple Macintosh users.

Adobe GoLive CS
www.adobe.com
Dreamweaver
www.macromedia.com
BBEdit
www.web.barebones.com

Microsoft Front Page
www.microsoft.com/frontpage
NVU
www.nvu.com

activity
INDIVIDUAL WORK
(8.5)

Visit at least three of the websites mentioned in Table 8.4 and note down at least three major features of each system.

Implementation issues

Implementation refers to how the business is proposing to develop an e-business operation. It requires a number of phases:

- Business planning – what problems will the e-business solve? How can the business best integrate any e-business with its existing information communication technology systems?

- Requirements of the e-business – what will the e-business need to be able to achieve? Will it simply be a catalogue or can customers purchase and make orders? How sophisticated does the ordering process have to be? How big will the website need to be?

- Customisation – there are standard software systems and website designs, but will these suit the purposes of the website?

- Installation – does the business already have a suitable information and computer network to cope with the demands of the e-business? What new hardware and software needs to be purchased?

- Integration – can the e-business systems be fully integrated into the current ICT system?

- Data conversion – what data needs are there for the new system? Can existing customer data be transferred to the new system?

- Testing – the e-business system needs to be thoroughly tested, even taking into account the most ridiculous thing a customer or visitor to the website might do.

- Training – a user training manual needs to be written and anyone that will be involved with the new e-business needs to be fully trained and shown exactly how the system works.

- Post-implementation – after the website has been up and running for a few days, but no more than a month, customers and employees using it need to be interviewed in order to assess their reactions.

- User support – customers and employees will need ongoing support, particularly if parts of the website are changed and processes differ.

remember

A poor website is worse than having no website at all.

activity
INDIVIDUAL WORK
(8.6)

Assume you are a small business wishing to establish an online presence. What would be the best way to detail chronologically all of the stages that you would have to work through in order to get the website up and running?

Desired speed of change

Switching from a predominantly offline form of business to an online business is the business itself something that cannot always control. In this section we will look at the various other factors that will influence and determine how fast the transition from offline to online can be.

Pace set by competitors

Some businesses are trend-setters or market leaders. They are the first businesses to move into new markets or devise new ways of selling their products or services. Other businesses take a different view and keep a close eye on developments within their competitors' businesses. As soon as their key competitors develop new systems online and are able to access a wider range of different customers they know that by not responding quickly they will lose some of their market share.

Adaptability of key staff

From the outset the business needs to ensure the support of its key members of staff and make plans to retrain them if necessary. The key members of staff in most modern organisations have the essential ICT skills. They may not be proficient in dealing with online business transactions and customer interaction. This can all be addressed with gradual but intensive retraining. A business would seek to include its key staff in the decision-making, particularly regarding how the online operation will work. It can learn from their experiences and the key members of staff may be able to suggest solutions or head off possible problems in the future before they have even occurred.

Potential redundancies and industrial relations problems

Some members of staff can be redeployed in other parts of the organisation, even if this means that they need retraining. Huge job losses, however, present a very different problem. If the majority of the employees realise that they have no part in the future plans of the business, they have nothing to lose from causing the maximum amount of disruption to the business.

We have also seen that when many businesses change to an online presence, they have a tendency to outsource many of their operations. This does leave existing employees without a job. Businesses need to support these employees and assist them in obtaining work elsewhere, as well as compensating them financially for their loss of work.

Timescale for effective transition to offline activities

Various parts of the transition can take place simultaneously. The sales department, for example, could be entering all of its customer records and sales histories onto databases while the warehouse changes to an electronic stock control system. Gradually the manual paper-based activities will be transformed into electronic versions.

Once all of the operations have been converted, the business will then be in a position to launch the online operation. It would be foolish to consider doing this before all of these necessary elements are in place.

Benefits

The obvious hope of a business transferring to an online operation is to have a greater market presence and the ability to attract a wider variety of customers. Businesses tend to look at the probable benefits of a radical change such as this in the short, medium and long term. They will not expect to cover all the costs of transition to an e-business immediately.

case study 8.10 — Building construction websites

In the UK around 42 per cent of construction businesses have their own company website and around 75 per cent of these sell their products and services online. Twenty-four per cent of them said that they had set up their websites to attract new customers. Nineteen per cent said the reason was to retain their customers, while 14 per cent thought it was an important part of providing a quality service.

Only 4 per cent of construction businesses thought that having a company website was vital for their success. Forty-seven per cent thought that having an e-business was good for their image as far as customers and suppliers were concerned. Forty-four per cent said that being online opened new markets and opportunities for them.

When asked where they would make a major investment, only 11 per cent said they would spend it on developing an e-business. Nineteen per cent said they would spend it on a new IT system and 29 per cent said they would spend it on buying new vehicles.

The most common reasons for not going online were lack of time (20 per cent) and eight per cent that said there was no need for them to go online.

activity
INDIVIDUAL WORK

Read the case study and then answer the following questions:

a) Do you think that lack of time is a sufficient reason for not establishing an online presence?

b) Do you think that some of the businesses are correct in saying that there is no need to have an online business?

c) Why might having a website be important for the business's image?

Competitive disadvantage of not going online

A business may choose not to totally commit themselves to an online presence because:

- It does not believe that the business would be more successful if it made this investment.
- The business is too small and already under pressure to meet its customers' needs.
- It believes that its entire computer system would be open to attack.
- It is quite happy with the processes as they already exist.
- It cannot forecast the level of demand and is unsure whether there would be any increased demand.
- Its profit margins may already be low and the additional costs of online transactions may not make new business cost-effective.
- It does not have sufficient resources to fund any switching costs from offline to online.

The Operations of an Online Business

Starting and running a traditional business is difficult enough. A retail store offering products and services to a local market needs to be well organised, well thought through and efficiently run.

Although online businesses do not need to have a physical presence, as it would be rare for customers to visit their premises, they do have a whole new set of concerns. In this part of the unit we look at how an online business operates.

Operation issues

Secure credit card payments

remember

Secure encrypted websites are essential to protect the credit card details of customers.

There are three main methods of online payment available. Credit card payments are the most popular, followed by Internet transfers and third-party payments. An Internet transfer is when a customer pays directly through their online banking system into the online store's account. A third-party payment involves a third party such as a bank, which enables the customer to make a payment directly into the online store's bank account. Although similar to Internet transfers, third-party payments occur at the same time that the customer makes their online purchase.

activity
INDIVIDUAL WORK (8.7)

Visit the Nochex website and answer the following questions:

a) What is the charge per transaction for a sole trader?

b) What are merchant tools?

Nochex
www.nochex.co.uk

Table 8.5 Online payment systems

Payment system	Website	Explanation and costs to business
PayPal	www.paypal.com	Paypal ensures a secure payment system with merchant accounts. The charges for this service are 2.2% + 20p on your transaction, so a £100 transaction would be approximately £102.40. This is the only cost that occurs with this service. PayPal also offers free listing on their index of shops. The PayPal shop index can be found at paypal.com. Customers can set up a PayPal account to pay for goods.
WorldPay	www.worldpay.com	For merchants that sign up to WorldPay Direct for their Internet payment system, the following transaction processing charges apply: £50 set-up fee + £145 annual fee + a transaction service charge, which also includes three free currencies (additional currencies by arrangement).
Credit cards		4.5% Merchant Service Charge on credit card transactions. Note that this is the only fee charged, there are no additional charges payable to banks or other third-party organisations.
Debit cards		50p charge per debit card transaction. There are no additional charges payable to banks or other third-party organisations.
Nochex	www.nochex.co.uk	This British payment system is a free checkout service for your website; they also provide email-based payment. The checkout is on an industry standard SECURE (128 bit SSL) web page, which can be branded to include a company logo.
Netbanx	www.netbanx.com	Entry level £75 + VAT. One product at a fixed price. Ideal for subscription services with one fixed price. NetBanx provides generic authorisation and decline pages. The merchant is responsible for maintaining the HTML payment form initially supplied by NetBanx. Intermediate level £125 + VAT. Set-up for two to 10 products, each at a fixed price, with one selectable for payment, e.g. a subscription to a service sold either monthly, weekly or annually would constitute three separate products.

PayPal
www.paypal.com
WorldPay
www.worldpay.com
Nebonx
www.netbronx.com

Exposure

Web defacement is just one of the many perils facing websites. It is carried out by hackers who gain access and change the contents of a website. The messages that hackers leave behind vary from merely placing their alias or logo to replacing the original contents with whatever content they wish, similar to how traditional graffiti is written.

Hostile chat rooms, negative publicity and defamation

Businesses may often find themselves victims of a very different form of attack – from hostile former customers, employees or activists who have a problem with either the products or services offered by the business or the way in which it operates.

Hostility and negative publicity can be very damaging to a business. Even if the root cause of the problem is based on facts, a business can find it very difficult to prevent rumours from circulating. The Internet has thousands of chat rooms, and a poor opinion of a business or a website expressed in a chat room can do immense damage. Worst of all, it is very difficult to stop the rumours from spreading.

> **activity**
> INDIVIDUAL WORK
> (8.8)
>
> Using an Internet search engine, find out about the *Noah* v *AOL* case in the USA.

Payment security and unfamiliar trading conditions

Some 90 per cent of Internet fraudsters get away with their crimes – the police are unable to deal with this new type of retail crime. Around 57 per cent of companies state that they have reported frauds to the police, but 53 per cent encountered a lack of interest. Only 9 per cent of frauds reported to the police by online retailers result in prosecution.

> **activity**
> INDIVIDUAL WORK
> (8.9)
>
> Find out the latest figures on Internet fraud and suggest reasons why customers might be frightened to leave their credit card details online.

Dealing with increased market interest

Flexibility is the key to dealing with increased market demand. It is a problem stepping up operations to cope with increased demand, but a problem that all businesses welcome.

Businesses tend to try and match any increased demand by either installing new systems or employing more staff. The business needs to be sure that whilst coping with increased demand, they are certain that this new level of demand will continue into the future. A business does not want the expense of purchasing new equipment and taking on more employees only to discover that the increased demand is temporary and that it falls back to the old levels of demand.

remember

Hostile attacks involve hackers try to break into businesses' systems to retrieve sensitive information and customer payment details.

Vulnerability to hostile attack

Contrary to what might be assumed, hostile attacks are currently the least significant cause of system crashes and problems. Environmental disruption and operator error are the biggest sources of problems followed by software issue and then hostile attacks.

On the other hand, the number of hostile attacks is increasing, roughly doubling each year. Occurrences of operator errors and design and implementation errors are increasing at a slower rate, while the occurrence of problems due to environmental disruption remains constant.

Denial of service

In a denial-of-service (DoS) attack, an attacker attempts to prevent legitimate users from accessing information or services. By targeting the business's computers and its network connection, or the computers and network of the sites they are trying to use, an attacker may be able to prevent the business from accessing email, websites, online accounts (banking, etc.), or other services that rely on the affected computer.

case study 8.11 — WorldPay under attack

In November 2003, the Internet payment system WorldPay was under attack from unknown hackers, disrupting thousands of online retailers around the world. WorldPay's payment and administration networks were flooded with computer-generated requests, which clogged its system and slowed transactions.

This was a denial-of-service attack. WorldPay said its service to customers had been 'adversely affected'.

However, WorldPay stressed that transactions were still being processed – albeit more slowly than usual – and that the security of data had not been compromised.

'We realise it is disrupting our business and our customers' business and we apologise unreservedly for that,' said a spokesman.

In an email to customers, WorldPay said it was doing all it could to combat the attack.

'While such attacks can be anticipated to some extent, it does take time to identify and deal with the exact nature of a particular attack which can also change several times, over several days,' the company said.

Owned by the Royal Bank of Scotland, WorldPay has 30 000 clients around the world. These range from multinational firms such as Vodafone and Sony Music Entertainment to numerous small online retailers. WorldPay operates in more than 70 countries. It accepts payments on credit cards including Visa, Mastercard and American Express.

activity
INDIVIDUAL WORK

Read the case study and find out what happened and how it was resolved. Have there been any other recent major denial-of-service attacks on businesses?

Operational risks

An online business's shop window is its website. This is where potential customers view the business's products and services. Based on the information they can see there, they will make their purchasing decisions.

An online business is completely reliant on its virtual existence. This means that the operational risks involved in running an online business are potentially even more disastrous than making a simple mistake in a traditional business. Typically, operational risks would include the following:

- Updating websites
- Wrong and out-of-date information
- Language difficulties
- Hardware and software failures
- Loss of service (ISP down)
- Global business regulations.

activity
INDIVIDUAL WORK (8.10)

Visit www.ametro.gr. This is the website of the city of Athens underground system. How many different language versions are offered on the website? Do you think they all contain the same information?

Attiko Metro
www.ametro.gr

Staffing issues

Many businesses are considering outsourcing work abroad. This means shifting jobs from the country in which the business is operating and developing a similar operation abroad. The first consideration is that the labour costs abroad can be a fraction of those in the home country, for example the cost of an average employee in the UK might be £14 000 per year but in India it could be as little as £1400.

Table 8.6 looks at the hidden costs of outsourcing abroad.

Table 8.6 Hidden costs of outsourcing abroad

Hidden costs	Explanation
Transition	A business cannot expect the overseas operation to work well from the beginning. The outsourcing service will need to understand the operations and processes and this may take some time.
Communications charges	If the business is videoconferencing or telephoning, their communications costs with the overseas office will inevitably be higher than for a local office, especially with a leased line.
Travel and accommodation	Interviews and meetings will require travel.
Staff management	Depending on the nature of the work being outsourced, offshore offices could leave local staff without work. Managing retraining or redundancy will create costs for the personnel department.
Management and governance	There will be new rules and regulations to deal with as different countries have different laws related to businesses.
Inflation risks	Wages and salaries for offshore staff will not stay the same forever. In addition, current salary rates in the emerging outsourcing markets, such as China, Vietnam or Mauritius, are increasing.
Business continuity	Political problems abroad may affect operations.
Security changes	Sending sensitive information overseas creates dangers.
Hidden labour costs	Bonuses paid by Indian companies to prevent staff leaving. Employee accommodation costs.

case study 8.12 Unions and outsourcing

A union spokesman said: 'We need to challenge some of the fundamentals. Global competition has undergone a step change. New technology makes many areas of work relocatable to anywhere in the world at, literally, the switch of a button. We now face a different competitive model than we thought. But this isn't going to fade away. Nor is it restricted to low-skilled work. It is wrong to think this is just a challenge at a low-skilled level. The challenge for us as unions, and for government, is how do we compete to maintain growth? All economies, including developing nations, are entitled to compete. Protectionism is not the answer. Raising the skills level is essential and necessary, but it is not in itself enough. We need to challenge the business model so companies can't unilaterally decide to follow the lowest-cost route. We don't accept that it is inevitable. This is not just happening in India. The challenge will also be from China, Africa and Asia – anywhere that can establish technology and a workforce.'

activity
INDIVIDUAL WORK

Read the case study.

a) What did the spokesperson mean by 'protectionism'?

b) What is meant by 'companies can't unilaterally decide to follow the lowest-cost route'?

Financial issues

A business which has either already established itself as an online operation or one that is expanding, faces financial uncertainties at every turn. A huge amount of new businesses fail in their first year simply due to the fact that they over-estimate their income compared with their actual spending.

Distribution issues

Unlike traditional businesses, which either simply put products into a carrier bag or box and let the customers take it away, an online business will nearly always need to post or organise the delivery of products. There is an entirely different set of problems that relate to the delivery of products and services.

Fragile goods need to be well packed and protected as they may have to travel thousands of miles to reach the customer. Businesses can arrange for courier services to pick up their parcels and take care of the distribution and delivery.

Businesses that provide services can often do this online and confirm information by post. Businesses offering online insurance quotations, for example, can request information from the customer and supply the quote online.

Online flights and hotel accommodation bookings can also be confirmed by the click of a mouse. The vast majority of flights require a hard copy of the booking, which will have to be shown at the airport.

In the case of hotels, once the booking has been confirmed and paid for online, the room is reserved in that customer's name. The customer will only need to turn up on the day of the booking and confirm their name.

activity
INDIVIDUAL WORK (8.11)
Visit www.easyjet.com and find out how easy it is to book a flight to Athens from London. What payment options are available? What do you receive as confirmation?

The Benefits of an Online Presence

The benefits of web presence for any business are increasing as more and more business communications are made online. The Internet has reached its full maturity to become the new medium of choice with huge advantages over the conventional media.

The Internet will see its next stage of development as businesses move their commerce activities totally online. Many creative marketing and sales approaches that use the power of online business have been proven in recent years, with great results, translating into increased productivity as well as profitability. The Internet offers great promise for businesses that are determined to be the pioneers in their industries in utilising it as the platform for conducting their businesses.

Market presence
Global market presence

The cost of a business acquiring its own domain name is a relatively simple and affordable investment which in turn gives the business vast and ongoing global exposure on the Internet.

The Internet simplifies internal and external communication through the use of email and the web. It allows any business to:

- Collaborate with colleagues and customers anywhere in the world.
- Publish information to a global audience.
- Gather information from global sources.
- Research competitors from anywhere in the world.
- Research and gain greater knowledge of potential customers anywhere in the world.
- Provide innovative and improved customer service and support 24 hours a day with FAQs (Frequently Asked Questions) and related answers.
- Sell products and services 24 hours a day, locally, regionally, nationally and globally.
- Purchase products and services 24 hours a day and enjoy 24-hour technical support from suppliers.
- Reduce information and distribution costs, as document files can be instantly transmitted around the globe via email and web.
- Increase market share without increasing advertising budget, by taking advantage of this low-cost, far-reaching, high-impact advertising medium. The Internet can deliver a real return on investment.

Remember that websites can be fully interactive; visitors read information on products or services and then fill in a form which automatically informs the business of their enquiries. This allows advertising, online order taking, online payments and customer support.

> **remember**
> Global market presence enabling businesses to sell for 24 hours a day, 365 days of the year requires customer service and support for a similar period in order to be successful.

activity
INDIVIDUAL WORK (8.12)
Visit www.approvedindex.co.uk. Find a web developer in your area and see what the costs are to develop a website.

Approved Index
www.approvedindex.co.uk

Rapidity of response to customer interest

E-commerce can help provide the business with additional profits. Not only will business make significant cost savings, but they will also have increased flexibility and rapid response to customers' needs, providing customers with new opportunities to enhance their activities and opening new market opportunities.

Customers now demand:

- Access to a service regardless of service provider
- The ability to give and receive information or to make a complaint
- The ability to carry out a transaction, book or pay for something
- An efficient response to enquiries
- Responsive helplines and extended opening hours.

Analysing online competition

Competitive Intelligence (CI) is an important task undertaken by all businesses. Competitive analysis allows a business to fill gaps in its knowledge about what competitors have been doing, are doing or even could be doing.

The Internet provides a wealth of free intelligence, including market reports, white papers and free research of every kind. Government sites are another excellent resource. Most countries maintain websites packed with information. Search engines, such as Google, provide some very useful results.

Marketing benefits

The key marketing benefits of having an online presence are:

- Attracting customers from remote locations – all a customer needs is access to the Internet.
- Customers with travel difficulties – there are many almost inaccessible parts of the world that do not have good transport links.
- Disabled customers – all the customer needs to be able to do is click and confirm a purchase.
- Mobile customers – increasingly customers are able to use not just wireless laptops and notebooks but mobile phones to make their purchases.

activity
**INDIVIDUAL WORK
(8.13)**

Go to a search engine such as Google and type in 'teaching in the outback'. Find out how education is brought to students hundreds of miles away from a town or city in Australia.

Google
www.google.co.uk

Level of response

The ability to operate an efficient and highly responsive, integrated supply chain is emerging as the key competitive advantage in business.

An efficient supply-chain network should provide:

- An ability to source globally
- Online, real-time information networked around the organisation
- Information management across the organisation
- An ability to offer products globally
- Improved customer response times
- Lower stock levels
- Shorter 'time-to-market' for new products.

Figure 8.1
Integrated supply chain

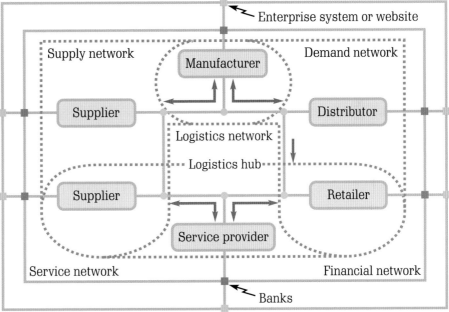

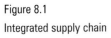

Extranet
– An extranet site is one that can only be accessed by a user group in the 'outside world', such as customers.

Electronic Data Interchange (EDI) has for a number of years allowed high-speed, secure, communication across such boundaries. For a number of reasons, EDI has only been adopted by the largest manufacturers – it seems to have been regarded as expensive and unfriendly. The **extranet**, the web-based information service, is now operating securely across a number of organisations.

activity
INDIVIDUAL WORK
(8.14)

Visit the Opportunity Wales website containing information on extranet services at: www.opportunitywales.co.uk (click on 'Online Guides' and 'Intranets and Extranets'). What are the main advantages for a business using an extranet compared to an intranet?

Opportunity Wales
www.opportunitywales.co.uk

Punctual deliveries

When a business becomes part of an integrated supply chain, it should have direct contact with all of its suppliers. It will know when the business might need additional raw materials, components, products or services, as it will be aware of its stock levels. This means, in theory, that the suppliers should always be in a position to deliver to the customer.

Access from a wide range of devices

One of the early developments was the laptop computer, which can be connected to the Internet via connections provided, for example in airport lounges, and of course mobile phones.

Mobile communications devices, such as the new-generation mobile phones and personal assistants, provide businesses with a means by which they can remain in touch with their suppliers and for their own customers to contact them.

MOST is a wireless sales management application designed to improve business efficiency. By using handheld PDAs (personal digital assistants, i.e. handheld computers), MOST ensures constant communication between the sales teams and the business itself.

> **keyword**
>
> **MOST**
> – Mobile Ordering and Sales Terminal.

E-procurement and sourcing

As we have seen, e-procurement is the purchasing of goods and services using the Internet. E-procurement systems are designed to simplify the procurement process. They reduce unnecessary administrative tasks and paperwork and improve the purchasing cycle process flow.

Electronic catalogues are loaded onto the online application to provide customers with a single searchable source of products and services. The orders created by users are sent electronically to the respective suppliers for action and delivery.

E-sourcing also involves the electronic procurement of products. The process is more automatic, especially dealing with contracts and processes. The systems include applications, decision-support tools and associated services used to identify, evaluate, negotiate and make purchases. E-sourcing's primary aim is to efficiently determine the mix of suppliers, products and services that can deliver the lowest total-cost solution while meeting business objectives.

> **activity**
> **INDIVIDUAL WORK**
> **(8.15)**
>
> Visit the Ariba website at www.ariba.com. Find out more about its e-sourcing options and solutions.

Ariba
www.ariba.com

Online order tracking

Being able to track orders from the moment they are placed to final delivery helps a business to control the way it operates. Depending on the particular system, benefits can include:

- Better service – customers and suppliers can check the progress of orders themselves.
- Cost savings – order tracking can interact with stock control processes, which means the business can reduce stock wastage (they are also likely to avoid over- and under-orders from their suppliers).
- Trust – offering the customer real-time online order tracking helps show that the business is an open and honest operation, thus increasing customer trust in them.
- Just-in-time production/delivery – shared order status lets customers and suppliers reduce lead times.

Integrated order tracking systems are useful if the business is supplying complex products. They will need to integrate their order tracking with their internal processes. This will allow the business to track orders from the moment the sale is made. The fully integrated system should allow the features outlined in Table 8.7.

remember

Websites such as Amazon give the customer the ability to see how far their order has progressed and whether it has been dispatched.

Table 8.7 Types of built-in order-tracking system

Type of built-in tracking system	Description
Delivery order tracking	Many online courier companies, such as TNT, UPS, etc., offer this as a free service. Customers will need email facilities to receive the shipment number and internet access to visit the courier company's website.
Website functionality	If the business already has a storefront website set up to handle sales electronically, then the 'shopping cart' software will usually be able to incorporate tracking data from a courier service.

Financial advantages

Reduced overheads and labour costs

By using the Internet and solutions provided by the Internet, a business can drastically reduce its costs in a number of different ways:

- Administration is reduced as the majority of the documentation needed is electronic.
- The premises used by the business can be located anywhere.
- The business may not need to purchase machinery to make products, as it may be cheaper to source them somewhere else in the world.
- Production machinery may not be necessary.

Reduced stockholding

Stock levels of products that sell well can be kept under control by using sales analysis and automatic order generation procedures.

Sales history can be used to identify products where there are excess stocks to satisfy customer demand. By identifying products that have not sold since a selected date, a business can evaluate the pricing in relation to different manufacturers' products within the same range.

Improved cash flow through fewer bad debts

A bad debt is an amount of money owed by a customer that the supplying business (the creditor) has no realistic chance of ever receiving. In theory, many businesses running online operations will not have customers who do not pay for products or services, unless they offer credit terms. Offering credit terms means offering the customer a specified period of time to pay the invoice for the products and services supplied.

Online businesses dealing with other businesses face the same kind of problems with bad debts as conventional operations.

case study 8.13   **Bad debts**

Scope Net Graphics is one of many small and medium-sized companies that suffers the problem of frequent late payments and, in the case of some customers, no payments at all.

'On a number of occasions, it has almost led to the company going under,' admits Michael Bowles, managing director of the small reproduction/graphics firm based in Kent.

With a turnover of £130 000, Scope Net Graphics always has to chase clients before receiving a settlement and is generally waiting on outstanding payments totalling between £25 000 and £30 000.

activity
INDIVIDUAL WORK

Read the case study and recommend a course of action for the business.

Freedom of low-cost location

Assuming that the business has access to good-quality Internet connections, then the actual physical location of the business does not have to be a great concern. The business also needs to have access to a reasonable supply of skilled employees and not be too far from major centres of population to make attracting new employees to the business a serious issue.

progress check

1. What is e-procurement?
2. What is a cross-channel shopper?
3. What do you understand by the term 'data conversion'?
4. Why might it be important for key staff to be adaptable as a business moves to an online presence?
5. What kind of hostile attacks could an online business experience?
6. Why is the adoption of the euro important to business in Europe?
7. Name a private distribution system.
8. What is an integrated supply chain?
9. What is MOST?
10. What is GPRS?

Exploring Business Enterprise

This unit covers:

- how to prepare for business
- how different aspects affect business preparation
- how to start and run a business

Many people wish to run their own business but the sad truth is that most people lack the expertise and the business will fail.

This unit looks at how to prepare to run a business operation.

You will look at your own strengths and weaknesses, which will give you an insight into whether you have, or can acquire, the skills required to run a business.

You will learn to understand regulations and laws that have an impact on businesses and how marketing and sales are of great importance. You will also investigate the various financial issues involved in running a small business.

Furthermore, you will look at how to prepare a proper business plan and at the wide range of advice and support that can be drawn upon to help make your business a success.

grading criteria

To achieve a **Pass** grade the evidence must show that the learner is able to:	To achieve a **Merit** grade the evidence must show that the learner is able to:	To achieve a **Distinction** grade the evidence must show that the learner is able to:
P1 describe how knowledge of personal strengths and weaknesses can be applied to preparing for and contributing to a business	**M1** explain, using examples, the benefits of running a business	**D1** evaluate the issues that need to be considered when starting and running a business
P2 describe how regulations and laws for small businesses can affect preparation for business	**M2** analyse the different aspects that will affect preparation for business	**D2** make and justify recommendations for starting a business

To achieve a **Pass** grade the evidence must show that the learner is able to:	To achieve a **Merit** grade the evidence must show that the learner is able to:	To achieve a **Distinction** grade the evidence must show that the learner is able to:
P3 describe how small businesses prepare to market and sell products or services	**M3** explain the components of a business plan and the reasons for preparing one	
P4 describe the financial issues that can affect preparation for business		
P5 outline the contents of a business plan when starting and running a business		
P6 describe the sources of advice and support available when preparing for business		

grading criteria

Although this unit is comprehensive, you should read Unit 10 Starting a Small Business for more detailed information and ideas about starting a small business.

How to Prepare for Business

Own strengths and weaknesses

A wide range of skills and qualities may be required by an individual or group of individuals that wish to start their own business. Although it may be a daunting list, remember that when more than one person is involved in the business their skills could complement each other.

Uniqueness of selling point or skill base

Most people who start their own business begin with a particular interest or expertise in the area related to the business's operations. An individual who enjoys music, for example, may wish to become a DJ or run a music shop, whilst someone interested in fashion may wish to open a clothes shop. These unique interests form

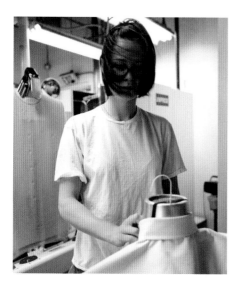

the basis of the skills and knowledge required to run a successful business in any given area.

Willingness to work long hours

Running a business can be a daunting task that will eat up an individual's time to the exclusion of almost everything else. The individual concerned will have to work long hours, they will need to devote most of their time and attention to their duties and ensure that they are available to step in to deal with any situation as and when it arises.

For someone starting their own business, a standard working week of 35 or 40 hours is not an option. The new business owner needs to be at the business before anyone else and will leave much later than the last customer or employee.

Professional standards and personal development

In addition to fulfilling the obligations required of a small business by government agencies, such as the Inland Revenue, customers, suppliers and employees will expect the owners of the business to show the highest standards of professional quality and commitment to the business. There are huge lessons to be learned by simply running the business, but there are also a large number of opportunities available for the owners to develop their own skills or undertake free or subsidised training. Local personal development and training opportunities will be available and these may be run by organisations such as Business Link or the Chamber of Commerce.

remember

By networking, even a small business can profit from the experience of other businesses, suppliers and customers.

Networking ability

Much business success can be put down to contacts. A small business needs to rapidly build up its list of suppliers, customers and other businesses that can provide them with services. Chambers of Commerce and other local business meetings provide a useful network forum to meet other local business people and exchange ideas and opinions.

Numeracy and interpersonal communication skills

The owners of the business will be the public face of the business to suppliers and customers. They will need to have developed good interpersonal skills and the ability to talk to people at all levels of society and for a huge variety of different reasons.

The business owners will also have to be able to carry out routine numeracy-related tasks, including working out costings, profit margins and, of course, totalling their income and expenditure.

Decisiveness

Business owners need to make decisions on a daily if not hourly basis. If the business is that of a sole trader, then there will be no one else to assist them in decision-making. Some decisions will have to be made instantly, whilst others will require a more considered approach. Decision-making is all part of the learning process in running your own business. Poor decisions will be made and the owner can only learn from the experience and not make a similar mistake in the future.

Willingness to develop or encourage market demand

If a business wishes to succeed in the long term, it needs sustained growth. It can only achieve this by constantly increasing its range of customers and encouraging those customers to recommend the business to others. This is a continuous process of growth and development which requires the owner to constantly look to the future rather than simply dealing with the present demands.

Efficient administration, honesty and business scruples

Although there are many laws, rules and regulations governing the correct running of a business, a small business should, from the outset, project itself in a positive manner. In addition to maintaining an effective administrative system that does not fail its suppliers or customers, the business must appear to be straightforward and honest with all groups with whom it deals.

The term 'business scruples' refers to ways of doing business that are fair and consistent throughout all the business's dealings. For example, if a customer has overpaid or been overcharged by a small amount then the small-business owner should highlight this fact and refund them.

Benefits of running a business

A small business will not only learn from its successes but it will also learn from its failures. Each day will present a new series of challenges that need to be overcome in order for the business to survive and ultimately become a success. The small-business owners will be able to recognise similar sets of circumstances and, on the next occasion they encounter them, remember how they dealt with that situation.

Small-business owners will continually be learning new ways of carrying out old tasks. They will know the pitfalls of dealing with particular suppliers or customers. They will learn to complete paperwork on time.

They will also begin to learn that sometimes situations may be beyond their current knowledge and that it is time to seek the advice of specialists or more

remember

Although the demands are high, the rewards, including independence, can far outweigh working for a salary or wage.

experienced advisers. Business Link or the Chamber of Commerce can provide the names and contact details of advisers and specialists such as accountants or solicitors.

Using either your local Chamber of Commerce or your local Business Link website, find the name and contact details for each of the following:

a) An accountant.

b) A solicitor.

c) A marketing specialist.

d) An adviser that could help with sales in Europe.

e) A computer specialist.

f) An employment agency that would provide temporary administrative staff.

Business Link
www.businesslink.gov.uk

Aspects for small businesses

There are many considerations for a business; in this section we consider the legal, financial, marketing and sales aspects.

Choosing an appropriate business structure

There are three basic types of business ownership: sole proprietorship (sole trader), partnerships and limited companies.

Sole traders

Around 63 per cent of all UK businesses are single-person enterprises known as sole traders. Many people choose this business structure as it can be the easiest to set up and run.

Table 9.1 The key issues of a sole trader

Key issues	Explanation
Management and raising finance	The owner makes all the decisions on how to manage the business. The owner raises money for the business out of their own assets, and/or with loans from banks or other lenders.
Records and accounts	The owner has to make an annual self-assessment return to the Inland Revenue. The owner must also keep records showing their business income and expenses.
Profits	Any profits go to the owner.
Tax and National Insurance	As the owner is self-employed, the profits are taxed as income. The owner also needs to pay fixed-rate Class 2 National Insurance contributions (NICs) and Class 4 NICs on profits.
Liability	As a sole trader, the owner is personally responsible for any debts run up by the business. This means the owner's home or other assets may be at risk if the business runs into difficulties.

Registration of a small business is very straightforward, the record-keeping is simple and the owner keeps all the profits after tax. Operating as a sole-trader gives the business owner a chance to test their market before getting involved in more complicated forms of business structure. The major drawback is that if the business fails, then any losses will have to be found by the owner. Sole-trader businesses have a single owner and that owner has complete control over the business.

Many sole traders operate under the name of the owner, but others choose a different name. It is not a legal requirement to register a business name.

As a sole trader, you must register as self-employed with the Inland Revenue within three months of starting up or you will pay a fine. The three-month limit starts from the last day of the sole trader's first month of trading.

Partnerships

A partnership is created when two or more people decide to form a business. There have to be at least two people and a maximum of 20 in a partnership. The partners receive a percentage of the profits in line with the percentage of the total investment they put into the partnership.

Table 9.2 The key issues of a partnership

Key issues	Explanation
Management and raising finance	Partners usually manage the business, although they can delegate responsibilities to employees. Partners raise money for the business from their own assets and/or with loans. It is possible to have 'sleeping' partners who contribute money to the business but are not involved in running the business on a daily basis.
Records and accounts	The partnership and each partner makes annual self-assessment returns to the Inland Revenue. The partnership keeps records showing business income and expenses.
Profits	Each partner takes a share of the profits.
Tax and National Insurance	Partners are classed as self-employed and taxed on their share of the profits. Each partner also pays fixed-rate Class 2 National Insurance contributions (NICs) and Class 4 NICs on their share of the profits.
Liability	Each partner is personally responsible for all debts incurred by the partnership. This means their homes or other assets may be at risk if the business runs into problems.

The partners are responsible for all of the debts of the partnership – not just the debts incurred by them as a partner, but the debts incurred by all partners. Creditors can demand that the partners surrender their own assets to cover the debts of the partnership.

Private limited companies

Many small businesses choose to set themselves up as a private limited company. A limited company is a separate legal entity, owned by its shareholders and run by the director(s).

There are two main ways of setting up a private limited company:

■ Ready-made company – you can buy an off-the-shelf limited company.

■ Tailor-made company – to set up a private limited company you will need to select a name for your limited company, then you will need to check if the name is available, and if it is available you should register with Companies House.

Table 9.3 The key issues of a private limited company

Key issues	Explanation
Management and raising finance	A director or board of directors must make all of the management decisions. Shareholders, borrowing and retained profits provide the finance. Public limited companies can raise money by selling shares on the stock market, but private limited companies cannot.
Records and accounts	The accounts must be filed with Companies House. An annual return (form 363s) is sent before the anniversary of incorporation each year. The form must be checked, amended and returned to Companies House with a fee. The directors and secretary are responsible for informing Companies House of changes in the structure and management of the business.
Profits	Profits are distributed to shareholders in the form of dividends.
Tax and National Insurance	Companies must pay corporation tax and must make an annual return to the Inland Revenue. Company directors are employees of the company and must pay Class 1 National Insurance contributions (NICs) as well as income tax. If the company or organisation has any taxable income or profits, it must tell the Inland Revenue that the company exists and that it is liable to tax.
Liability	Shareholders are not personally responsible for the company's debts, but directors may be asked to guarantee loans to the company.

The main advantages of setting up a limited company are:

■ Limited liability – the shareholders will not be held personally liable for company debts.

■ Separate entity – the company has its own legal identity separate from the shareholders and officers.

Franchises

One option in setting up a business is to buy a franchise. This means that you buy the right to run a business that the franchisor has set up. Typical examples of franchises are McDonald's, The Body Shop and KallKwik. For small businesses, the franchise tends to involve retailing and eating establishments or providing a service such as cleaning.

When choosing a franchise, many people use the services of an independent adviser. It is important to make sure that the franchisor is a member of the British Franchise Association. An accountant can check the forecasts of sales given by the franchisor.

British Franchise Association
www.britishfranchise.org

Table 9.4 Advantages and disadvantages of franchises

Advantages	Disadvantages
■ You get more help and advice starting up and running the franchise than you would get starting your own business. ■ You start with a reputation and under a well-known name. ■ You get a ready-made product or service that is established.	■ You may be less free to develop in your own way. ■ You may have to start fairly big – maybe too big for you if you have no experience. ■ You have to pay an ongoing management fee.

Table 9.5 The key issues of a franchise

Key issues	Explanation
Management and raising finance	The franchise agreement usually sets out how the franchised business should be run. The franchisors usually provide management help and training to franchisees as part of the overall package. The franchisee has to find the money needed to start up the business. In some cases, the franchisors offer a loan.
Records and accounts	The records and accounts depend on the business structure chosen by the franchisee. In addition to the regular legal requirements, the franchisors will need to see detailed financial records.
Profits	Franchisees usually pay a share of their turnover to the franchisor. This reduces the profits and these are distributed according to the legal structure of the business.
Tax and National Insurance	This depends on the business structure chosen by the franchisee.
Liability	This depends on the business structure chosen by the franchisee.

activity
INDIVIDUAL WORK
(9.2)

a) Investigate at least five partnership firms in your local area and try to discover the number of partners in each of these businesses. What advantages do they have over sole traders?

b) If you were starting a business, what qualities would you be looking for in your partners?

Business registration

It is quite simple to form a company. Ready-made companies can be bought for quite a small sum of money and although the company may already have a name, this can be changed for an additional small fee.

Companies House holds the public records of more than a million companies. Its four main functions are to:

- Incorporate and dissolve companies.
- Examine and hold documents presented under the Companies Act 1985 and 1989 and other legislation.
- Make this information available to the public.
- Exercise certain powers in relation to companies on behalf of the Secretary of State for Trade and Industry.

keyword

Incorporation – The procedure by which a business registers itself at Companies House and becomes a legal entity. It is also known as registration and formation.

Once the registration of the business (**incorporation**) has been completed, every business is required to provide the following information to Companies House:

- An annual return
- Its registered address
- Notification of a change in the company's directors
- Notification of a change of company secretary
- Details of its directors and shareholders
- Annual (yearly) accounts.

Companies House attempts to ensure that this information is available to any individual wishing to gain access to it. In doing this, the organisation helps to provide peace of mind for its customers, suppliers, creditors and shareholders.

activity
INDIVIDUAL WORK (9.3)

Visit the website of Companies House at www.companieshouse.gov.uk.

Click on 'WebCheck'. Type in the name of a business local to you and this will enable you to click on the name from a list.

When was this company formed? What is its official address and company number?

Companies House
www.companieshouse.gov.uk

Use of solicitors

For a new business, choosing the right solicitor can be as important as choosing the right bank. Solicitors tend to specialise in different areas of the law, but most partnerships have a small-business specialist and one that can give advice on starting a new business. Sometimes businesses choose larger firms of solicitors in order to benefit from the combined skills and expertise of the individual partners.

Key legal constraints

Using a solicitor will assist a business in ensuring they comply with the required laws that are in force for anyone that begins trading or starts their business operation. Businesses are required to ensure that they have complied with various legal guidelines.

Employment law requires that particular attention should be paid to providing a contract of employment for all those who work for the business and that they pay attention to the laws concerning discrimination.

Health and safety regulations have become an increasingly complex area for businesses to consider. A business must ensure that it complies with the Health and Safety at Work Act 1974 in the following respects:

- Providing safe machinery and equipment.
- Ensuring that regular maintenance is undertaken.
- Ensuring that all operating procedures for machinery and equipment are carefully monitored.
- Ensuring that safe methods of handling potentially dangerous or hazardous materials are adhered to.
- Ensuring that employees are well supervised at all times.
- Providing healthy and safe working conditions.
- Ensuring that the access to and exit from the premises is safe, unblocked and clearly marked.
- Ensuring that any visitors to the premises encounter a safe environment.

remember
Businesses must comply with a wide range of laws aimed at ensuring it acts properly and responsibly.

Employer's liability insurance covers a business against claims that may be made by employees who have suffered injury in the course of their work. The term 'employee' is a broad one in this respect, as it covers all of those individuals that are under contract in some way to the business.

The Trade Descriptions Act 1968 relates to the products and services that a business supplies. This legislation states that:

- A product must comply with its description.
- A product must be capable of performing to the levels claimed by the manufacturer.
- Faulty products should be replaced or a refund made to the customer without exception.
- Products should meet all existing safety standards.
- An organisation faces prosecution if it is found to be selling unsafe products.

activity
INDIVIDUAL WORK
(9.4)

Another piece of legislation that governs the activities of a business is the former Sale of Goods Act 1979 and 1995 that has now been replaced by the Sale and Supply of Goods to Consumers Regulations 2002.

Find out what a customer can now demand if products they have bought from a business are faulty.

Financial implications

Planning the financial resources of a new business involves considering:

- The amount of capital available from the owners of the business
- The source of any additional finance needed.

Before any business can begin its operations it needs start-up finance to pay for essential items. The organisation will need a variety of different pieces of equipment or assets, such as vehicles, premises, shop fittings, machinery, land and working capital.

Initial start-up capital

The majority of small businesses do not require significant funding to get started. Around 25 per cent only need about £10 000 for their initial start-up capital. This reflects the fact that very few new small businesses are involved in manufacturing. Most small businesses use a combination of funding rather than one single source.

Many young business owners are unlikely to have the assets to provide a guarantee against a loan, as they will not have a lot of their own capital to invest and will not have the track record to be an attractive proposition for funding. At the same time, their business ideas can be quite innovative and as a consequence they are often viewed as risky.

Working capital and reserves

Broadly speaking, the business will need finance to cover the cost of the essential assets required for their activities. Essential assets are the items needed to enable the business to operate, such as premises, shop fittings, equipment and transport. All of these are key items that the organisation must have obtained before it can start its business activity.

remember

Working capital is the money that is available immediately and which is needed to pay for daily expenses.

Working capital is needed to finance the day-to-day running of the business. Working capital is used to pay for the running costs and raw materials, to fund credit offered to customers and to pay a business's immediate debts. If these debts cannot be paid, a business is considered to be insolvent, or not in a financial position to continue to trade.

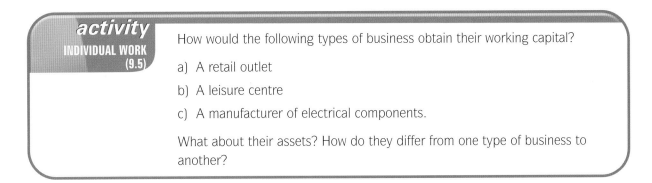

activity
INDIVIDUAL WORK (9.5)

How would the following types of business obtain their working capital?

a) A retail outlet

b) A leisure centre

c) A manufacturer of electrical components.

What about their assets? How do they differ from one type of business to another?

Identifying appropriate sources of finance

In order to fund the purchase of capital assets, the business will use a number of methods to raise capital, including:

- Trade credit – this refers to the payment terms agreed between the supplier and the business.

- Overdraft – the size of an organisation's overdraft depends upon its working capital requirements. Generally, the amount is agreed each year with the bank.

- Factoring – this is a cash advance given by a bank or financial service provider. The amount of the cash advance is usually calculated as around 80 per cent of the total of money owed to a business by its customers.

- Leasing – if an organisation chooses to lease its equipment then it is never the legal owner of that equipment. The equipment remains the property of the leasing company. The equipment is leased in return for a regular schedule of payments. The business can buy the equipment at the end of the lease period at a reduced rate.

- Hire purchase – this is different from leasing in that a finance provider buys the equipment and hires it to the business. The business has to agree to make regular payments until the full cost has been repaid.

- Loans – loans are often negotiated with a bank or finance provider in order to acquire an agreed sum of money, which may be earmarked for the purchase of a particular piece of equipment. The loan is usually paid back over a fixed period of time, with agreed levels of interest and regular payments.

- Mortgages – a mortgage is a legal agreement between a bank or financial service provider and the business, which gives the lender certain legal rights over the property being purchased via the mortgage.

- Profit retention – this means that the business would put aside a certain portion of any profits they have made to ensure that they have sufficient working capital.

- Grants – these may be available to a business from central governments, local authorities and the EU. Grants are often linked to social and regional development and the grant provider will offer assistance for projects relating to various business activities.

---

activity
GROUP WORK
(9.6)

If you were partners in a business and only had a limited amount of working capital available to you, which of the available finance options listed here would you consider to be the most beneficial for your business's cash flow if you needed to purchase a piece of equipment? Discuss this as a group and then list the advantages and disadvantages of each option.

---

activity
INDIVIDUAL WORK
(9.7)

Visit the following websites:

www.businesslink.gov.uk

www.dti.gov.uk (on the 'Select a DTI site' menu, click 'Regional').
These websites should provide you with information about the many different types of grant available to business in your region.

DTI	Business Link
www.dti.gov.uk	www.businesslink.gov.uk

Using accountants

In choosing an accountant, particularly at the start of the business's operations, the owners will need to make the decision as to whether or not they wish to use the services of a large or small concern. While larger firms of accountants may be unwilling to provide basic bookkeeping services, a small accountancy firm may not be able to offer assistance in raising finance. It is, therefore, a balancing act that needs to be based on the business's particular requirements.

Generally speaking, accountants offer a business the following advice or services:

- Bookkeeping.
- Setting up an accounting system.
- Advice on the use of computerised accounting software.
- Auditing – where the accountant checks the records of the business to make sure they are in order and are a true record of the business's transactions and activities.

- Managing cash flow.
- Raising start-up capital.
- Negotiating additional finance.
- Payment of tax to the Inland Revenue.
- Payment of National Insurance.
- Payment of VAT HM Revenue & Customs.
- Payment of business tax.
- Production of the financial elements involved in business plans (covered later in this unit).
- Production of budgets and forecasts or predictions.

---

activity
INDIVIDUAL WORK (9.8)

Accountants that are qualified with particular associations, or examining boards, have letters after their names. Using the Internet, find out what the following letters mean:

a) ACA.

b) FCA.

c) ACCA.

d) FCCA.

VAT and income tax

Self-employed people will normally pay their income tax at the end of January and July every year. The tax is assessed and paid on the previous year's activities. This arrangement is somewhat different to that of employees, who pay their tax on a weekly or monthly basis.

In a partnership, the taxable income is worked out in a very similar way to that of a sole trader. Business expenses can be deducted and tax relief applied for on capital expenditure, National Insurance contributions and losses. The tax burden placed on each partner is in proportion to the profit share of each individual partner.

In the case of a limited company on the other hand, taxation is not assessed against a particular individual. The limited company will pay capital gains tax and corporation tax.

remember
The amount of VAT increases as the value of products rises from raw materials to finished goods.

The VAT (Value Added Tax) system is a method of using businesses to act as tax collectors for the government. VAT is an indirect tax in that it is only paid when a customer buys an article. A business pays VAT on their purchases and also charges VAT on the products or services they sell. If the business has charged more VAT on the products or services it has sold than it has paid on the goods it has purchased, then it will owe HM Revenue & Customs the difference between the two amounts.

Visit the website of HM Revenue & Customs at www.hmrc.gov.uk. Under the Business and Corporations menu, click on the 'Learn about VAT' icon and choose the 'Introduction to VAT' option, then answer the following questions:

a) How many rates of VAT are there?

b) What are the rates?

c) Which products or services have reduced rates of VAT?

HM Revenue & Customs
www.hmrc.gov.uk

Insurance requirements

Sorting out insurance should be one of the high-priority jobs of any new business. If businesses fail to obtain the correct insurance, they could lose money. Insurance basically fall into two categories:

- Insurance required by law
- Insurance that is desirable in order to cover possible risks or accidents.

Asset insurance attempts to ensure that the business is protected against loss or damage to stock, equipment or processes as a result of various uncontrollable factors. There are four main types of asset insurance:

- Damage and loss insurance
- Theft insurance
- Interruption of business activity insurance
- All-risk insurance.

A business will also have to have public liability insurance. This covers it against injury to a member of the public as a direct or indirect result of any occurrence or event related to the business. This insurance will also cover loss or damage to the customer's property. Related to this is the need for the business to obtain employers' liability insurance. It is the responsibility of the employer to compensate an employee who may have been injured or become ill as a result of working for the business. The certificate of insurance for employers' liability should be visible and accessible to all employees.

Visit the website of the Norwich Union, which is an insurance company, at www.norwichunion.com. Click on the 'Business' link and then on the 'Self-employed insurance' link. Now answer the following questions:

a) What kind of businesses does small-business insurance cover?

b) What does the website define as being the insurance needs of a small business?

c) What cover does the self-employed policy provide?

Norwich Union
www.norwichunion.com

Monitoring finance

Financial data and forecasts form the basis of a business's ability to raise finance, negotiate the purchase of premises and order raw materials. If a business is inaccurate in its forecasting then there would be insufficient money available to the business. If a business fails to meet its projected forecasts, it may be difficult or impossible to acquire further finance. A provider of finance will often reject a business that asks for more money because its forecasting has proved inaccurate.

A business starting out for the first time does not want to have to cope with financial problems created as a result of poor or ill-conceived financial forecasts. It must attempt, therefore, to estimate sales, costs and cash balances.

Businesses may choose to detail their financial data and forecasts using different time periods: weekly, monthly or yearly. For cash-flow forecasts, it is the monthly time period that is the biggest concern. Totals will have to be calculated for cash received and cash outgoing for each month. It is probable that certain assumptions will have to be made, particularly in the case of forecasts relating to months in the future.

Potential problems regarding cash flow or profitability must be considered at every stage. If there are shareholders, they will demand to know the true state of affairs within the business. It may be necessary for them to make additional share capital available to finance short-term cash-flow problems on long-term investments.

A profit and loss account is used to calculate the total income derived from invoices issued during the month and the costs of any expenses during the same period. This document, produced by an accountant, will give a balance per month which indicates the profit or loss in that month.

Balance sheets, on the other hand, tend to be drawn up on a yearly basis, working from information derived from actual cash flow and profit and loss. A balance sheet shows what an organisation owes and what it owns at a particular time on a particular day. A projected balance sheet will show an estimate of what the business will owe and own on a particular day in the future.

A cash-flow forecast in its simplest form is a record of cash received by the business and an indication as to when cash will be needed to pay bills. Within a business plan, it is usual to make a cash-flow forecast that extends for two or three years. Providers of finance may require a business to extend that forecast for up to five years.

A start-up balance sheet can only contain items of income and expenditure of which a business is already aware. It is advisable for a new business to use an

> **remember**
>
> Profit and loss accounts are essential in order for a business to know how they are performing at any given time.

accountant to help produce a balance sheet at this stage of its operations. The key headings of a balance sheet include:

- Fixed assets – all equipment received, even if this has not yet been paid for.
- Current assets – cash, debtors and stock.
- Capital – which the owners have put into the business to start it up.
- Liabilities – money owed by the business, such as overdrafts, tax or VAT and other businesses they owe money to, such as suppliers.

A profit forecast can be made in order to establish the level of profit that the business hopes to produce at the end of a specified period. The projected profit and loss and balance sheet should indicate whether the business will be in a position in the future to either **break even** or show a small profit.

By constructing a monthly profit and loss account and a monthly balance sheet, an organisation will be able to monitor its adherence to its start-up business plan. This control mechanism should be able to identify any causes for concern and allow the business to react in time. The normal procedure is for a business to create a cash-flow forecast which includes budgeted figures for various items. Then, as the figures become available, the business can compare these with the budgeted figures.

Own drawings

Many owners of new businesses, as well as the self-employed, choose not to take very much money out of their business in its early stages. Drawings are, effectively, the wages that the small-business owner or the self-employed person pays to themselves. Obviously these individuals do have other financial commitments, mainly to run a home, pay bills and support their family. By minimising the amount of drawings they take from the business in the early stages, they can reinvest the maximum amount of money in the business to ensure its long-term survival and, ultimately, its success.

> **keyword**
> **Break even**
> This means a business has been able to cover its costs by the products or services they have sold, but they have not made a profit.

> **remember**
> Own drawings are in effect wages paid to the owner of the business.

> **activity**
> **INDIVIDUAL WORK (9.11)**
>
> It is now time to think about the financial considerations involved in launching and selling a product or service.
>
> a) What kind of start-up capital would you need?
> b) Where could you go to find appropriate sources of finance?
> c) What kind of grants might be available?
> d) How would you find an accountant, solicitor or an insurance provider?
> e) What contact would you have to make with the Inland Revenue and HM Revenue & Customs?
> f) How would you monitor and control your finances?
> g) How much would you have to pay yourself each month in order to meet your domestic financial requirements?

Marketing, sales and the competition

A business will also constantly evaluate its own position, both in terms of what it is doing now and what it might do in the future. It will then compare this with its competitors. Ultimately, as we will see, a business will seek to strengthen its position, deal with threats before they emerge and take advantage of any opportunities that may arise by planning for those opportunities in advance.

Competition

As far as customers, or consumers, are concerned, the higher the level of competition for products and services, the higher the level of quality and the lower the price paid. Increased competition drives down prices as more businesses are competing for sales.

Pressures on a business are very strong and the business must ensure that they not only offer the broadest possible range of products and services, but that they are competitively priced and of high quality. They also need to be available in as many different outlets or places where customers can purchase them as possible.

---

activity

GROUP WORK (9.12)

Many standard products and services are available from a wide range of competing businesses, even in a relatively small area. Think about the following products. Write beside each one how many different stores, within walking distance of one another, sell the same product.

a) A bag of chips.

b) A bottle of cola.

c) A local newspaper.

d) A bottle of nail varnish.

e) The details of a two-bedroomed house for rent.

f) A pair of football socks.

g) A bag of two-inch nails.

h) A fountain pen.

i) A pair of tights.

j) A diary for next year.

Range of comparable businesses

Most businesses are concerned with competitors that supply broadly similar products and services to broadly similar customers. 'Broadly similar' in terms of products and services means that an estate agent would be concerned with the activities of all other estate agents in the immediate area. A supermarket would be concerned with not only other supermarkets and grocery outlets in the immediate area but also regional ones and certainly online supermarkets that deliver to the local area.

'Comparable markets' mean broadly similar types of customer. In a typical high street there may be a dozen or more clothes outlets. Whilst all of them sell clothing and accessories, they do not all have the same market. Some will be aimed at younger age groups and have fashionable clothing. Others may be catering for children or older people. This means that simply looking in the *Yellow Pages* under clothing might reveal a number of clothes shops in a particular area. But what it does not reveal is the nature of those clothes shops and which markets they are attempting to sell their products to.

Identifying the competitive market

In order to understand the difficulties businesses face in identifying their competitors, the following headings in this section ask you to look at a particular case – a florist shop. Initially you will discover that it is relatively easy to identify competitors. But the further afield you look for competitors, the more difficult it is to assess what impact they might have on a business.

activity
GROUP WORK
(9.13)

Before you read on, you need to imagine that you and your partner wish to set up a florist shop in your local area. You will offer cut flowers and plants to customers who pass your shop. You will also take telephone orders for weddings, funerals and special occasions and you will set up a website that allows customers to purchase plants and flower arrangements online. You will offer a full delivery service free of charge.

Think of a name for your shop and imagine the ideal location in your local area.

activity
GROUP WORK
(9.14)

Using the *Yellow Pages* or your local *Phone Book*, identify the number of florists in your immediate area. For example, the city of Norwich has 26 florists. This is in addition to petrol stations and supermarkets, as well as market stalls and garden centres, which sell cut flowers or potted plants.

Local

The most obvious competitors are in a business's immediate local area. These competitors offer either exactly the same or very similar products and services and could easily attract customers who would otherwise purchase from the business. Normally businesses know a great deal about their local competitors.

Regional

In some parts of the UK particular areas are regional centres where you will find the majority of businesses including retail outlets. These businesses cater for the whole of the area and draw customers in from the outlying towns and villages.

National

Gauging the number of competitors nationally is more difficult. Many businesses, although not located anywhere near their customers, can supply products and services and are direct competitors with local businesses.

European and global

For florists, European or international competitors may not be a great threat, unless of course a customer wishes to have flowers delivered to an overseas location. They are competitors in the broadest sense, but the complications of payment, delivery charges and additional time concerns may well mean they are not as serious a threat as local, regional or national competitors.

activity

**GROUP WORK
(9.15)**

Using the *Yellow Pages* again, look at the florists in the region. If you live in a county, your *Yellow Pages* will cover the whole of that county. If you live in a city, you should include all the boroughs and the outlying towns. How much more competition is there regionally compared with locally for your florist shop?

This is not necessarily the case for all businesses. It is sometimes considerably cheaper for customers to buy products from overseas businesses. In the manufacturing industry, countries such as China can produce products at far lower cost than businesses in the UK due to their low wage rate.

---

activity
GROUP WORK
(9.16)

Summarise your findings from the previous group work activities. What was the total number of local competitors? What was the total number of regional competitors? Which were the five major national competitors? Why do you think they were serious competitors to your florist business?

---

case study
9.1

Tesco's online rival

Tesco launched its online shopping service in 1998. It has around 1.5 million registered users. Its service provides delivery to over 95 per cent of the UK population. Iceland is the only company that covers more of the population with 97 per cent coverage. Asda's home delivery service only caters for around 10 million households. In 2002, Waitrose, part of the John Lewis Partnership, launched a new home delivery service. Initially it tested its systems just in Hertfordshire, but in June 2002 it expanded into London. It has a warehouse that can process the same amount of groceries as 20 large supermarkets. Unlike Tesco, Ocado, a new business in partnership with Waitrose, promises to deliver within a one-hour time slot and rewards customers with gifts if deliveries are late.

---

activity
INDIVIDUAL WORK

Read the case study and then answer the following question:

For a home-delivery service, why might the maximum population coverage be important?

How Different Aspects Affect Business Preparation

A detailed knowledge of the marketplace and the possible opportunities and threats to a business is essential. Knowledge of the marketplace allows a business to plan for likely issues that could affect the running of the business, its sales and its profitability.

Approximate current market share

Market share is a notoriously difficult figure to calculate. Normally a business will attempt to assess the total value of a particular market and then work out its own share of that market. The problem arises with actually measuring that market in the first place.

A mobile-phone manufacturer, for example, may calculate its market share by calculating the total number of mobile phones sold in a particular country in a specific year. It will then look at its own sales and compare this with the total sales. Unfortunately this does not show the whole picture. It is better to try to calculate a value, in terms of total sales figures for a particular market, and then to compare this figure with the total value of sales that the business has done in that market. In this way the actual value of the market, in income terms, can be calculated by the business.

As a simple example, if a particular market is worth £10 million and a specific business has £1 million of sales in that market, then they have 10 per cent of the market.

Degree of competition

The more complex a business and the more markets in which it operates, the more complicated the situation regarding competition becomes. It would be fairly straightforward for a local toy shop to be able to assess the degree of competition it faces in the market. It would begin by looking at other toy shops in the immediate area, larger toy shops that may be based in the region (such as Toys R Us), and it will then look at online toy shops, toys sold through catalogue showrooms (such as Argos), and supermarkets and other outlets that have a limited toy selection.

Theoretically the small, local toy shop competes with all of these different businesses. But, on a Saturday afternoon, when children visit the high street, they will not have a huge amount of competition for pocket-money spending. The competition may only arise with major purchases, such as for birthdays and Christmas.

Supermarkets selling an organic food range have hit many health-food stores, which were once the only source of organic food, extremely hard. If customers can purchase organic food with their other shopping, then the likelihood is that they will not bother to visit the health-food store at all. This problem facing health-food stores has been mirrored by many of the other independent outlets such as toy shops and chemists.

activity
GROUP WORK (9.17)

Thinking about organic food, list at least three reasons why a supermarket might choose to offer these types of products. Why might selling them add to their attractiveness to customers?

Past market history and likely developments

One of the most common ways in which a business will attempt to predict future trends in the market is to look at the past history of the market in terms of sales and trends. A business that sells luxury goods could confidently expect that if the country's economy is strong, then its sales will be high. If the country's economy is weak and people are reluctant to spend money in an uncertain time, then company sales will fall. It will be able to see these trends having occurred in the past and, if there is the likelihood that these factors will repeat themselves, it can be prepared for that eventuality.

Most markets tend to follow a regular pattern. Sometimes they enjoy periods of growth, followed by a levelling off of demand and then, perhaps, a fall in demand. By recognising what stage the market is at during any given period, the business will not be caught unaware and either left with stock that cannot be sold or have insufficient stock to satisfy increased demand.

For many businesses, technology has a drastic impact on either their operations, their products and services, or the customers that they serve. Banks, for example, have witnessed tremendous changes in technology that have seen **debit** and **credit cards** replacing cash and cheques in many transactions. Improved information communication technology has allowed online banking and telephone banking, neither of which were even thought of 10 years ago.

Other industries, such as the music trade, have seen a shift from vinyl records to CDs and then to downloadable MP3 music files. All of these developments have been driven by changes in technology.

Debit card
– A modern alternative to a cheque. The funds are taken out of the account of the cardholder immediately after having been approved by the issuing bank.

keyword

Credit card
– A card that allows the user to make purchases on credit, up to a limit specified by the issuing bank, building society or finance provider.

keyword

Market concentration is the degree to which the top businesses in any particular industry control the lion's share of the market. In the UK food retail market in 1980 the top 14 retailers had a 23 per cent market share between them. By 2000 the top nine retailers had captured 63 per cent of the market. This gradual process resulted in smaller businesses being squeezed out of markets, as they could not compete with the sheer size and financial strength of the larger businesses. Although there are laws that prevent businesses from totally dominating a particular market, the gradual process of a handful of businesses controlling most of a market continues.

Evaluating market position

Having identified the key customers and their attributes, along with recognising market demand and trends, a business should have a clear idea of the market and its competitors. The next logical step is for the business to look at what it does and make a comparison between its efforts and those of its competitors. This section looks at the types of activity and concerns that the business would need to examine in order to evaluate its own market position.

SWOT analysis

SWOT (Strengths, Weaknesses, Opportunities and Threats) analysis is a means by which a business can describe the factors that may have an impact on operations.

- The strengths and weaknesses of the businesses are best described as its internal resources and capabilities, such as management skills or product or service quality.

- The opportunities and threats are the external factors that can affect the business. Competitors would be classed as a threat, and a new market an opportunity.

The purpose of SWOT analysis is to produce, in the easiest and most understandable way, a list of the key issues. Normally SWOT analysis is presented in the form of a straightforward grid, as can be seen in Figure 9.1.

remember

Strengths and weaknesses are internal, opportunities and threats are external.

Figure 9.1
SWOT analysis

Strengths	Weaknesses
Opportunities	Threats

The business will usually start a SWOT analysis by listing the internal factors, starting with its strengths and listing them in the Strengths box. It will ask itself a number of questions, including:

- What makes the business good at succeeding?
- What does the business do well?
- Why are customers pleased with the business's products and services?
- What advantages does the business offer customers and suppliers?

Above all, the business needs to be honest. If it is not objective, then the SWOT analysis will have no value.

Having looked at the strengths, the business now turns its attention to its weaknesses and lists them in the Weaknesses box. These are issues that affect performance and typically it will ask itself the following questions:

- What could be improved about the business?
- What problems does the business constantly encounter?
- What does the business do that could be improved?
- What must the business avoid?
- What does the competition do that is superior to what the business does?

Again the business needs to be honest. It needs to list its weaknesses as clearly and as honestly as possible.

Having looked at the internal factors, the business must now look at the external issues that impact on the business. It will begin by looking at opportunities and list them in the Opportunities box. It will ask itself a number of questions, including:

- What market opportunities are available to the business?
- What customer needs are not being fulfilled by the business or its competitors?
- What important trends are taking place in the market?
- Are there any technological, legal or social changes happening that the business could take advantage of to improve its position?

remember

A business needs to think about possible negative impacts that could be caused by the competitors.

The final issue is the threats facing the business, listed in the Threats box. Some of the threats will be more obvious than others and the business needs to consider both the actual threats and the possible threats in the future. Typical questions would include:

- Would a period of poor sales or a major customer going out of business seriously affect the business's future?
- What is the competition doing and is it taking sales away from the business?
- What would the competition do if the business tried to exploit an opportunity it has identified?
- Are there any trends or changes in the market that could have a negative impact on the business's products or services?
- Are there any technological changes that could have a negative impact on the business's products or services?

The main aim of SWOT analysis is not only to identify key issues but also to organise them in such a way that the business can:

- Build on its strengths
- Minimise its weaknesses
- Take advantage of opportunities
- Deal with threats.

GROUP WORK (9.18)

In pairs, draw up your own SWOT analysis grid and try to identify the strengths, weaknesses, opportunities and threats for your school or college.

Product quality

Perhaps the most fundamental internal factor is an analysis of the business's products and services. A business will need to examine and make a judgement about whether its current products and services are of sufficient quality to remain attractive to potential customers. It will do this by comparing its products and services with not only the competition's products and services but also with the expectations of its customers. It may be the case that the majority of products and services offered by the business and its competitors do not meet its customers' expectations. Therefore, simply comparing the business's products and services with those of its competitors is not sufficient to be sure that they are of good quality.

Consistency

The term 'consistency' refers to the average quality of the products and services offered by the business, and it is also a measure of all of the services provided by the business. Consistency therefore means regular and guaranteed high-quality products and services, backed up by high-quality customer and after-sales service.

Customer service

Many businesses recognise that in the majority of markets, where products and services offered by a variety of different businesses are similar, the only real difference is the quality of the customer service. It is no longer the case that businesses can simply sell their products and services to a customer and then sit back and count their profits. Customers demand a far more extensive relationship with a business. They need to be able to contact the business should they have a problem and that problem needs to be resolved quickly and efficiently. In ensuring that customers are dealt with in a prompt, efficient and more than satisfactory manner, businesses can establish a strong relationship with the customer, which means that next time they wish to purchase a similar product or service they will remain loyal to that business.

activity
INDIVIDUAL WORK (9.19)

Are you a loyal customer? Do you have any store loyalty cards? Do you always shop in the same place for your clothes, CDs, takeaway food or other regular purchases? What is it about the business that you buy from that makes you loyal to them?

Image and branding

Businesses spend millions of pounds establishing an image for their products and services. The main purpose of developing an image or a brand for a particular product or service is to make it instantly recognisable to the customers. Having created an image and a brand name, the business will be keen to ensure that it retains its customers by constantly reminding them that the products and services connected with that brand are of a high quality.

Reputation

Once the business has established a brand name and an image for its products and services, it will seek to remind customers that its quality, reliability and usefulness are guaranteed. Over a period of time the product or service will achieve a reputation for its standard of quality, reliability and usefulness, which the business will ensure remains at a consistently high level.

Unique selling points

remember

USPs are sometimes called unique selling propositions; these are things that set a product or service apart from the competition.

Unique selling points, or USPs, are characteristics of a particular product or service that sets them apart from any other product or service offered by a competitor. The business will use a product's USPs in its advertising or promotion of the product or service. They will use the USPs in order to compare the product or service with that of the competition, so that it is clear that the product or service is superior in some way.

It is the USP that will help customers to choose the business's products or services over those of the competition. In the majority of markets, there are tens or even thousands of businesses offering broadly similar products and services.

activity

GROUP WORK (9.20)

Look at the following list of products and try to think of the USP of at least three of them:

a) A KFC meal.

b) A pair of Nike trainers.

c) Jamie Oliver's range of cookware.

d) Your favourite football team's club shirt.

e) Body Shop cosmetics.

Competitive pressures

The issues already covered in this section deal primarily with the strengths and weaknesses of a SWOT analysis. Competitive pressure is the first issue that addresses potential opportunities and threats. Competitive pressures relate not only to the amount of competition in the market but also to the impact on the business of their activities. Each time a competitor launches an initiative to take advantage of an opportunity that it has identified, it becomes a threat for all of the other businesses in that market. Competitive pressure may come from a number of the largest businesses in the market, which, as we will see, may be more able to use their resources to gain market share. Competitive pressure may also come from smaller competitors, or indeed businesses that have just joined the market and have become new competitors.

Competitor resources and strengths

In many markets, the size of a business may determine the extent of its resources, which in turn could be its major strength. If a market is dominated by a handful of large businesses, they may be more concerned about fighting over market share with the larger competitors than with the smaller ones.

It is certainly the case that in the retail food markets the larger businesses, such as Tesco, Asda and Sainsbury's, are more concerned with countering one another's activities than trying to force a small corner shop out of business. Unfortunately their activities, such as longer opening hours, price cuts, home deliveries and a wider product range, while aimed at dealing with their larger competitors, have had a huge impact on their smaller competitors.

If a major business has more customers, higher sales and profits, better-trained staff and a more convenient location, then it has a huge advantage over its competitors. In reality, this is rarely the case, and in most markets a competitor may have superior resources and strengths in certain areas but a lack of resources and some weaknesses in others. This is not to say that they are balanced out, but it does give the smaller competitor a chance to compete even with the largest businesses. Many customers would actually prefer to buy from a smaller, more local business than a large impersonal business even if the local business is slightly more expensive.

> **activity**
> **INDIVIDUAL WORK**
> **(9.21)**
>
> Do you have a local store? If so, how often does your family use it? What do you buy there that you could obtain from a large supermarket? Why do you choose to use the corner shop rather than visit the supermarket for these products?

How to Start and Run a Business

Support

There is a huge amount of support and guidance available to those wishing to start a new business. This section focuses on the key areas where potential small businesses could seek assistance. Remember that you will need assistance in a huge number of different areas from different specialists. Not all of the information is necessarily related to financing the business. Some of the information may provide business contacts, relay personal experiences about starting a business or provide assistance in marketing.

Business Link partnerships

> **remember**
>
> Each area of the country has its own Business Link office, with national contacts.

Business Link is a nationwide service that provides practical advice for businesses and particular expertise in assisting new businesses. Initially the advice provided by Business Link will be free, but additional advice and information can be bought at a discounted price using various grants and schemes offered by local and central government and the EU.

> **activity**
> **INDIVIDUAL WORK**
> **(9.22)**
>
> Following the instructions in the 'Want To Find Out More?' box, click on your local Business Link website address and find out what events or seminars are being held in your area, and which would be useful to a new business.

Small business services provided by banks

Banks are not merely sources of possible finance for a small business, they also provide useful business advice. All of the major high-street banks and some online banks offer specific help to small businesses.

> **activity**
> **INDIVIDUAL WORK**
> **(9.23)**
>
> Find the 'Business banking' section of the Barclay's website. What is included in its start-up package for small businesses? Click on 'Starting up with us?' to find out more information about the kind of services that this bank provides.

Barclays Bank
www.barclays.co.uk

Trade associations

There are a huge number of different trade associations related to each particular type of business or the market the business serves. They can provide realistic and practical assistance for small businesses.

Chambers of Commerce

Chambers of Commerce are a nationwide network of organisations that represent 100 000 businesses of various sizes which employ 4 million people. The Chamber of Commerce claims that it is the voice of UK business and it provides useful information and guidance.

---

activity
**INDIVIDUAL WORK
(9.24)**

Follow the instructions on the British Chamber of Commerce website and click on the option 'Contact your local chamber'. This will reveal a map of the UK. Click on the relevant region and find your local Chamber of Commerce.

British Chamber of Commerce
www.chamberonline.co.uk

Friends, family, personal contacts and investors

Anyone that may eventually have a financial interest in the small business may be able to offer useful guidance and assistance. Many members of your family or close friends may have experience of running a small business, although not necessarily in the area that you wish to develop. They will be able to inform you about many of the pitfalls that they encountered in the early stages of their own business.

Government agencies and funding agencies

The Department of Trade and Industry (DTI) is a good starting point for any investigation into relevant government agencies or funding agencies. The DTI's website contains a huge amount of information related to all forms of support and assistance for businesses of any size.

---

activity
**INDIVIDUAL WORK
(9.25)**

From the DTI website choose the 'Business solutions' option and click on 'Raising finance'. There is a section designed for small businesses and new businesses. The page link details loans, grants and consultancy available. Identify anything that would suit a proposed new business.

Department of Trade and Industry
www.dti.gov.uk

Business plans

In order to fulfil this unit's requirements you have to create a draft business plan. A business plan is a written statement about a business. It is written by the owners or the managers and states what they intend to achieve and how they intend to achieve the objectives.

As we will see, a basic business plan needs to cover:

- The structure of the business.

- The products and services offered.

- The types of customer and how they will be approached to offer the products and services.

- The growth potential of the business.

- How the business intends to finance the operations.

As well as stating the business's main objectives and identifying its financial requirements, the business plan will also include a section on its marketing plans. This marketing plan will assist the owners of the new business by focusing on:

- The main factors that need to be addressed in order to remain competitive.

- Identifying and examining the business's expansion opportunities.

- Preparing a series of measures to address any future problems.

- Setting identifiable goals and results that it is hoped that will be achieved by them.

- Identifying criteria to be met in the achievement of the business's goals and objectives.

- Setting out a series of measures to allow the monitoring of progress.

- Providing the information required by providers of finance.

Action planning

Action planning requires a business to set its own targets and decide how it will achieve them. Often it involves making difficult decisions about plans for the future, and a business needs to be focused about what it wants to do, as well as being realistic about what it will be able to do.

An action plan looks at where the business is now and where it wants to be in the future. Having established these basic facts, it must identify how it intends to get there. What steps will it have to take? How many smaller steps will this involve? There will often be several different routes that the business can take, or in some cases is forced to take, before it reaches it goals. The next important consideration is the timescale. The business needs to establish a series of dates at which it could confidently expect progress to have been made. On these dates, the business will review the situation and see whether it has progressed as far as it anticipated towards its goals. The business may have to revise its plans at the review dates and, perhaps, add new goals or rewrite its plans to reflect any changes that have occurred. The main reasons why a business would action plan are as follows.

Consolidating and strengthening market position

keyword

Consolidation
– In this context consolidation means maintaining the current market share.

Having achieved a particular market share, a business cannot rest on its successes as there will undoubtedly be a large number of competitors that are working to take away that market share for themselves. Achieving a market share, therefore, is not the end of the business's work. It now has to protect that market share, a process known as consolidation. A business can achieve **consolidation** by ensuring that its current number of customers remain loyal to them.

The second phase is to strengthen or increase the market share that has already been achieved. A business can do this by continuing to market its products and services and making more people aware that they are available. If the business can get itself into a strong position in the market, where the majority of potential customers have heard of the business, then it is less likely that new competitors will be able to take away the business's market share.

Identifying opportunities for expansion

Expansion can be achieved in a number of different ways. One of the most common ways is for a business to gradually increase its sales, which allows it to reinvest its profits into growing the business in terms of its range of products and services, as well as taking on more employees. A business needs to choose the correct time at which to expand and not choose a time when the market is experiencing difficulties. Having said that, if the market is strong and the competitors are doing well, they will be seeking to expand at the same time.

keyword

Acquisition
– When a business buys another business.

keyword

Merger
– When two or more businesses decide to become one business.

An increasingly popular way of expanding is known as **acquisition**. This means that a business will seek to buy another business, either in its own market or in a market similar to that of the purchasing business. If two or more businesses choose to join together, then this is known as a **merger**. This means that the two businesses will now have a common management and structure and will be able to benefit from the expertise of both of the original businesses.

keyword

Takeover
– When one business gains the total ownership of another business.

Another form of acquisition is known as a **takeover**. This is often referred to as a hostile takeover, as the business being acquired does not actually wish to be purchased by the other business. There are other forms of takeover, when the owners of the business being acquired are prepared to be bought by the other business.

case study 9.2 — Morrisons take over Safeway

In the spring of 2004 the Bradford-based Morrisons supermarket chain completed a £3 billion takeover of its rival, Safeway. The other big three supermarket chains, Tesco, Asda and Sainsbury's, along with the owner of Bhs, Philip Green, had all made bids for Safeway. Morrisons now have around 550 stores throughout the UK and have begun a process of converting 180 of the medium-sized Safeway stores into full Morrisons supermarkets.

The family-run Morrisons chain hopes to make annual savings of some £215 million from the takeover.

activity
INDIVIDUAL WORK

Read the case study and then answer the following questions:

a) How might the fact that four other businesses were trying to buy Safeway have affected the final price Morrisons paid for the company?

b) As far as customers are concerned, give two advantages and two disadvantages of there being one less independent supermarket chain in the UK.

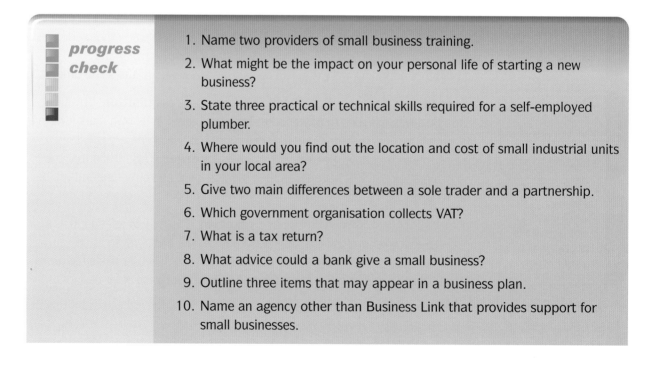

progress check

1. Name two providers of small business training.
2. What might be the impact on your personal life of starting a new business?
3. State three practical or technical skills required for a self-employed plumber.
4. Where would you find out the location and cost of small industrial units in your local area?
5. Give two main differences between a sole trader and a partnership.
6. Which government organisation collects VAT?
7. What is a tax return?
8. What advice could a bank give a small business?
9. Outline three items that may appear in a business plan.
10. Name an agency other than Business Link that provides support for small businesses.

Starting a Small Business

This unit covers:

- how to present the initial business idea using relevant criteria
- the skills and development needed to run the business successfully
- the legal and financial aspects that will affect the start-up of the business
- being able to produce an outline business start-up proposal

This unit looks at how good an initial business idea is and whether it provides the basis for a successful business. The unit also looks at funding, potential markets and the competitors.

This unit aims to help you consider your idea within real business parameters, including the type of business, how good the business idea is, the target market and how to balance personal and business needs. You will also look at your own ability to run the business and how you would acquire any new skills or expertise to assist you in this.

The unit also looks at the legal status of business and trading terms, as well as considering legal issues and finance.

Ultimately you will have the opportunity to outline your own proposal for a new business, drawing on the expertise of professionals, in order to help you pull together the necessary information in an effective manner, using communication skills and information technology.

grading criteria

To achieve a **Pass** grade the evidence must show that the learner is able to:	To achieve a **Merit** grade the evidence must show that the learner is able to:	To achieve a **Distinction** grade the evidence must show that the learner is able to:
P1 present the initial business idea using relevant criteria	**M1** explain and justify methods used to identify the target market for the proposed business	**D1** present a comprehensive business proposal that addresses all relevant aspects of business start up
P2 describe how to identify the target market	**M2** analyse the development needed to run the business successfully	

293

grading criteria

To achieve a **Pass** grade the evidence must show that the learner is able to:	To achieve a **Merit** grade the evidence must show that the learner is able to:	To achieve a **Distinction** grade the evidence must show that the learner is able to:
P3 describe the skills needed to run the business successfully and what areas require further development	**M3** assess the implications of legal and financial aspects that will affect the start up of the business	
P4 describe the legal and financial aspects that will affect the start-up of the business		
P5 produce a written outline proposal for starting up a new small business, following an acceptable business model		

The Initial Business Idea Using Relevant Criteria

A niche market is a specialised market that is not often targeted by larger organisations. The products sold to a niche market are often tailor-made so competition is low and high prices can be charged. Marketing and selling products and services to a niche market often requires a very different approach to that adopted for larger markets or mass markets. There are likely to be fewer customers in a niche market and this means that they will require the product or service to be precisely what they require.

activity
INDIVIDUAL WORK (10.1)

You now need to consider the feasibility of a proposed new business. Your tasks are:

a) Consider who your likely customers are.

b) What are your likely start-up requirements in terms of skills and resources?

c) Draw something that represents what your product will look like or explain how your service will be of use to the customers.

Market trends

It is vital for a business to understand its markets and its customers. Providing they do understand who they are selling to and why those customers purchase products and services from them, the business can begin to understand how future demands might move.

Markets and customer tastes and demands change constantly. A business needs to keep track of these movements to ensure that they can match the predicted market trends as and when they occur. This is difficult to do as it requires the business to invest time, money and effort in market research.

Use of primary and secondary market research

To find out about market trends, consumer confidence and what the competition is doing, a business will carry out market research. This research can be broken down into two types: primary research and secondary research. When a business has to obtain the information themselves, this is known as primary research or field research. There are four methods of primary research:

- Personal interview
- Telephone interview
- Postal survey
- A panel.

So, primary research can be expensive and time-consuming. Before an organisation goes to this expense, it should consider what information is already available. Secondary data, which is already available and known, can be sourced from a variety of different places and can be much cheaper than carrying out primary research.

activity

INDIVIDUAL WORK (10.2)

Visit the website of the Office of National Statistics at www.statistics.gov.uk. What information does it supply that could be useful to you in determining the current trends related to your idea for a new business?

Office of National Statistics
www.statistics.gov.uk

Current business and consumer confidence and market competition

In carrying out market research, a business will try to make some kind of judgement about its potential share of the market. In other words, it will need to

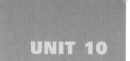

Table 10.1 Advantages and disadvantages of primary research

Methods of primary research	Advantages	Disadvantages
Personal interview	■ There is a high response rate as people do not often refuse to answer. ■ A questionnaire is easy to analyse. ■ Any questions misunderstood can be explained. ■ The respondent does not have time to consider their answer so responses are likely to be more truthful.	■ The cost is often high because of the cost of the interviewer's time. ■ If the respondent is in a hurry they may not give full consideration to the questions. ■ Interviewers will need training. ■ Collecting the information can take time.
Telephone interview	■ It is a quick way of getting through a lot of interviews. ■ The interviewers can stay in one place. ■ Costs are relatively low because travel is not involved. ■ People are easily accessible.	■ You cannot interview people that do not have a telephone. ■ You cannot tell a respondent's approximate age without asking. ■ People may be annoyed at being disturbed and may not pay attention. ■ The interviewer cannot provide identification.
Postal survey	■ A wide selection of the population can be reached. ■ It is relatively cheap. ■ Interviewers do not have to be trained. ■ Specialist groups, such as readers of particular magazines, can be reached. ■ Answers may be more considered and not rushed.	■ Not everyone will respond. ■ Questions could be misunderstood. ■ It is expensive to keep an up-to-date mailing list. ■ It can take a long time for all responses to come back. ■ The person that the questionnaire was intended for may not be the one in the household to complete it.
A panel	■ It gives a good indication of trends. ■ Valuable background information about the members of a panel can be obtained. ■ It is easy to judge whether or not external factors have influenced the members of the panel.	■ External factors, such as a death or a family problem, could affect the respondent's opinions. ■ The respondents may not behave as they normally do because they are being observed. ■ It is expensive because panellists will have to be rewarded and/or replaced if they leave.

seek information about competitors' businesses and their products. This will enable it to position its product and set pricing levels. Many small businesses operate in a market where there are lots of suppliers and no single organisation has more than about a five per cent share.

It is important for a business to measure their market potential, which is different from market size. Market potential refers to the probable growth or lack of growth of the markets. In order to find out about potential customers, a business will:

■ Send questionnaires to potential customers.

■ Follow leads from a list of individuals that may have approached the business as a result of receiving correspondence from it in the past.

■ Follow leads from existing customers who may have referred potential new customers to the business.

Before a business can collect statistical data on its market for a product or service, it needs to know which market that is. To define what the market is, it needs to decide:

- Whether the market is a consumer, industrial or professional one.
- Whether age, sex, family size or marital status is the basis of the customer target group.
- Whether the product or service relies on the local area alone.
- Whether a customer's social status is important.
- Whether the customer's frequency of purchase is an important factor.
- Whether the target market is influenced by fashion or current trends.
- Whether the target market is influenced by the price of the product or service.
- Where the target market currently purchases their products or services.
- Whether the target market requires fast and frequent deliveries.
- Whether the target market requires a high level of after-sales service.

Identifying the target market

Market opportunities represent chances for businesses to be able to identify demand (need) for products and services and then supply them. The identification of particular demands can be complicated and the business needs to be sure that it is geared up to be able to satisfy these demands should it find a worthwhile opportunity. A business will begin, as we will see, by looking at its own strengths and weaknesses. It will then examine the opportunities and threats presented by the market and the competitors. The business needs to understand as much as possible about the market and in particular the trends of the market. It will achieve this by carrying out research. Some research can be purchased or is available on the internet through government agencies. Other more focused research may need to be undertaken by the business itself.

activity
GROUP WORK
(10.3)

You now need to think about a product or service in terms of the market will it be aimed at.

a) What do you think are some of the characteristics of your potential customers?

b) Is your product or service aimed at a market that has lots of competition?

c) If so, who would be your main competitors? What do you know about them?

Carry out some research within your own group and some of the staff at your school or college. Design a questionnaire aimed at finding out whether your product or service would be attractive to the respondents. Ask them how much they would be prepared to pay for it and whether or not they already use a similar product or service. If so, where do they buy it and why do they do so?

Products and services in potential demand

Customers' needs, wants, desires and requirements change all the time. Anticipating what will be needed in the future is quite an art. The first task of an organisation is to try to identify what the customers want and not what the organisation thinks they want.

The overall market demand for products and services is often beyond the direct control of an individual organisation. Needs are generated by the public in any region or market and they are often unique to that market. They are quite easy to measure. The main factors affecting demand can be categorised as follows:

- Economic factors – the influence of the economy.
- Geographical factors – wether, for example, can have an effect on which products or services are demanded.
- Demographical factors – for example the age, average household size and composition of the market.
- Socio-cultural factors – trends that affect a customer's motivation.
- Comparative price factors – the value of the product or service to the customer in relation to their spending power. Factors in this category include inflation, wage levels and the cost of raw materials in the market.
- Mobility factors – the customers' willingness or ability to travel in order to visit a particular retail outlet or location.
- Government or legislative factors – the legal consideration as to whether there are government rules and regulations about particular product or service development.
- Media communication factors – the media has a powerful influence over the demand for products and services.

Demand also responds to changes in the supply of products and services. Supply is an important consideration of demand and demand is an important consideration of supply.

Customers demand that their requirements are met. They are always looking for the benefits that a product or service can offer them. A business will want to ensure that it has the right product:

- Available
- At the right price
- In as many places as possible
- In stock at all times, both in the warehouse and in the retail outlets.

Some of the more obvious expectations of customers can be addressed as a matter of course. Organisations can identify the key expectations relating to their particular area of business, including:

activity

**INDIVIDUAL WORK
(10.4)**

If you worked for a business that offered holidays abroad to its customers, which of the following would you consider important?

a) Better-quality furnishings in hotels.

b) Soundproofed rooms.

c) Better heating and ventilation in rooms.

d) Better bathroom facilities.

e) Bigger rooms.

f) Better lighting in rooms.

g) Better food on the plane.

You probably think that all of these are important. But not all can be done immediately. Put them in order of priority.

- Accurate and reliable information about the product or service.

- Prompt and courteous advice and feedback regarding questions about the product or service.

- Wide availability of the product or service.

- Consistency in the quality, style, colour or other standardised features of the product or service.

- Reliable and responsive **after-sales service**, maintenance or technical back-up after the purchase of the product or service.

- Good, competitive prices that encourage customers to return to the same organisation for their products or services.

- A consistent public image of the business that does not undermine or embarrass the customer.

keyword

After-sales service – A customer service provided by a business after the sale of the product or service has taken place.

So, to ensure that there is potential demand for its products and services, a business will need to make sure that what it produces is what the market wants and needs. It will want to do this for a number of reasons, including:

- To generate income from sales or produce a profit for the business.

- To maximise the benefits to the business of increased sales, more profit and creating a good image.

- To manage the effects of any forthcoming changes, such as political, legal, economic, social or technological.

- To allow them to coordinate their activities in order to meet their aims and objectives.

- To enhance customers' perceptions of the organisation, product or service.

Skills and Development Needed to Run the Business Successfully

At the outset it will be important for a new business's owners to assess their skills and to be aware of the resources available to them. They may have ideal visions of what they want to do in the future, but without adequate skills and resources they will not succeed in such a competitive world. Essentially, the skills they would need are the ability to:

- Evaluate their own strengths and weaknesses
- Work independently or with other people
- Plan
- Manage their time effectively
- Set targets
- Review progress
- Make decisions
- Solve problems.

Set targets   Review progress   Solve problems

remember
> Not all business owners are skilled in sales, marketing, finance and distribution and they may need experts to assist them.

Resources are even more fundamental. Resources can be:

- Human – the person starting the business and the skills of others needed.
- Physical – including premises, machinery and equipment, stock and materials.
- Financial – how much capital it has available and where it would get any additional finance that might be needed.

Legal and Financial Aspects that will Affect the Start-Up of the Business

The legal and financial considerations for a business very much depends on the type of business, or in other words, the legal status of that business.

All businesses will have similar legal responsibilities, such as those that control the way in which they deal with customers. For some, employment law may not be relevant if they do not actually employ anyone. Generally, however, the laws related to consumers, the environment, employment, taxes and VAT will be the same, regardless of the size or nature of the business itself.

The key legal aspect is liability. This means the business, or owners of the business, have a legal responsibility for the actions and the finances of the business itself. There are key differences in this aspect of legal consideration:

- A sole trader has unlimited liability, this means that the sole trader is fully responsible for the debts of the business and its actions.
- A partnership means that all partners have equal responsibility for the debts of the business.
- A private limited company has shareholders that are only responsible for the business debts up to the value of the shares they have invested. In other words, if the business fails they only stand to lose the shares that they own.
- A franchise may be any of the above types of business and, as a result, the owners may have unlimited or limited liability. It is also important to remember that a franchisee (the people who have bought the franchise) will have a legal commitment to the franchisor (the individual or people who have licensed the franchise) and this will be included in a legal agreement.

link See Unit 9, pages 280–83

The main point about liability is whether the business is considered to be a separate entity. In other words, whether the business has a separate legal identity from the shareholders of the business. If it does have a separate identity then the liability falls on the business and not on the owners.

This is not to say that the owners of the business do not have any legal responsibilities if the business has a separate legal identity. They cannot simply walk away and blame the mistakes on the business. They must act according to the law and, in some cases, if they do not, they will be held personally responsible. In some cases they could face criminal or civil charges in court, which could lead to them being banned from owning a business or, in extreme cases, they could be given a prison sentence.

As far as financial considerations are concerned, again the nature of these is dependent on the legal structure of the business:

- A sole trader has to make all of the financial decisions for the business, raising money themselves through loans and any existing finance they may have.
- Partners can take responsibility for certain aspects of the business. One could focus on financial aspects. Partners can contribute finances from their own assets or they may raise money singly or as a group. Some partnerships have 'sleeping partners' who contribute to the setting up costs or any expansion plans of the business. In return they take a share of the profits, but they do not usually have any input into the business on a daily basis.

- Limited companies have specific directors responsible for the monitoring and reporting of financial figures. Limited companies raise money through the sale of shares. This can allow the business to start up or later additional shares can be sold in order for them to expand. They may also use a share of the profits, rather than paying out a full share of the profits to shareholders. This is known as a retained profit, as the business holds onto the profit that they have made in order to reinvest it.

- Franchises raise cash for launching the business according to the type of legal structure they have used. They could be a sole trader, a partnership or a limited company. The other major consideration for franchises is that they will have to pay the franchisor a set up fee to use the name. They will probably have to buy fixtures, fittings, products and services from the franchisor, pay a marketing budget (contribution to advertising) and a share of the profits. A good example of this is the franchised McDonalds around the country.

See Unit 9, p280–283 for further information

Business Proposal

Researching a market that the business believes to contain profitable opportunities is a vital task. A business will want to find out:

- The size of the market.
- Whether the market is growing.
- Whether the market is supplied by out-of-date or inefficient businesses.
- Whether the market is a niche that has not been considered by the competitors.
- Whether the market is dependent on certain pricing levels, which determine whether or not customers buy.
- Whether the market is already supplied by a competitor's branded products or by products that do not command considerable levels of customer loyalty.
- Whether the market is dominated by lots of competitors or just a few large ones.

Identifying customer thinking

As we discovered earlier in this unit, a business will want to know what products the customers are buying, why they buy them, what they are prepared to pay for them and who they are currently buying them from. A new business will do its utmost to identify its particular target group of customers and meet their needs, wants and preferences. It will also want to make its products or services more appealing to the customers than those of the competition.

Many businesses, before they spend time and resources in developing products and services, look for what is known as a market gap. A market gap is an opportunity for a business to step in and provide a product or service that at present no other business or competitor is providing.

Expectations of trading success

All parties involved in the start-up of a business will want to have an optimistic view of what the future holds. They will have high expectations of a successful trading business in the future. The business plan offers the business owners an opportunity to identify a series of objectives with the aim of improving the overall state of the business in the future. For new businesses, this essential objective setting may be not only a basic requirement of any providers of finance, but also of fundamental importance to the eventual success or failure of the enterprise.

For an organisation entering the market as a new business, its first objective may be to supply its products or services. An analysis of present market conditions and the comparative success of existing businesses operating in related areas will be of prime importance in meeting this objective. The business will also have to look at distribution and see whether it can identify cost-effective methods of bringing products and services to potential customers. A great deal of basic information can be provided in statistical form by the government or agencies working on behalf of the government. A careful analysis of competitors' activities and their published materials, such as company reports, may also prove to be valuable. Trends in customer spending can also be useful data on which to base the criteria needed to establish objectives in relation to the supply of products and services.

Another objective of the organisation may be to achieve particular levels of sales in terms of units sold or to obtain a financial advantage by being able to sell lots of products or services. This level of sales objective could be met by a business supplying their own-label products to wholesalers and retailers. The need to achieve high sales levels is particularly important to a business that produces inexpensive products.

activity

**GROUP WORK
(10.7)**

You should already know from the mandatory units of this book that there are some other common objectives of business. Write a short explanation on the following four:

a) Achieving sales value.

b) Making a profit.

c) Breaking even.

d) Meeting timescales.

Small business vulnerability

It is generally accepted that the first three years, and in particular the first year, present the greatest risk to a new business. So many things could potentially go wrong. The business may lack sufficient resources, finances or skills and expertise to be able to make it successful. Many small businesses are over-optimistic about how they will perform once they are up and running and they will have made serious financial commitments that they simply cannot cover from the revenues received.

In addition to having to cope with its expected costs, a business may often encounter costs that it could not have reasonably predicted. It may need to seek new suppliers, the premises may need to be refurbished, key members of staff may leave, and their financial providers may lose confidence in the business's ability to pay back any loans it may have borrowed.

Whilst the business needs to keep a careful eye on income and expenditure, there are other stronger forces that could influence its success. Established and probably larger competitors will move quickly to try to snuff out new businesses as they emerge. Existing businesses are aware that small businesses are vulnerable in the first year or so of their existence. The small business is still learning and it may make costly mistakes that the competition can exploit. Larger competitors can afford, at least in the short term, to reduce their prices and therefore make the small business follow, in the knowledge that this loss of income will have a greater effect on the new business than it will on the existing one.

Contingency plans

Many new small businesses have very few staff. They will rely on the expertise of this handful of people in order to carry out all the tasks and duties related to the smooth operations of the business. The loss of a key individual at the early stages of a small business could be disastrous. A business would find it difficult to run if the sole specialist in a particular area was unavailable due to sickness, accident or injury. This means that at the very beginning of a new business, in order to offset the negative impact of the loss of one of these key members of staff, the others need to be able to step in to fulfil their roles. This can be difficult if the business is that of a sole trader, particularly if it has to have specialist skills or qualifications in order to run the business. It would not be appropriate or desirable, for example, for a sole trader that has been trained to mend computers to be replaced by a sales assistant that has little or no experience in this field.

One possible solution is to encourage multi-skilling between those involved in the business. At the earliest point, the owners or key members of staff need to be trained to do one another's jobs. So, in the event of one of the key individuals being absent for a prolonged period, one of the others could step in and take over their duties.

Developing the resource base

An essential part of a business plan is to identify the cost and sources of necessary resources, including premises, equipment and material that will be essential to run the business. The business needs to examine a number of different premises to discover which would be the most suitable. Depending on the type of business, the new business may need a constant amount of passing trade, which means being close to where customers shop. Other businesses may need to be close to their business customers in order to make it simple to deliver products and services as required.

Equipment needs differ from business to business, but any providers of finance would need to see carefully considered and costed breakdowns of all equipment needs of the business. They may be able to suggest cheaper or more effective substitutes.

Materials refer to consumable items that may be needed by the business. A retail store, for example, would need carrier bags, a mail order business would need packaging material and a craftsperson would need tools to carry out their work. Again, any advisers or providers of finance would need to see that the business has broken down all of its material needs and costed each of these out precisely.

Presenting information to key audiences

Before we look at the way in which a business plan appears, it is important to understand that various groups or individuals will be interested in ensuring that all of the major areas have been covered. Banks, external investors, grant providers and business advisers will all be interested in how professional the business plan looks and how reliable the information is that is contained within it.

Ideally, a business plan should include the following features:

- An executive summary – an overview of the business. This is vital because many lenders and investors will only read this section of the plan.

- A description of the business opportunity – what the business plans to sell or offer and why, and who the customers are.

- The business's marketing and sales strategy – why customers will buy from the business and how the business plans to sell products and services to them.

- The business's management and key personnel – the qualifications and experience of all key members, including owners, involved with the business.

- The business's operations – including the proposed premises, work facilities, management information systems and IT.

- Financial forecasts – which essentially translate all of the previous parts of the business plan into numbers in terms of income, expenditure and profit.

Above all, the plan should be short. If it is of a manageable length, it is more likely to be read. A well-presented plan will encourage the audience to have a positive impression. The key points are:

- Number the pages.

- Include a contents list.

- Start with the executive summary.

- Use a sensible and large enough font.

- Write the plan so it addresses an external audience.

- Edit and re-edit the plan to make sure it makes sense.

- Show the plan to expert advisers, such as accountants, and ask for feedback.

- Avoid using jargon.

- Put all data, such as balance sheets and other tables, at the back of the report as appendices.

Above all, the business plan needs to be realistic. It may need updating at a later stage and it is a useful tool to judge the relative successes of the business.

activity

INDIVIDUAL WORK (10.7)

Your teacher or lecturer will provide you with a blank business plan format. It will have a number of headings that roughly correspond to the areas discussed in the section above. Complete the business plan, following on from your work in the previous activities in this unit relating to your product or service.

progress check

1. What is a USP?
2. What are market trends?
3. Identify three of your own key strengths.
4. Identify three of your main weaknesses.
5. What is a skills gap?
6. State two financial liabilities a business may have.
7. Why might it be important to consider fire regulations?
8. Why is it important to set targets and goals for a new business?
9. Why is it important to include information about the market in a business proposal?
10. What is a profit forecast?

Glossary

Acquisition – When a business buys another business.

Aerospace – Manufacturing industry that produces parts and products for the aircraft industry, including rockets, engines and other equipment.

After-sales service – A customer service provided by a business after the sale of the product or service has taken place.

Application – A written response to an advertisement, asking to be considered for a named vacancy.

Asset – An item that has a cash value. In the case of machinery, this asset used to produce products. Other assets could include land, buildings or patents.

BACS – The abbreviation for Bank Automated Clearing System – employees' wages are paid straight into the bank and they can have access to the money immediately.

Break even – This means a business has been able to cover its costs by the products or services they have sold, but they have not made a profit.

Call centre – An office environment in which staff have access to telephones and computers and use computer software to make calls to potential customers.

Candidate – A potential employee who has applied and been selected to attend for interview.

Charities – Organisations that exist to provide a service or to support a particular cause.

Consolidation – In this context consolidation means maintaining the current market share.

Constitution – The rules made when the business was first started up that state the procedures and policies of the organisation.

Cookie – A small text file that is placed on the user's hard drive by a web server. It is a code that is uniquely the user's and can only be read by the server that sent it.

Credit card – A card that allows the user to make purchases on credit, up to a limit specified by the issuing bank, building society or finance provider.

Debit card – A modern alternative to a cheque. The funds are taken out of the account of the cardholder immediately after having been approved by the issuing bank.

Disciplinary procedures – A series of warnings or actions that can be taken against an employee.

Domain name – A website's address on the Internet. It needs to be registered by a business, organisation or service, just like a business name. It allows potential customers to find the business's web address and website easily.

Domestic consumers – Household buyers rather than businesses.

Exported – Goods or services that are produced or provided by a UK organisation and sold to an overseas country.

Extranet – An extranet site is one that can only be accessed by a user group in the 'outside world', such as customers.

Gender – Relates to the sex of the customer: either a male or a female.

Guarantees – These are usually given free of charge by the manufacturer of a product, guaranteeing to the customer that the product will work for a set period of time.

Imported – Goods or services that are produced or provided by an overseas country and brought into the UK.

Income – Cash or funding received by an organisation as either payment from customers for goods and services or as a grant of money from another organisation, such as central or local government, to provide those goods and services.

Incorporation – The procedure by which a business registers itself at Companies House and becomes a legal entity. It is also known as registration and formation.

Invoice – The document that gives full details of the products or services sold and the price of those products/services.

Job description – A statement prepared by the business that identifies the nature of the job, including the tasks and responsibilities involved.

Media – The general term used to describe newspapers, television, radio, magazines and, increasingly, Internet news and information services. The media also includes marketing, public and community relations.

Merger – When two or more businesses decide to become one business.

Minutes – A written record of what took place, what was discussed and agreed, including actions to be taken before the next meeting and by whom.

Mission statement – An organisation's vision of what it wants to achieve in the future. A good mission statement needs to be easy to understand, relevant to the organisation, ambitious and useful in motivating staff.

MOST – Mobile Ordering and Sales Terminal.

Multinational – A business that runs operations in at least two different countries.

Opportunity cost – The true cost of something when measured in terms of what you have to forego (forfeit) in order to get it.

Output – The total number of products or services produced or offered by a business in a given period of time.

Person specification – This is also sometimes known as a job specification. It identifies the characteristics of the successful individual needed to carry out the job.

Point-of-sale (POS) – The physical location in a store where the customer purchases products and services, such as a cash register or payment point.

Profit – The ability of a business to sell its products and services for more than it cost to acquire or provide those products and services.

References – Statements made by independent individuals that comment on the character and/or abilities of the candidate.

Revenue – The income received by a business in exchange for selling its products and services.

Screen-saver – A moving image on the computer screen that appears if the computer is not used for a few minutes.

Shift – A period of non-standard working hours, such as starting at lunchtime and working through into the evening or beginning earlier in the day and finishing after lunch.

Shortlist – When the top candidates are identified and invited to attend for an interview.

Spam – unsolicited, unwanted, irrelevant or inappropriate messages, usually advertising, sent to large numbers of email addresses. Also known as 'junk mail'.

Takeover – When one business gains the total ownership of another business.

Telecommunications – The manufacturing and service industries that produce or provide communications equipment.

Telesales – Also known as telephone sales, involves calling customers, either at home or at their workplace, and attempting to sell them products and services.

Warranties – These are similar to guarantees, but normally the customer pays for the extra protection. They are often known as extended warranties or insurance policies against repair and replacement costs.

Index

Index

Index